Frank Stewart is Associate Editor of the ACBL *Bulletin,* a Life Master player, and a noted bridge teacher.

WINNING DEFENSE

for the Advancing Bridge Player

MORE CONSTRUCTIVE THINKING AT THE BRIDGE TABLE

FRANK STEWART

Author of
Better Bridge for the Advancing Player

Prentice-Hall, Inc., Englewood Cliffs, New Jersey 07632

Library of Congress Cataloging in Publication Data

Stewart, Frank, 1946 Oct. 16–
    Winning defense for the advancing bridge player.

    "A Spectrum Book"—T.p. verso.
    Includes index.
    1. Contract bridge—Defensive play. I. Title.
GV1282.42.S74   1985   795.41'53   84-22327
ISBN   0-13-960691-2
ISBN   0-13-960683-1 (pbk.)

Interior design and production
   coordination: Fred Dahl
Buyer: Frank Grieco

This book is available at a special discount when ordered
in bulk quantities. Contact Prentice-Hall, Inc., General
Publishing Division, Special Sales, Englewood Cliffs, N.J. 07632.

A SPECTRUM BOOK

10 9 8 7 6 5 4 3 2 1

Printed in the United States of America

ISBN 0-13-960691-2

ISBN 0-13-960683-1 {PBK.}

Prentice-Hall International, Inc., *London*
Prentice-Hall of Australia Pty. Limited, *Sydney*
Prentice-Hall of Canada Inc., *Toronto*
Prentice-Hall of India Private Limited, *New Delhi*
Prentice-Hall of Japan, Inc., *Tokyo*
Prentice-Hall of Southeast Asia Pte. Ltd., *Singapore*
Whitehall Books Limited, *Wellington, New Zealand*
Editora Prentice-Hall do Brasil Ltda., *Rio de Janeiro*
Prentice-Hall Hispanoamericana, S.A., *Mexico*

This book is dedicated to the best writer in the family . . .

my mother

CONTENTS

PREFACE

The scope of this book assumes that you are a player of at least moderate experience and that you feel like putting in some effort in the interests of self-improvement. As in the companion work, *Better Bridge for the Advancing Player,* I've tried to minimize the presentation of endless rules in the text and to concentrate instead on the *logic* on which some of the better known rules are based, the times when you'll feel impelled by your card sense to disregard a rule, and the situations when you must *reason out* the right answer to a problem when there is no handy rule to guide you.

Whereas the previous volume dealt with winning dummy play and good judgment in the auction, the subject here is defense. Many ambitious players need help with this area of their games more than any other. It is on defense that the more advanced techniques of counting and logical inference become essential, and the delicacy of proper signalling must be understood. There is ample opportunity for partnership confusion and individual error.

If you are a player who invariably relies on rules to guide you, prepare to look at defensive play from a different standpoint. My intention is to emphasize thought processes instead of rules. This is, after all, a thinking person's game. Nobody can get the most from the time they spend at the bridge table unless they learn to think for themselves when the necessity arises.

In each chapter, there are instructive introductory deals. Then, six problems are posed so that you may test your comprehension of the ideas that have been presented. Most of the problems are fairly difficult, especially in the later chapters. They are intended to stimulate your thought by enhancing and expanding upon the basic ideas in the introductory section.

To make the text more readable, I hope, I have again inserted each problem into a real-life situation from the world of bridge and bridge players. In places, I may have offered views and commentary with which the reader will not agree, and for that I have to ask his or her indulgence. My purpose is not really to singlehandedly change the course of the (bridge) world but only to provide a diversion that might make the instruction less tedious.

In any case, when a problem is posed and asterisks follow (*******), you are advised to try to think out some sort of answer before proceeding. The book will be most useful to you if you do so. Don't be disappointed if many of the problems stump you. The truth is, if you get as many as half of them right, you probably don't need any help from me!

ACKNOWLEDGMENTS

I have several nice people to thank:

Edgar Kaplan and Jeff Rubens, at *Bridge World* magazine, who kindly gave permission for me to reproduce material from my own *Bridge World* articles, as well as certain other illustrative deals. I have found *Bridge World*, which enjoys an international reputation for excellence in the expert community, a constant and valuable source in writing this book.

Robert Wolenik, of *Popular Bridge* magazine, for his gracious permission to reuse some material from articles of mine that originally appeared in that very fine and colorful publication.

The indefatigable Henry Francis and Sue Emery, at the ACBL *Bulletin,* who granted me permission to use some material that first saw print in my ACBL *Bulletin* column.

Andy Bernstein, of Devyn Press, who gave his assistance, which is much appreciated.

Thanks, as always, go to my wife Charlotte for her support; and finally, a big thank you to my editors at Prentice-Hall, for their faith in my ability to produce a readable and rewarding bridge book that I hope you, the reader, will find justified.

Frank Stewart
Birmingham, Alabama
(that hotbed of bridge)

FOREWORD

Frank Stewart's newest book addresses the very core of expert bridge, namely, the ability to play consistently fine defense. His thrust is simple: How do we set this hand? His emphasis is on thought processes in real situations, not rules committed to memory. Each chapter is followed by illustrations "at the table" and the reader is asked to participate.

Frank has found a way to attack the most important advanced areas of defensive play with simplicity, practicality, and, incredibly, humor. Bridge is a young game. Bridge is a difficult game. Frank has proven that bridge is the best game.

I heartily recommend this book to all of you who want to improve your table thinking on defense.

Bobby Wolff

(*Author's note:* A four-time Bermuda Bowl Champion and a winner of the Olympiad Open Pairs, Bobby Wolff serves on the ACBL Board of Directors and writes the nationally syndicated column, "The Aces on Bridge." No one in bridge is better liked or more respected. Thanks, Bobby.)

PROLOGUE

So you think playing tight defense is a piece of cake, huh? Second-hand low, third-hand high, lead through strength and up to weakness, and cover an honor with an honor, and you're ready for the world.

The aim of this book is simple. I want you to set more contracts than you do now. (Really, I'd be satisfied if you only cut down on letting unmakable contracts slip through.) To start with, I must get you to realize that there is a lot more to good defense than rigid adherence to any set of axioms, like the ones above. Winning defense requires things like constant counting, frequent use of logical inference, and a well-developed card sense, as well as ferocious concentration, a pliable imagination, and a good partnership rapport.

For a little shock therapy, let's look at a few defensive problems. In each case, the game is rubber bridge.

One

Dlr: South
Vul: N–S

♠ Q75
♥ 63
◇ AQ10643
♣ 32

♠ K94
♥ Q10742
◇ K8
♣ 764

☐

Bidding:

South	West	North	East
1♣	Pass	1◇	Pass
2NT	Pass	3NT	(All Pass)

You, West, lead the four of hearts. Partner obliges with the King, which holds. He continues with the heart Jack and another, and declarer takes his Ace on the third round. Now the two of diamonds is led toward dummy. Plan your defense.

☐ ☐ ☐

Two

Dlr: South
Vul: N–S

♠ J95
♥ 763
◇ K94
♣ AQ105

☐

♠ Q763
♥ J1094
◇ A2
♣ K62

Bidding:

South	West	North	East
1NT	Pass	3NT	(All Pass)

West, your partner, leads the two of spades. Declarer, a well-known expert, puts up dummy's Jack. Plan your defense.

Three

Dlr: South   ♠ AK105
Vul: none   ♡ 842
               ◇ Q94
               ♣ J104

♠ Q983
♡ QJ753   □
◇ K2
♣ 83

Bidding:	South	West	North	East
	1 ◇	Pass	1 ♠	Pass
	3 ♣	Pass	3 ◇	Pass
	3NT	(All Pass)		

You, West, lead the five of hearts. Declarer ducks partner's King, and wins the return of the heart ten. At trick three, declarer leads the spade Jack. Plan your defense (in a hurry).

□   □   □

Four

Dlr: South   ♠ K952
Vul: E-W   ♡ A94
               ◇ AQ10
               ♣ 743

                   ♠ 874
                   ♡ K7
      □   ◇ 87432
                   ♣ QJ10

Bidding:	South	West	North	East
	1 ♡	Pass	1 ♠	Pass
	2 ♣	Pass	4 ♡	Pass
	4NT	Pass	5 ♡	Pass
	5NT	Pass	6 ◇	Pass
	6 ♡	(All Pass)		

West, your partner, leads the Queen of spades, won by declarer's Ace. At
trick two, declarer runs the Queen of hearts to your King. What do you
return?

□   □   □

SOLUTIONS

One

If you played second-hand low, declarer is probably going to make *four*.
The full deal is:

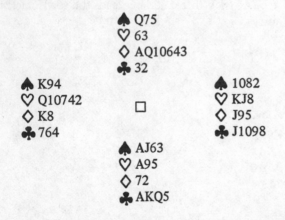

♠ Q75
♡ 63
◇ AQ10643
♣ 32

♠ K94　　　　　　　♠ 1082
♡ Q10742　　□　　♡ KJ8
◇ K8　　　　　　　◇ J95
♣ 764　　　　　　　♣ J1098

♠ AJ63
♡ A95
◇ 72
♣ AKQ5

If declarer held the diamond Jack or partner had the doubleton Jack, your
position would be hopeless. But if declarer has a small doubleton diamond
(not unlikely), you must put up your diamond *King*. What is declarer
to do? If he ducks, you are in to cash your good hearts. If he wins, he
cannot establish the diamonds without ruining his communication with
dummy. You are bound to get in again, with the King of spades, to take
your winners.

　　　If you fail to play the diamond King, declarer will beyond doubt
play dummy's ten, passing his diamond loser to your partner, who has no

more hearts. If, on a spade return, he judges to go up with the Ace and lead another diamond, he will be able to claim the rest of the tricks.

□ □ □

Two

You should play the *seven* of spades, not the Queen. Declarer is an expert, remember. Think about his play of the spade Jack. Would he choose this play if he held Ax of spades? No, he'd surely make the percentage play of the *nine* from dummy. This would gain if opening leader's spades were headed by Q10 or K10, and would lose if he had underled KQ. The odds in favor of declarer's playing the nine would be two to one. Suppose declarer had Kx of spades. He'd still try the *nine*. The Jack could never gain him anything, but the nine might induce a helpful defensive error.

Could your partner have both Ace and King of spades? No way. Declarer must have at least one honor to have enough points for his 1NT opening.

The full deal is:

```
                ♠ J95
                ♡ 763
                ◇ K94
                ♣ AQ105
♠ A842                        ♠ Q763
♡ 85                          ♡ J1094
◇ 8765            □           ◇ A2
♣ 873                         ♣ K62
                ♠ K10
                ♡ AKQ2
                ◇ QJ103
                ♣ J94
```

Declarer was trying to *induce you* to cover when he played dummy's Jack. Note the probable outcome if you oblige him by putting up your spade Queen.

□ □ □

Three

If you covered the Jack of spades, declarer claimed 3NT and hurriedly dealt the next hand. This is the full deal:

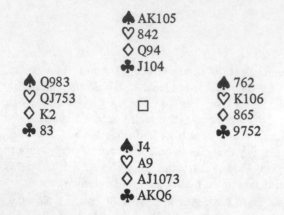

```
                    ♠ AK105
                    ♡ 842
                    ◇ Q94
                    ♣ J104
  ♠ Q983                         ♠ 762
  ♡ QJ753           □            ♡ K106
  ◇ K2                           ◇ 865
  ♣ 83                           ♣ 9752
                    ♠ J4
                    ♡ A9
                    ◇ AJ1073
                    ♣ AKQ6
```

Look at the problem from declarer's point of view. He has eight top tricks and can make at least one more if he guesses which of two finesses is going to work. Once you covered the Jack of spades, his worries vanished. But what if you had ducked and looked happy about it? Declarer would have had an uncomfortable guess. Suppose he had decided to stake everything on the *diamond* finesse!?

After partner produces the heart King at trick one, you should be able to figure out the entire hand. If declarer holds the 19 HCP that his jump shift to three clubs suggests, he must have every outstanding face card. And if he has a five-card club suit, he has nine tricks, so you might as well assume he has only four clubs. Therefore, it is a clear error to cover any honors this time. Not when declarer has options in the play, and a cover will help him out.

Are you starting to get the drift of this discussion?

□   □   □

Four

This is not an easy problem. The correct return is a *diamond*! Look at the full deal.

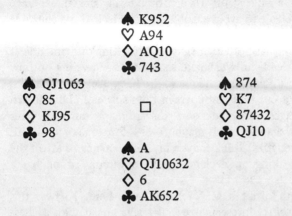

When the deal was actually played, East returned the Queen of clubs up to dummy's weakness. Declarer won, led a trump to dummy, and took the King of spades. He ruffed a spade, cashed the club King, and ran trumps.

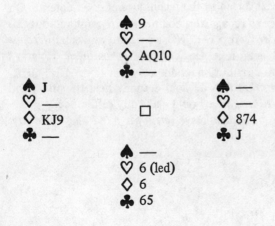

West had to keep the spade Jack, since dummy's nine was a threat, so he discarded a diamond. Declarer then threw the spade from the table, and followed with a diamond to the Queen, making three diamond tricks and his slam.

There was really no hurry for a shift to clubs at trick three, since declarer would never be able to avoid a club loser if he lacked the club Ace or King, regardless of the rest of his hand. East might have reasoned this way instead: "If declarer has both high clubs and the King of diamonds, it doesn't matter what I lead—he will make six or fail, depending on how many heart tricks he has. But West could have the King-Jack of diamonds, and then he would hold our side's stoppers in both spades and diamonds. Is there a chance he might come under some discarding pressure? Declarer is likely to have a very shapely hand, maybe 1-6-1-5, to make up for his minimum high-card strength. I think maybe my only chance to affect the outcome is to try breaking up declarer's link to dummy if he has a singleton diamond."

"Through strength" isn't a very reliable guide here. To beat this hand, you'd have to *think*, foreseeing several tricks ahead, like a chess player planning his moves. Note how the diamond return leaves declarer with no chance to make his slam.

These four hands are difficult, but surely not insoluble. None are "tricked up." (Would I do that to you?) The best defense can (and would) be found by any player well-versed in the techniques of good defense. On hand ONE, it was necessary to recognize a common card combination; this means having a *practiced card sense*. On TWO, we had to draw an *inference* from declarer's play and act on it. On THREE, we *counted* declarer's high-card points, tricks, and distribution, and knew what to do. On FOUR, we defended on the *assumption* that declarer actually held the only hand on which the line of defense we chose would make any difference.

But on none of the hands could we settle for blind allegiance to a set of aphorisms.

Let's look at one more hand.

```
Dlr:  South      ♠ K864
Vul:  Both       ♥ Q4
                 ♦ KQJ106
                 ♣ Q10

      ♠ A5
      ♥ J1098          □
      ♦ 842
      ♣ KJ74
```

Bidding:	South	West	North	East
	1 ♣	Pass	1 ◇	Pass
	1 ♡	Pass	1 ♠	Pass
	1NT	Pass	3NT	(All Pass)

You, West, lead the Jack of hearts. Declarer surveys dummy for a moment, and puts up the heart Queen, which wins. At trick two, dummy leads a spade, declarer plays the Queen, and you take your Ace. What should you do now?

□ □ □

Think it over carefully. Declarer has the heart Ace-King left, for three heart tricks. How about diamonds? Who do you think has the Ace? *Declarer* surely has it. Put yourself in his place. If you were playing this hand and you were missing the diamond Ace, what would your play to trick two be? A *diamond*, I hope. Surely you'd hasten to set up your best suit. The only reason declarer isn't establishing his diamonds is that they're good already. (Another clue: would declarer win the heart *Queen* at trick one, removing what might be his only entry to dummy, unless he could run diamonds whenever he wanted?) So, you can "give" declarer five diamond tricks. The spade King is now a winner, so he's about to make 3NT, unless you can win four fast tricks in clubs.

Now, be careful here. *Which* club you lead may be critical. The full deal is:

                ♠ K864
                ♡ Q4
                ◇ KQJ106
                ♣ Q10
♠ A5   ♠ J972
♡ J1098   □   ♡ 765
◇ 842   ◇ 953
♣ KJ74   ♣ A82
                ♠ Q103
                ♡ AK32
                ◇ A7
                ♣ 9653

You must start with the club *King* or they'll still make it. Partner will get his club eight out of the way on this trick. You can continue with a club to his Ace, and now his return of the club two will go through declarer's 96 to your J7.

Note that declarer's opening bid would have been *1NT* had his club nine been the Ace. He played well by trying to steal his ninth trick in spades before running his diamonds. He would have succeeded had you not been alert and thinking.

To defeat this contract, you must count declarer's tricks and high cards, draw an inference from his play, and assume that partner has the Ace of the first suit declarer bid to give your side a chance to set him. Then, as if all that isn't enough, you must handle a tricky suit combination correctly. Quite a workout!

The rules we mentioned at the beginning are better described as "tendencies." As very general advice, they are sound enough. But as you read through this book, you should begin to see that correct defense is often based on logical and simple *reasoning*. That's what bridge is supposed to be all about. It's a beautifully *logical* game, a game for thinkers.

Ready to put Rules in their proper place and start learning to think for yourself? Good. Now we can go ahead. Why don't we start by looking at one of the concepts we touched on in this discussion, the idea of *assumption* on defense?

chapter one

DEFENSE CAN BE EASY

PRELIMINARIES

I expect you may feel a twinge of skepticism at the title of this very first chapter. Bridge writers before me have invariably commented on the difficulty of playing tight defense. Their premise is that the defenders, burdened by a lack of knowledge of each other's hands, are obliged to make many unpleasant guesses during the play. Weighty decisions about proper signalling, to mention only one aspect of partnership cooperation, must be made in combatting this natural handicap. Plenty of deductive reasoning, much of it delicate (and perhaps apt to awe and dismay the less experienced player), will be needed. On most hands, there will be chances enough for the defenders to lose their way.

     I am able to deny none of this, but nevertheless there is an encouraging word or two I can offer. Look, first, at the following deal.

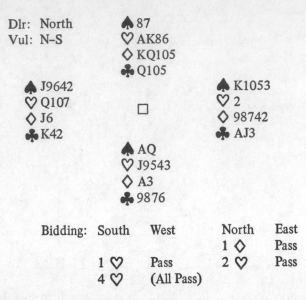

Dlr: North
Vul: N–S

♠ 87
♡ AK86
◇ KQ105
♣ Q105

♠ J9642
♡ Q107
◇ J6
♣ K42

□

♠ K1053
♡ 2
◇ 98742
♣ AJ3

♠ AQ
♡ J9543
◇ A3
♣ 9876

Bidding:

South	West	North	East
		1 ◇	Pass
1 ♡	Pass	2 ♡	Pass
4 ♡	(All Pass)		

West leads the four of spades, to the seven, King, and Ace. South, the declarer, cashes the Ace and King of hearts and then begins to run diamonds. He discards a club on the third round, as West ruffs in with his good Queen of trumps.

At this point, the handwriting is strictly on the wall for West. East's play of the spade King denies the Queen, so declarer has no loser in that suit; and there are no further red-suit tricks to be had; so if four hearts is beaten, the defense must cash three (fast) club tricks. *East must hold specifically AJx in the suit.* There is no other hope.

Therefore, West should bang down his King of clubs and continue with a low one. This time, his optimism will be rewarded.

The entire basis of defense rests on this idea of *assumption*. In defending most contracts, your idea will be to visualize a possible hand for declarer (consistent with the bidding, your partner's signals, and declarer's approach to the play of the hand) that gives you a chance to set him. You then base your defense on the assumption that declarer *actually has* that hand or one virtually identical, at least until some further information comes your way that disproves or weakens your original assumption. (Of course, we are dealing here with defense at rubber bridge or IMP scoring, where the defeat of the contract is normally the goal; when we get to matchpoint duplicate defense (Chapter Twelve), we'll see that possible overtricks and undertricks can affect making your assumptions at that form of scoring.)

Now, the reason Defense Can Be Easy is that, on many hands (especially when the contract is a *high* one), your options will be severely limited. There may even be just *one* sort of hand you can reasonably expect declarer (or your partner) to hold that will allow the defense to prevail. In such a case, you need only proceed on the assumption that the most favorable lie of the cards is the one that actually exists. If you find that declarer holds some other hand, and the contract is unbeatable, all you can do is cut for another deal. You just don't want to see declarer steal his contract when he holds a hand where there is a successful defense available.

```
Dlr: South        ♠ J976
Vul: none         ♡ 97
                  ◇ KQ5
                  ♣ AQ107

♠ 5                              ♠ A83
♡ Q10532                         ♡ AK86
◇ 104          □                 ◇ J9876
♣ 96432                          ♣ 5

                  ♠ KQ1042
                  ♡ J4
                  ◇ A32
                  ♣ KJ8
```

South opened one spade, North raised to three spades (forcing), and South went on to four spades. The opening lead was the three of hearts, won by East's King. East knew that another heart would cash (since the lead of the *three* indicated that West had no more than a five-card suit); and the trump Ace was a sure trick. But the setting trick would have to be a ruff, since declarer needed both the diamond Ace and club King for his opening bid. East therefore shifted to his club. Declarer won and started trumps. East won the second round and *underled* his Ace of hearts to West's Queen, obtaining his club ruff for down one.

The underlead was a risk, of course, and could have cost an overtrick had declarer turned up with the heart Queen. But East could see that there was no other way of *setting* four spades, so he *assumed* that his partner had the Queen of hearts.

You can see from this deal that *counting your potential defensive tricks* is a prelude to making your assumptions. You don't want to have to make any more assumptions than necessary, so you need to keep track of what defensive tricks seem more or less likely. To give the simplest example:

```
Dlr: West        ♠ AJ95
Vul: E-W         ♡ KJ
                 ◇ 742
                 ♣ AQJ4
   ♠ 62                      ♠ K4
   ♡ 10983          □        ♡ Q762
   ◇ J985                    ◇ AK3
   ♣ 1072                    ♣ 8653
                 ♠ Q10873
                 ♡ A54
                 ◇ Q106
                 ♣ K9
```

Bidding: South   West   North   East
                  Pass   1NT   Pass
          3 ♠   Pass   4 ♠   (All Pass)

West led the heart ten, and dummy's Jack was covered by the Queen and won by South's Ace. The ten of spades was then passed to East's King. East could see that the defense needed three diamond tricks for a set. Declarer clearly had no more major-suit losers, and he could finesse against the club King if necessary. East therefore had little to lose by returning a *low* diamond away from the Ace-King! Of course, declarer put in his *ten*, taking the percentage play, and promptly found himself down one.

(If you're thinking that declarer's play of the hand was questionable, I agree. He could have tried for a fast discard on the clubs before drawing trumps, banking on the 62 percent shot that the suit would split 4-3; or he could have played to the Ace of trumps and followed with three rounds of clubs, giving himself some additional chances. As he actually played, he would still have succeeded against most Easts.)

The next example of assumption on defense is a little more complex.

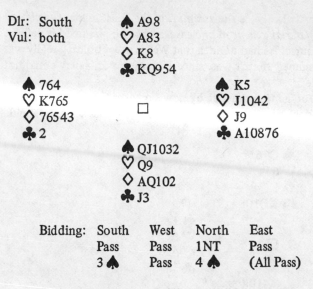

Dlr: South
Vul: both

♠ A98
♥ A83
◇ K8
♣ KQ954

♠ 764
♥ K765
◇ 76543
♣ 2

♠ K5
♥ J1042
◇ J9
♣ A10876

♠ QJ1032
♥ Q9
◇ AQ102
♣ J3

Bidding:

	South	West	North	East
	Pass	Pass	1NT	Pass
	3 ♠	Pass	4 ♠	(All Pass)

Opening lead: two of clubs.

East won the first trick with his club Ace, and considered carefully before mechanically returning the suit. He could see three sure tricks: a club, a club ruff, and the trump King. There would be no problem, whatever he returned, if partner had the Ace of diamonds (or perhaps the King-Queen of hearts). If declarer held the heart King and diamond Ace, the contract was probably unbeatable. The critical case seemed to be where partner held the *King* of hearts and declarer the Queen. Then an early heart play would be needed from *East* if the defenders were to establish their heart trick before declarer had time to draw trumps and discard his (assumed) heart loser on dummy's clubs.

Certain that he would regain the lead with the spade King before declarer could get all the trumps in, East shifted to the Jack of hearts at trick two. Declarer covered with his Queen, and West's King forced the Ace. Declarer played Ace and a trump hopefully, but East won the King, led a club for partner to ruff, and won the setting trick with his heart ten.

If East had given partner his club ruff prematurely, West would have been unable to lead hearts from his side, and the defenders would never have gotten a heart trick. Note the *assumption* that East made. *His play to trick two was immaterial except in one case,* and so he planned his defense accordingly. Of course, he had no idea that West's heart holding really was Kxx(x), but he assumed that it was, since if it was not, his play could not affect the outcome.

You should be getting the idea by now, so cover the West and South cards on the next deal if you wish, and figure out how East should defend.

Dlr: South
Vul: N-S

♠ Q96
♥ 65
♢ KQ4
♣ KQ1084

♠ K75
♥ QJ1072
♢ 1085
♣ J9

□

♠ 43
♥ A83
♢ AJ62
♣ 7653

♠ AJ1082
♥ K94
♢ 973
♣ A2

Bidding:	South	West	North	East
	1 ♠	Pass	2 ♣	Pass
	2 ♠	Pass	4 ♠	(All Pass)

West leads the Queen of hearts, and our first assumption is that you win the Ace as East.

If South has solid spades and the club Ace, this will quickly turn into a very dull hand. To have a chance for a set, you must place your partner with either a trump trick or the Ace of clubs. It is, however, too much to expect him to have *both* of these features—South did open the bidding, after all—so you will need two tricks from diamonds. To get them, you must find partner with the diamond ten and no more than three cards in the suit, or a doubleton diamond plus the Ax or Kxx of trumps, so that he can take a ruff. In either case, you return a low diamond.

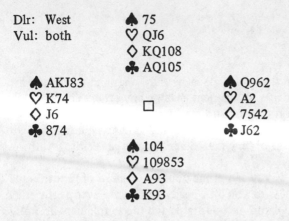

Dlr: West
Vul: both

North
♠ 75
♡ QJ6
◇ KQ108
♣ AQ105

West
♠ AKJ83
♡ K74
◇ J6
♣ 874

East
♠ Q962
♡ A2
◇ 7542
♣ J62

South
♠ 104
♡ 109853
◇ A93
♣ K93

West opened one spade and North doubled for takeout. East raised to two spades, and South's competitive three hearts ended the auction. This was a potentially correct decision in the bidding by E–W, since three spades is down off the top. However, they still had to beat three hearts.

West started with his two high spades, East following with the nine and deuce. East's encouraging spade signals made it unlikely he was interested in a club shift (with both the King and Jack), so West figured that he needed partner to hold an Ace to beat the contract. At trick three, he shifted to the Jack of diamonds. Declarer won in hand with the Ace and led a low heart. West carefully hopped up with his King and played his other diamond. When East won the trump Ace, he was able to give partner a diamond ruff for the fifth defensive trick.

If East had held the *diamond* Ace (instead of the heart Ace), he would have had to *duck* the first round of the suit, playing West for Jx of diamonds, to preserve communications for a later ruff.

Note, again, that West was an optimist. He assumed a lie of the cards that would produce a set, and defended as if things were really as he hoped.

□   □   □

AT THE TABLE

One

I'd be willing to wager that more mistakes, silly ones and otherwise, are made on the first board of a tournament than on any other. You wouldn't think bridge players need to warm up just like athletes, but they do. The ferocious concentration, attention to fine detail, and convoluted thought processes that are typical of the tournament expert are hard to turn on and off at will.

You're better off if you can prime your brain ahead of time in some way and get things in gear so you'll be ready to operate at top efficiency when the first board is placed on your table and the tournament abruptly gets started. In a team-of-four event, you and your teammates might play a deal or two while you are waiting for the first round to be called. At the least, you and your partner could talk over some of the more disastrous hands from your last session together, or straighten out an ambiguous point or two in your bidding system. Anything to get into the right state of mind to play bridge (and hopefully, to play *winning* bridge). Avoid, however, an intense discussion of the opposite sex, the stock market, or whether the Padres can repeat, unless you want to risk leaving your bridge game in the starting gate.

Playing in a Swiss Teams, you look at the first hand of your opening match. (This is an especially good time for a cold-engine error; the Swiss is held on the last day of a typical tournament and invariably starts at some ungodly hour, like 10:30 AM, to let the out-of-town players get an early start for home. So be extra alert.)

```
Dlr: West        ♠ 10876
Vul: N–S         ♡ KQ765
IMPs             ◇ A8
                 ♣ 94
    ♠ K3
    ♡ A102        □
    ◇ QJ104
    ♣ AQ83
```

Bidding:	South	West	North	East
		1NT	Pass	Pass
	2♣	Pass	3♠	(All Pass)

You, West, lead the Queen of diamonds. Declarer wins the King in his hand, as partner plays the deuce. At trick two, South pushes out the Jack of hearts. You take your Ace, and partner plays the nine. Plan your defense.

☐ ☐ ☐

This isn't a difficult problem if you count your tricks. You have a heart in the bag, there are no diamonds tricks for your side, and you will be able to take at most two clubs. So you simply need two tricks in trumps to beat it, and this will be impossible unless partner has the trump Ace. You should shift to the *three of spades*. The full deal is:

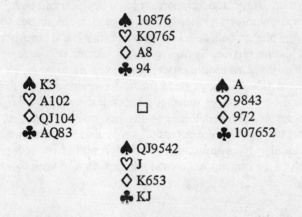

```
              ♠ 10876
              ♡ KQ765
              ◇ A8
              ♣ 94
♠ K3                        ♠ A
♡ A102                      ♡ 9843
◇ QJ104          ☐         ◇ 972
♣ AQ83                      ♣ 107652
              ♠ QJ9542
              ♡ J
              ◇ K653
              ♣ KJ
```

If you fail to put partner in right away for a club return, declarer will discard his clubs on dummy's hearts and make four instead of going down.

Hopefully, this is a mistake you avoided. Sometimes an error on the first board can be doubly costly; it can prey on your mind and cause fatal lapses in concentration for the entire balance of the session.

☐ ☐ ☐

Two

One of the most frequent questions social bridge players ask me is whether I take along a partner when I go to a big tournament, or find (or maybe get assigned) another single player when I get there. In fact, my partnership arrangements are usually made far in advance.

It is an obvious advantage to play in a partnership of long standing. The more you and your partner have discussed your bidding system and defensive carding agreements, the bigger edge you will have on your less-practiced competitors. (Some of the most successful pairs, like Peter Weichsel-Alan Sontag, probably spent *hundreds* of hours in discussion of their methods.) Also, you're clearly better off to play with somebody you know, like, and can get along with at the table. Bridge is an emotional game, and good partnership rapport will help you handle the inevitable bad result smoothly.

There are plenty of people, however, who do take off for a tournament without a partner. Every large tournament has a "partnership desk," where a staff of local volunteers earnestly tries to pair up the singles to best advantage. Bridge players being such as they are, this is a *lot* tougher job than running a dating service. Trying to match players of the same level of skill, who like the same bidding style, who have a similar temperament, and all of whom vehemently demand the best available partner for their own—well, you'd do best to get somebody lined up ahead of time!

Your regular partner pleaded illness at the last minute, and your teammates for a local team game were depending on you, so you borrowed a fifth person from another team and struck up an impromptu partnership. Unfamiliar partnerships do turn up occasional winners. One of your early hands is:

Dlr: West ♠ AK54
Vul: N–S   ♡ 5
IMPs   ◇ 873
     ♣ AQ1082

♠ 987
♡ Q10962   □
◇ A9
♣ 963

Bidding:	South	West	North	East
		Pass	1 ♣	Pass
	1 ♠	Pass	2 ♠	Pass
	2NT	Pass	4 ♠	(All Pass)

You, West, finger the Ace of diamonds for a moment, but finally settle on the ten of hearts. Partner puts up the King, and declarer's Ace wins. Declarer draws three rounds of trumps, East discarding a heart. When the club Jack is led and passed, partner produces the King and returns the four of diamonds, declarer playing the two. What should you do here?

☐ ☐ ☐

This hand is really too easy when presented as a problem on paper. If you want four fast tricks, you have no options. You must win the diamond *Ace* and return the nine, playing partner for KQxx. Perhaps the full deal is:

```
                    ♠ AK54
                    ♡ 5
                    ◇ 873
                    ♣ AQ1082
    ♠ 987                        ♠ 62
    ♡ Q10962           ☐        ♡ K864
    ◇ A9                         ◇ KQ104
    ♣ 963                        ♣ K74
                    ♠ QJ103
                    ♡ AJ3
                    ◇ J652
                    ♣ J5
```

Partner's good play of leading a low diamond (even though he had a sequence in the suit) was automatic, since he had to assume you had the diamond Ace.

If you won thriftily with the nine of diamonds and disappointed your new partner, you can bet that *he* might resort to the partnership desk next time.

☐ ☐ ☐

Three

It was a holiday, and since you were off from work, you took in the morning duplicate at your bridge club. About halfway through the session (almost time to get out your brown bag lunch), you get to apply what you know about making assumptions.

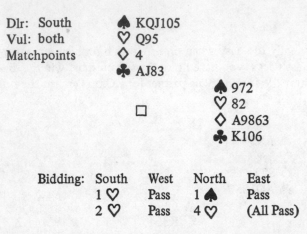

Dlr: South
Vul: both
Matchpoints

♠ KQJ105
♡ Q95
◇ 4
♣ AJ83

♠ 972
♡ 82
◇ A9863
♣ K106

Bidding:	South	West	North	East
	1 ♡	Pass	1 ♠	Pass
	2 ♡	Pass	4 ♡	(All Pass)

West, your partner, leads the two of diamonds to your Ace. What do you return?

□   □   □

Declarer is about the claim the rest if he has the Ace of spades and both top hearts, so you must hope partner has one of those cards. He can hardly be expected to have two of them, however, in addition to his marked diamond honor.* So it looks like you need two club tricks to beat this. Partner will have to hold the club Queen, and you certainly need to lead a club right now, before declarer can draw trumps and take club discards on dummy's spade suit. The full deal:

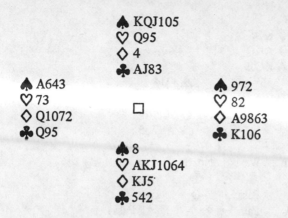

```
              ♠ KQJ105
              ♡ Q95
              ◇ 4
              ♣ AJ83
♠ A643                        ♠ 972
♡ 73            □            ♡ 82
◇ Q1072                       ◇ A9863
♣ Q95                         ♣ K106
              ♠ 8
              ♡ AKJ1064
              ◇ KJ5
              ♣ 542
```

* Possibly, declarer could have opened on: x, AJxxxx, KJx, Qxx. But he can always make his contract if he has that hand.

Four

When I teach bridge, a frequent problem I face is coping with a class that is poorly motivated to think and learn. Alas, bridge is not yet one of life's necessities. My students aren't taking bridge for college credit or as a requirement to land a better job. Basically, they're just out looking for a good time. My philosophy, that having fun at bridge is a product of putting out some effort to learn the game well, can meet with opposition. I often find myself wishing I were the imposing Professor Kingsfield of "The Paper Chase," able to intimidate his terrified law students into learning their lessons with the dreaded Socratic Method. I can still hear John Houseman intoning sternly, "We use the Socratic method here. I ahhsk a question, and you . . . (pause) . . . *answer*."

Well, if it's good enough for Socrates. . . . Look at this defensive problem and then I'll indulge my secret aspirations by trying the Socratic method out on you.

Dlr: North   ♠ 87
Vul: N–S   ♡ KQ6
IMPs   ♢ AKQ
             ♣ KQJ94

                      ♠ QJ4
                      ♡ 4
           □   ♢ 10876
                      ♣ A8765

Bidding:	South	West	North	East
			1 ♣	Pass
	1 ♡	Pass	2 ♢	Pass
	2 ♡	Pass	4 ♡	(All Pass)

West, your partner, leads the two of clubs. You play your Ace on dummy's King, and declarer follows. Plan the defense.

□   □   □

Answer each question before you peek at the answer. This is a classroom situation, remember. Use a piece of paper to cover the page.

Q. *How many tricks will it take to beat this contract?*
A. Four. Very good.

Q. *Can you give partner a club ruff?*
A. Sure. The real question is, should you do so immediately?

Q. *What are the crucial missing honors on this deal?*
A. The Ace and King of spades and the Ace of hearts.

Q. *If partner has any two of them, will the contract be defeated regardless of what you do?*
A. Yes. Say, for example, that partner has the Ace of hearts and the spade King. You can either give him his club ruff right away, after which the obvious spade shift will set up a trick that he can cash when he wins the trump Ace; or, you can shift to the spade Queen at trick two. He will put you back in with the spade Jack when he wins his trump trick and now you give him his ruff.

Q. *Suppose partner has only one of the three key cards. What then?*
A. It depends on which one he has.

Q. *Can we beat them if he has the heart Ace?*
A. You'd have to give partner his club ruff just to hold them to four.
Q. *What if he has the spade King?*
A. The best you can do is hold them to *five* with a club ruff.
Q. *Any hope if he has the spade Ace?*
A. Aha! We've finally found a situation where your defense is critical.
The full deal actually was:

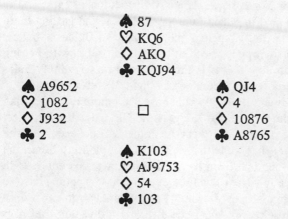

You must return the spade Queen if the defense is to get all its tricks. Give partner his ruff prematurely on this lie of the cards, and you'll never be in again to come through South's King of spades. Since the hand above is the only one declarer can have where your play makes any difference, assume that's what he has.

This piece of analysis may seem pretty involved to you. All I can do is reiterate my approach to bridge by paraphrasing Mr. Houseman in his television commercials: "Good bridge players get their good results the old-fashioned way—They *earn* them."

Five

In 1968 I was invited by Uncle Sam to visit beautiful South Korea as a two-year guest of the 8th U.S. Army. I was lucky, since it could have just as easily been Vietnam.

There was, in all of South Korea, just one bridge club. But it was a member of the Far East Bridge Association and faithfully sent a team to the Far East Championship every year. In 1968, in what I'm confident will be my only foray into international competition, I played for my adopted country in the Far Eastern championship! The "Korean" team that year could safely be called an unlikely aggregation. There were a Thai and a Yugoslav (both in Korea on business), an American who was a naturalized Korean citizen, an Air Force sergeant, an Army lieutenant, and I. The 1968 tournament was held in Kuala Lumpur, Malaysia, and getting there from Seoul was half the fun. I caught a military flight to Okinawa, bussed to another air base on the opposite end of that island, and flew to Penang Air Base in Thailand on an old C-141. From there, a taxi(!) ninety miles into Bangkok to the airport, and a commercial flight to Kuala Lumpur.

As for the tournament itself, it would have been more rewarding had I known something about how to play bridge. In 1968 I was a brash novice, and here I was pitted against the great Australian, Tim Seres, and the talented Formosan team that went to the World Championship Finals the next year. Somehow, our team finished fifth (of ten teams entered) in spite of me. Now, so many years later, I'd give every master point I have to relive those few days in Malaysia. It would be, at this stage, an experience I could appreciate a little more. And I could resolve a question that nags occasionally. Could the 1968 South Korean team have *won* the Far East Championship, earning a shot at the World Title(!), if I could have played with these sixteen years of experience behind me?

The hands from that tournament have almost all vanished. But I learned a couple of lessons that stayed in my memory. There was a deal something like this one:

```
Dlr: South        ♠ 964
Vul: N-S          ♡ KQJ5
IMPs              ◇ 9852
                  ♣ A10

   ♠ KJ82
   ♡ 10873          □
   ◇ AQ
   ♣ KJ5
```

Bidding:

	South	West	North	East
	1◇	Dbl.	Redbl.	Pass
	Pass	1♠	Pass	Pass
	1NT	Pass	2NT	(All Pass)

You, West, choose a passive heart lead, and have mixed emotions about it when you see dummy. (They bid 'em up in Hong Kong, hence North's raise.) Declarer wins the King on the table, partner playing the deuce. Next, he leads the nine of diamonds to the seven, three, and Queen. How should you proceed?

□   □   □

This is a matter of counting your tricks and defending on an assumption to get them. To beat 2NT, partner must have one of two features: either the Axx(x) of spades, which will let you take four spades and two diamonds; or five clubs to the Queen, in which case you take four *clubs* and two diamonds.

Which suit should you attack first? Clubs, obviously, since you will get another chance to switch to spades later. Your best play is the club Jack. If declarer ducks this around to his Queen, you try a spade when you win the diamond Ace. But if South plays dummy's club Ace and partner signals encouragement, your continuation will be King and another club.

The full deal is:

```
                  ♠ 964
                  ♡ KQJ5
                  ◇ 9852
                  ♣ A10
   ♠ KJ82                      ♠ Q107
   ♡ 10873          □          ♡ 962
   ◇ AQ                        ◇ 74
   ♣ KJ5                       ♣ Q9732
                  ♠ A53
                  ♡ A4
                  ◇ KJ1063
                  ♣ 864
```

It would not be good enough to switch to a spade first on this layout, as your count of tricks should have indicated (or, I dimly recall through the mists of time, as *my* count of tricks should have indicated).

□   □   □

Six

A National Open Pairs is usually a huge game. Sometimes over a thousand pairs are entered, and even after two qualifying sessions reduce the field by half, the event still seems like a lottery. To finish high in a field this large, you need lots of good results and you can't afford to miss any chances.

Dlr:
Vul:
Matchpoints

♠ AQ
♡ KQ95
◇ 1087
♣ KQJ4

□

♠ J987
♡ A6
◇ K9654
♣ A5

Bidding:	South	West	North	East
		Pass	1NT	Pass
	2♡	Pass	Pass	Dbl.
	Pass	2♠	3♡	(All Pass)

West, your partner, leads the Ace of diamonds. You signal your liking, and he continues with the two of diamonds to your King, declarer dropping the Jack and Queen. How do you proceed?

□   □   □

Since it appears you could have made three spades, for +140, it behooves you to get +200 against three hearts. There are four tricks in top cards, and despite declarer's attempt at deception, you can give partner a diamond ruff. (Even if partner had chosen to start a diamond from A32, his second lead would have been the *three*.) The crucial sixth trick will have to be a club ruff you take yourself. But partner's only entry to give you a club ruff must be the diamond ruff you give him, so you have to switch to clubs at trick three. Say you lead the five. You can win the first trump lead, cash your club Ace, let partner ruff a diamond, and hope to receive your club ruff. You'd like for the full deal to be:

```
              ♠ AQ
              ♡ KQ95
              ◇ 1087
              ♣ KQJ4
♠ K10654                    ♠ J987
♡ 87           □            ♡ A6
◇ A2                        ◇ K9654
♣ 9876                      ♣ A5
              ♠ 32
              ♡ J10432
              ◇ QJ3
              ♣ 1032
```

You'll need plenty of +200s in part-score situations to do well in this event.

chapter two

PART ONE: THE MOST IMPORTANT QUALITY

PRELIMINARIES

This chapter, like the first one, deals with basic ideas. First, I want us to look at some basic thought processes that should guide your defense of a *suit contract*. In particular, there is one Essential Principle of defensive play vs. suits that you must be able to understand and apply, else you will find yourself being greeted warmly by all prospective declarers who oppose you.

Let's start examining this Principle by looking at two very different hands.

One

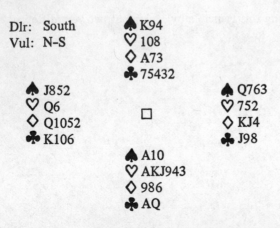

Dlr: East
Vul: both

♠ J93
♡ Q104
◇ KQJ94
♣ AJ

♠ 1054
♡ 85
◇ 8765
♣ Q952

♠ AKQ76
♡ A2
◇ 103
♣ K864

♠ 82
♡ KJ9763
◇ A2
♣ 1073

Bidding:

	South	West	North	East
				1 ♠
	2 ♡	Pass	4 ♡	(All Pass)

West led the four of spades in response to his partner's opening, and East was able to cash the Queen and King, West playing the five on the second round. Declarer ruffed the spade Ace continuation, and knocked out the Ace of trumps. Winning the trump return, he ran diamonds and threw two club losers away, making his contract.

Two

Dlr: South
Vul: N–S

♠ K94
♡ 108
◇ A73
♣ 75432

♠ J852
♡ Q6
◇ Q1052
♣ K106

♠ Q763
♡ 752
◇ KJ4
♣ J98

♠ A10
♡ AKJ943
◇ 986
♣ AQ

Bidding:

South	West	North	East
1♡	Pass	1NT	Pass
4♡	(All Pass)		

I don't care for South's four heart rebid. With his semi-balanced pattern and broken heart suit, perhaps 3NT would have been wiser. However, West led the two of diamonds against the heart game. Declarer ducked the first trick and won the diamond continuation. He ran the eight of hearts, losing to the Queen. After cashing the Queen of diamonds, West decided to break some new ground by leading a spade. Declarer played low from dummy, won East's Queen with his Ace, and ran the spade ten, setting up a discard for his Queen of clubs. Making four again.

Our declarers seem to do pretty well, don't they? Well, both of these contracts can be set easily, and they *would* have been set had the defenders operated under our Essential Principle. Let me quote you a passage from Marshall Miles' classic book, *How to Win at Duplicate Bridge*: "More important than any other quality of a defender is the ability to tell which tricks will vanish unless a vigorous effort is made to obtain them, and which tricks declarer is bound to lose eventually. A good defender must know when to be aggressive, attempting to establish or cash tricks, or when to be passive, waiting for them to fall into his lap while declarer does all the guesswork." Read this quote at least twice. On the first hand, dummy's strong diamonds furnish declarer with a rich and obvious source of tricks. It should have been apparent to East that the defense had to set up a club trick *early*, before declarer had time to draw trumps and use his diamonds. So a club return at trick three, hoping West could produce the Queen, was a move that had nothing to lose and much to gain.

Think about it in terms of our first chapter, on *assumption*. From East's point of view, if West has the Ace of diamonds or a trump trick, the contract is always down. If he holds neither, declarer surely has at least four heart tricks, five diamonds, and the club Ace. That's ten tricks. He'll make his bid *unless the defense is able to win four tricks first*. So East has no choice but to take a chance and lead a club. (For a similar situation, look again at the third problem hand in Chapter One.)

Now, what about the second hand? The crucial fact is that *once declarer won the diamond Ace, the dummy was left without a good source of tricks:* Only one high card (an almost certain trick, true, but just one—the defense could mentally shrug this off); no good suit declarer could set up; no possibility of ruffing tricks. Nothing much at all! Therefore, there was no hurry for West to lead spades. In fact, it was a grave error to do so. If declarer had spade losers, *there was no way he could avoid them.* West should have been interested in getting out of the lead as safely as possible (with his other trump) leaving declarer to struggle with his anemic dummy and lose his inevitable losers. (Yes, I see that West could have saved himself by leading the spade *Jack* instead of a low one.)

Try to contrast these two hands: the first one, on which it was vital for the defense to *set up a club trick before it was too late,* with the second hand, on which they were called upon to do nothing but *wait* patiently. On almost every hand you defend, you should think in these terms. You should have a . . . well, in deference to the computer-word processor on which I'm writing this book, I'll call it a *PROGRAM.*

□   □   □

IF THE DUMMY HAS A READY SOURCE OF TRICKS . . . for declarer, and it is clear that he has the tricks available to make his contract, *your PROGRAM is ACTIVE.* You go out looking for tricks of your own in a hurry. You lead away from Kings and Queens; you lay down or even underlead Aces; you get busy.

IF THE DUMMY IS FLAT AND WEAK . . . with little help for declarer, *your PROGRAM is PASSIVE.* This means "safety first." You might lead from a sequential holding. You could lead trumps, a suit in which your play probably won't give declarer anything that he can't make on his own anyhow. You could lead something that declarer will have to trump, spending one of his sure winners. Or, if declarer breaks a new suit and you win a trick there, leading the same suit right back to him may be safe. What you must *avoid* is taking risks. If you lead away from your Kings and Queens here, you may help declarer avoid a guess he has, give him a helpful free finesse, or generally eliminate some of his worries.

□   □   □

In an Active program, it may be necessary to get really desperate:

Dlr: South   ♠ 852
Vul: both   ♡ AJ4
              ◊ 74
              ♣ AKJ105

♠ AJ104   ♠ Q73
♡ 92   □   ♡ 86
◊ QJ1085   ◊ A962
♣ 73   ♣ 8764

              ♠ K96
              ♡ KQ10753
              ◊ K3
              ♣ Q2

After South's one heart opening, N–S reached four hearts with no problem. West led the diamond Queen to East's Ace. It was clear to shift to spades, and another time East would have led a low one. But with dummy's clubs a potent threat, he chose instead to return the spade *Queen*. As it happened, this was the only card to give E-W four tricks.

Again, contrast the next hand.

Dlr: South   ♠ 1053
Vul: E-W   ♡ AJ105
              ◊ A53
              ♣ J84

♠ Q84   ♠ K962
♡ 73   □   ♡ 98
◊ KQ108   ◊ 642
♣ A952   ♣ Q1073

              ♠ AJ7
              ♡ KQ642
              ◊ J97
              ♣ K6

Bidding:	South	West	North	East
	1 ♡	Pass	2 ♡	(All Pass)

This hand was dealt in a rubber bridge game. The vulnerability and the fact that he had only three spades induced West to sell out conservatively. At matchpoint duplicate, he would no doubt have balanced with a double.

He led the King of diamonds to dummy's Ace and East played the deuce. Declarer drew two rounds of trumps, and tried a club to his King. West won and *got out with a club* to East's Queen. A diamond return let West win his ten and Queen, and he led another club, forcing South to ruff. Declarer was then obliged to open up the spade suit, and he lost two tricks there, for down one. This was a perfect Passive program by West. After the first trick, dummy was virtually barren, so there was no need for him to do anything except try hard to give nothing away when he was obliged to lead.

(No doubt you realize that declarer's play left a lot to be desired. With so many potential problems, his aim should have been to *force* the defense to help him. For instance, he could have exited with a diamond after drawing trumps. After winning his two diamond tricks, West must play something to declarer's advantage.)

It may be a little less obvious to get Active when declarer's side-suit tricks are located in the *closed* hand instead of dummy.

Dlr: North
Vul: none

```
                    ♠ AK
                    ♡ 10964
                    ◇ 943
                    ♣ Q754
   ♠ 83                              ♠ 10542
   ♡ KQ5                             ♡ J
   ◇ K1062          □                ◇ Q875
   ♣ J1083                           ♣ AK92
                    ♠ QJ976
                    ♡ A8732
                    ◇ AJ
                    ♣ 6
```

Bidding:	South	West	North	East
			Pass	Pass
	1 ♠	Pass	1NT	Pass
	2 ♡	Pass	3♡	Pass
	4 ♡	(All Pass)		

Bold bidding by South. It looks like he fell in love with his fifth heart when the suit was raised. West led the club Jack and a second club was ruffed. Declarer tried Ace and another heart. West won, and carefully *shifted to a diamond without cashing his other trump*, setting up the fourth defensive trick. Had he defended passively, leading another club, declarer would have been a tempo ahead, with time to discard dummy's diamonds on his spades.

(Declarer misplayed again. He should have started on spades after cashing his trump Ace, conceding two heart tricks, but avoiding a diamond loser. To beat the hand legitimately, the defense must switch to diamonds at trick two.)

Reread this part of the chapter until you have the idea of Active vs. Passive defense firmly in mind. *Perhaps the most common error made on defense is failure to distinguish when the proper program should be applied.* In particular, my experience is that many players are reluctant to sit back and do nothing. They seem to think that some dynamic stroke is required of them on every hand. They snatch winners when a passive policy would serve them best. If you can resist the temptation to get active when there is no need, you begin to demonstrate some maturity as a bridge player.

There are, of course, a few other "programs" that may be appropriate in the defense of a suit contract. Here are three common ones.

If the look of dummy suggests that declarer will make extra tricks only by *ruffing* some of his losers, you may wish to *LEAD TRUMPS*.

```
Dlr: South        ♠ 8
Vul: none         ♡ K652
                  ◇ J8542
                  ♣ K87

♠ Q5                          ♠ K10962
♡ Q1087                       ♡ J9
◇ AK106     □                 ◇ Q97
♣ 964                         ♣ A32

                  ♠ AJ743
                  ♡ A43
                  ◇ 3
                  ♣ QJ105
```

Bidding:	South	West	North	East
	1 ♠	Pass	1NT	Pass
	2 ♣	(All Pass)		

West led the Ace of diamonds, which held the first trick. Dummy had no good side suit declarer could establish and little high card strength; but it did contain some club length and not many spades. So West shifted to trumps, and East played Ace and another. Declarer could make only three trumps in his hand, one ruff in dummy, and his three top cards in the majors, for down one. Note that West could place his partner with five spades on the bidding, so declarer was likely to have some spade losers, losers that he could *only* get rid of by ruffing them. Imagine for yourself how the play would go if West continued diamonds at trick two.

Another possible program is a *FORCING GAME*. In this approach, the defenders try to make declarer use up all of his trumps by making him ruff repeatedly, so that *control* of the hand passes to the defense.

When the defenders are concentrating strictly on damaging declarer's trump holding, the side suits may be disregarded. Look at this example, on which best defense requires giving declarer a *ruff-and-discard,* usually considered a heinous crime.

Dlr: South   ♠ J1096
Vul: N-S   ♡ KQ9
                ◊ A963
                ♣ 76

♠ A543   ♠ 2
♡ 105   ♡ 8762
◊ J5   □   ◊ 10872
♣ KQ1085   ♣ A942

                ♠ KQ87
                ♡ AJ43
                ◊ KQ4
                ♣ J3

Bidding:	South	West	North	East
	1NT	2♣	3♣	4♣
	4♠	(All Pass)		

When West climbed in with his overcall, North's three clubs was the Stayman convention. South guessed to bid the right major, and East, not knowing what his partner's spade holding might be, decided not to sacrifice in five clubs.

When West held the first two tricks with the King and Queen of clubs, he knew that declarer must have every outstanding face card, save the club Ace. Since there were no possible side-suit tricks for the defense, West continued with a third club. Declarer took the ruff in dummy and started trumps. But West ducked the first two trump leads, placing declarer in a dilemma. If a third trump was led, West would win and force the *closed hand* to ruff with a further club lead, gaining control. He would be able to win his long trump and a long club as well, for down two. The best declarer could do was abandon trumps in favor of cashing his red-suit winners, keeping control, but allowing West a ruff with his low trump, for down one.

The forcing game is most attractive when you have some unexpected length in trumps (perhaps as many as four cards, as West had above) or when you suspect that your partner may have length. This is an approach you must use with some caution, however. There will be times when declarer will look with favor on such a defense, because it will help him *scramble* in several tricks with his small trumps that he would not be able to take without your help.

Note this well: The purpose of a forcing game is to make it impossible for declarer to draw trumps and safely cash his side-suit tricks. If your side may have a strong trump holding, be wary of letting declarer score several tricks with his small trumps, especially if his side tricks are in *top* cards (which can be cashed whether trumps are drawn or not), and not long cards or intermediates.

The last "program" we will discuss here also involves tricks in the trump suit. Somehow, there seems to be a psychological barrier to taking tricks in the suit the declaring side has staked out as its own. Nevertheless, the trump suit may be the only suit in which the defense can hope to accomplish anything.

There are two possibilities. In a *TRUMP PROMOTION*, declarer is placed in a position in which he must either ruff low and be overruffed, or ruff high at the cost of strengthening a defender's trump holding. Here is an example:

```
Dlr: North          ♠ K53
Vul: none           ♡ 32
                    ◇ AK65
                    ♣ A432
♠ 92                              ♠ AQJ764
♡ Q874          □                ♡ 9
◇ J432                           ◇ 1098
♣ J97                            ♣ Q108
                    ♠ 108
                    ♡ AKJ1065
                    ◇ Q7
                    ♣ K65
```

Bidding:	South	West	North	East
			1 ◇	1 ♠
	2 ♡	Pass	2NT	Pass
	4 ♡	(All Pass)		

West led the nine of spades, and three rounds of the suit put South in the middle. Ruffing low would have been immediately fatal, so he ruffed with the trump Jack. But West discarded a diamond, and his Q874 of hearts turned out to be worth *two* tricks when East turned up with the trump nine.

Refusal to overruff with a natural trump winner is a common technique in playing for a trump promotion. Notice that if West had overruffed the Jack with his Queen, the effect would have been the same as if declarer had merely taken a finesse to his Jack; and the defense would gain nothing.

A similar idea is known picturesquely as the UPPERCUT.* In this situation, a defender ruffs in with a significant trump intermediate, so that declarer must weaken his trump holding if he overruffs. Say the trump suit is:

```
                    ♠ 84
♠ 1093          □                ♠ Q2
                    ♠ AKJ765
```

West leads a club, in which both East and South are void. If East trumps with the spade Queen and South overtrumps, West's 1093 will suddenly be worth a trick.

We have looked briefly at some general ways you may conduct your defense against a suit contract. Most of the defenses you play will fall into one of the programs we discussed (or perhaps consist of two or more of them combined). One point bears still more repetition: The key question on most hands is whether you must launch an Active program or whether you can afford to go Passive. In Chapter Five, we will look once more at how you might determine which of these two programs is correct.

*It is common practice, if not at all accurate, to use the terms "trump promotion" and "uppercut" interchangeably. In fact, the first situation above shows a trump promotion while the second one illustrates an uppercut.

AT THE TABLE

One

You arrived at the club in the mood for rubber bridge with set partners, but there were not four but six interested players on the premises, so courtesy demanded a cut-around game of Chicago, with four people in the game at a time. Many people nowadays would rather play Chicago anyway. To tell the truth, I can't remember the last time I played in a rubber bridge game! Chicago scoring is based on matchpoint scoring, with every deal a separate entity. Most players are familiar with it, and its simplicity is appealing. You don't have to worry about forgetting you have a leg up (embarrassing!), nor must you distort your bidding to cater to a part score. That's one aspect of rubber bridge I always hated. There are enough pitfalls in the bidding, it seems to me, without a whole new set of rules for a 40-partial, a 60-partial, and so forth. I used to see many rubber bridge disasters, like passed jump shifts resulting in slams played below game, because of the subtle intracacies of part-score bidding. Maybe a lot of other people feel the same way, judging from the popularity of Chicago.

Anyway, when your turn to play comes, you have this problem to cope with:

Dlr: North
Vul: N-S

♠ 842
♡ KJ3
◇ 8753
♣ K103

♠ AK103
♡ 76
◇ KQ106
♣ 986

Bidding:

	South	West	North	East
			Pass	Pass
	1 ♡	Dbl.	2 ♡	Pass
	3 ♣	Pass	4 ♡	(All Pass)

You, West, lead the Ace of spades (suggesting the King as well): two, five, seven. Next, you try the King of diamonds. This time partner plays the nine and declarer the two. What do you do now?

□   □   □

Look at dummy. It's flat and weak. Declarer wasn't strong enough to jump to four hearts directly; he had to settle for a game try. Clearly, this is a borderline game, and no doubt you should defend as passively as possible.

When the hand was actually played, West continued routinely with a diamond, which forced declarer to ruff. This looked safe enough at the time, but the full deal was:

♠ 842
♡ KJ3
◇ 8753
♣ K103

♠ AK103   ♠ J95
♡ 76   ♡ 852
◇ KQ106   □   ◇ AJ94
♣ 986   ♣ 752

♠ Q76
♡ AQ1094
◇ 2
♣ AQJ4

After ruffing, declarer continued with a club to the ten and ruffed another diamond. He went back to the club King for another diamond ruff. He then played the trump Ace, overtook the Queen, and drew the last trump with dummy's Jack. Two more high clubs brought his trick total up to ten. He made four clubs, three high trumps, and three diamond ruffs in his hand.

The *super* safe exit of a trump (or even a club) at trick three would have been a killer. Declarer is an entry short of pulling off the dummy reversal without help, and he'd have to lose three spades in the end, for down one. (Try it.)

I guess this is an appropriate hand for 1984. It might be said that all passive exits are equal, but some of them are more equal (and effective) than others.

◻   ◻   ◻

Two

I find physically imposing opponents intimidating at the table. Not some nice-looking wench with a 40-inch bustline. I mean the gruff-looking hulk of a man who must surely weigh upwards of 235 and looks fit enough to play a full quarter against the Redskins or Raiders despite his bulk. People like that invariably get the better of me because their burly physical presence upsets my concentration. Silly, isn't it, to yield to such an irrational feeling at a strictly mental game?

We have a guy like this, John Sledge, nicknamed Big John, at our club. Although John must be nearing forty, and a tinge of gray has crept in around his temples, most of him is still muscle. He often wears a sleeveless shirt, and with his tanned and sinewy arms exposed, you can get the idea you're sitting down to play bridge against Doc Savage. Nobody seems to know much about John's background, although there are rumors connecting him to everything from the CIA to the NHL. My guess is that he was an African mercenary, and spent most of his pre-bridge days dashing into enemy guerilla camps with a Thompson submachinegun under one arm and a belt of ammunition draped over the other.

Big John, as you might expect, loves to overbid. He enters the auction at the drop of a hat, and accepts all game invitations. And he gets away with it. Quite often, the defenders find a way to let him make his pushy contracts, because they are too happy to take a trick, *any* trick, against John.

Here's an example from not very long ago. Defend it yourself.

Dlr: South
Vul: E-W
IMPs

♠ 3
♡ AJ53
◇ A8753
♣ 974

♠ AJ1094
♡ 987
◇ QJ9
♣ 82

	Big John			You
Bidding:	South	West	North	East
	1 ♣	Pass	1 ♡	Pass
	2 ♠	Pass	2NT	Pass
	3 ♠	Pass	6 ♣	(All Pass)

North likes the way John plays 'em, hence the leap to slam. West, your partner, leads the King of hearts, won by the Ace. At trick two, declarer calls for dummy's spade. What do you return?

☐   ☐   ☐

The full deal was:

♠ 3
♡ AJ53
◇ A8753
♣ 974

♠ 65
♡ KQ1064
◇ 1042
♣ J103

♠ AJ1094
♡ 987
◇ QJ9
♣ 82

♠ KQ872
♡ 2
◇ K6
♣ AKQ65

When the hand really came up, the terrified lady in East flew with the spade Ace and returned a heart. Big John then played accurately to produce the twelfth trick on a *double squeeze*. He ruffed the heart, ruffed a spade, and cashed all his black-suit winners. As he laid down his last trump, the position was:

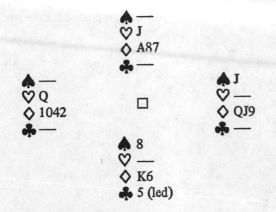

```
                    ♠ —
                    ♡ J
                    ◇ A87
                    ♣ —
♠ —                                 ♠ J
♡ Q                                 ♡ —
◇ 1042          □                   ◇ QJ9
♣ —                                 ♣ —
                    ♠ 8
                    ♡ —
                    ◇ K6
                    ♣ 5 (led)
```

West had to save the heart Queen, so she threw a diamond. John then discarded dummy's heart Jack. East had to keep the spade Jack, since South's eight was a threat, so *she* let a diamond go. Dummy's eight of diamonds won trick thirteen!

Of course, you saw through the hoax of this problem. *You didn't return anything*, because you passively *ducked* the spade lead from dummy! There is no big hurry to win your spade Ace; declarer can't ruff *all* his spades, and you are bound to get your Ace eventually. If you duck, declarer will score one of his high spades, but you won't set up *both* of them for him. And he won't be able to recover the difference by ruffing an extra spade in dummy, since West can overruff twice. The result will be down one.

The lesson is, when you're defending a pushy contract, don't panic. Play bridge. A passive defense will often work well when declarer has no extra values to work with. Even if your strapping opponent glares at you menacingly, remember: the bigger they come . . .

□   □   □

Three

This is a hand from the semi-finals of the 1983 Grand National Teams, an event that starts with nationwide eliminations at the grassroots level. Eight teams survive to play off at the Summer National tournament. The West player here was Peter Pender, a member of the San Francisco squad that captured the title in 1982 and 1983. See if you can duplicate his excellent defense.

Dlr: East
Vul: none
IMPs

```
              ♠ 973
              ♡ KJ532
              ◇ 4
              ♣ J942
♠ KJ
♡ Q84          □
◇ AQ6
♣ AKQ105
```

Bidding:	Hamman South	Pender West	Wolff North	Ross East
				Pass
	1♠	Dbl.	Pass	2♡
	2♠	3♣	Pass	4♣
	4♡	Dbl.	4♠	Pass
	Pass	Dbl.	(All Pass)	

Pender, West, led the King of clubs against South's four spades doubled, and all followed low. What did he play to trick two?

□   □   □

Pender knew that his partner had one good card for the raise to four clubs; but if East held the heart Ace, and declarer's four heart cue-bid was based on a heart void (and a really freakish 7-0-5-1 pattern), the contract was probably unbeatable. Finally, Pender put down the *Jack of spades*. And East proved to be a very good partner indeed. The full deal was:

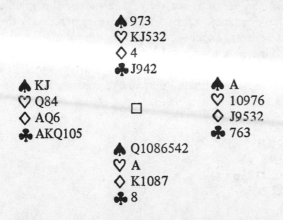

```
                    ♠ 973
                    ♡ KJ532
                    ◇ 4
                    ♣ J942
♠ KJ                                ♠ A
♡ Q84              □               ♡ 10976
◇ AQ6                               ◇ J9532
♣ AKQ105                            ♣ 763
                    ♠ Q1086542
                    ♡ A
                    ◇ K1087
                    ♣ 8
```

Pender's reasoning was sound. He figured that, even if his spade play lost a trump trick, he would at worst break even by stopping some diamond ruffs in dummy. As it was, E–W were able to clear two rounds of trumps, leaving declarer with a second diamond loser, for down two. When the board was replayed, four spades doubled was reached again, but this time West continued clubs at trick two, and declarer was able to get out for one down. Five IMPs to San Francisco.

It helps to be single-minded at bridge. If you are sure your best program is to lead trumps, the chance that your play might give up a trick in the trump suit should not necessarily discourage you.

□ □ □

Four

Most professional baseball players would tell you they feel more pressure in the League Championship Series than the World Series. If they reach the World Series, they are assured of substantial recognition and a fat paycheck, win or lose. For many players, it is a career highlight just to compete for all the marbles.

Bridge players might say roughly the same thing about an event like the Grand National Pairs. This is another event with local, sectional, and regional qualifying, and the tension can weigh heaviest in the middle stages, where only a couple of pairs (out of a big field) may qualify for the national Finals, and there is an expense-paid trip to the tournament up for grabs. (In 1983, this meant a few free days in Hawaii.) However, once you get to the Finals, you can relax and enjoy it.

Playing in the GNP Regional finals, you feel like you may be in contention.

Dlr: North   ♠ K107
Vul: both   ♡ 95
Matchpoints   ◇ QJ1086
           ♣ Q105

                       ♠ 85
             □   ♡ AJ8642
                       ◇ K7
                       ♣ K93

Bidding: South   West   North   East
                               Pass   1 ♡
          4 ♠   (All Pass)

West, your partner, leads the two of hearts, and declarer's King falls under your Ace. How do you proceed?

If partner has the Axx of diamonds, you can beat them with a diamond ruff; but this is assuming a very specific lie of the cards. If you lead the diamond King and find declarer with the Ace, he will probably make the rest of the tricks, giving you a matchpoint bottom. (Declarer certainly has at least one side Ace in addition to his solid spades. With two Aces, partner would have doubled four spades.)

A better shot is to get busy in clubs. Partner might have the club Ace, of course, but even the Jack could be good enough. The full deal:

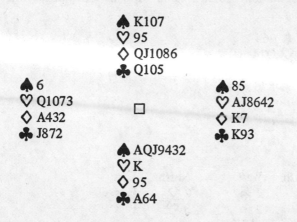

♠ K107
♥ 95
♦ QJ1086
♣ Q105

♠ 6
♥ Q1073
♦ A432
♣ J872

♠ 85
♥ AJ8642
♦ K7
♣ K93

♠ AQJ9432
♥ K
♦ 95
♣ A64

On your low club lead, declarer ducked and partner's seven forced the ten. Declarer drew trumps and led a diamond. Partner jumped up with the diamond Ace and returned a club. Your nine forced declarer's Ace, and you were able to cash the club King for the setting trick when you won the King of diamonds.

When you play an Active defense, you're willing to lead away from Kings, right? Sometimes even if you can see the Queen in dummy!

□ □ □

Five

When I teach a bridge class, there are certain attendance figures I look forward to seeing. Multiples of four are best of all—full tables and no stragglers. One extra person isn't bad—he can kibitz a deal or two and then take somebody's place for a while. Two extras is a problem. And three is worst of all—that's when I have to draft myself to make up a full table.

Filling in with three of your pupils in an advanced class, you find yourself thrust into the crucial seat. This would be a bad time to have an "accident." Your reputation couldn't stand it. Can you practice what you've been preaching?

Dlr: South
Vul: none

	♠ 964
	♡ Q74
	◊ KQ96
	♣ KJ3

♠ AKQ872
♡ J93   □
◊ A5
♣ 104

Bidding:

South	West	North	East
1 ♡	1 ♠	2 ◊	Pass
2 ♡	2 ♠	3 ♡	Pass
4 ♡	(All Pass)		

Sitting West, you cash your Ace and Queen of spades. Partner high-lows to show his doubleton, and declarer drops the ten and Jack. Where do you go from here?

□   □   □

The dummy is quite strong, and there will be no more side tricks except the diamond Ace. So the setting trick will have to come in trumps. If you can just find partner with as much as the heart *ten*, you can do it. *Cash your Ace of diamonds* and lead a *low* spade. All is well, because the full deal is:

	♠ 964	
	♡ Q74	
	◊ KQ96	
	♣ KJ3	
♠ AKQ872		♠ 53
♡ J93	□	♡ 10
◊ A5		◊ Jł08743
♣ 104		♣ 8752
	♠ J10	
	♡ AK8652	
	◊ 2	
	♣ AQ96	

Declarer has to overruff partner with one of his high trumps and must lose a trump trick to your J93.

There are two points here. First, you led a *low* spade, *forcing* partner to ruff. No doubt he should put in his ten of trumps even if you lead your high spade King, but who knows, he may be sleepy today. Also, it was essential to cash your diamond Ace *early*. If you did not, declarer could discard his singleton diamond on the third spade, as a loser-on-loser play, instead of overruffing partner at the cost of a trump trick. This is a cardinal principle of trump promotions and uppercuts: The defense prefers to *cash their side suit winners* before they try to promote their trump holding, else declarer may be able to counter by discarding a loser instead of weakening his trumps.

Here's hoping your students are now beaming at you with pride.

Six

Many years ago, I had a partnership (I really did) with a fellow named, aptly enough for a bridge player, Steve Diamond. We always got along fine, though I secretly wished I could see him harness up with another friend of mine, Dave Hart. I figured if they could enlist Sam Spade and then locate a guy named Joe Club, they'd have a—well, a suitable team-of-four.

In my seventeen years of tournament bridge, I've seen it all, or most of it, anyway. I once played a team match against Bernstein, Feldstein, Silverstein, and Goldstein. Silverstein and Goldstein played together. I've opposed Black-White, Long-Short, Knight-Day, and even Nixon-Ford. There was a piscatorial tandem of Salmon-Troutman, who told me they got along swimmingly at the table (I doubt they'd ever get a good result from Dr. John Fisher of Dallas); the agricultural pair of Corn-Cobb; and a guy named Will Rogers, who probably never met a hand he didn't like.

I knew a Mrs. Passmore, whose overcalls were legendary for their soundness, and I occasionally played against a man named Bidwell, who was noted for his remorseless accuracy in the auction. In college, there was a professor at the bridge club who justified his name, Ponder, by searching the depths of his soul for what seemed an eternity before he made a move.

Getting down to basics, I've played against Paul Deal, Jeff Hand, and various and sundry Cards and Sessions. There have been some Singletons, but no Doubletons; a Majors, but no Minors; Wests and Norths, but not any Souths or Easts that I can recall; a Grand (but no Small); and a deckfull of Kings, one or two Queens, and even a few players named Ace somebody-or-other.

A fellow named Don Stack, out of Kansas City, complains that his trumps always break 5–0, Georgian Wayne Counts usually remembers to do just that, and when I sat down against GNP champ Ivan Scope of San Francisco, he confided to me that he uses Listermint. One of Canada's fine women players is Joan Eaton. I always thought she should be paired up with another lady named Moth. Wouldn't that be great? A Moth-Eaton partnership!

I suppose I'll never see the diminutive expert Bobby Nail and fictional detective Mike Hammer in harness; but surely there's a way to get Texan Charlie Weed and British champion Nicola Gardener together. I'm betting they'd really dig each other, especially if Oregon's Ross Rainwater would lend assistance as a coach.

And, I've even met up with a few just plain Smiths and Joneses.

Playing in a Sectional Non-Mixed Pairs, you are up against two ancient ladies, perversely named Masters and Johnson.

```
Dlr:  North          ♠ J4
Vul:  none           ♡ 10853
Matchpoints          ◇ KQ10
                     ♣ 8542
                                 ♠ KQ98
                     □           ♡ J72
                                 ◇ A953
                                 ♣ K10
```

Bidding:	South	West	North	East
			Pass	1◇
	1♡	Dbl.*	2♡	2♠
	4♡	(All Pass)		

*A "negative" double, which conventionally suggests length in the unbid suits.

West, your partner, leads the Ace and deuce of spades to your Queen. Your play to trick three?

This is one of those occasional deals that you can't pigeonhole into a generalized program. The full deal is:

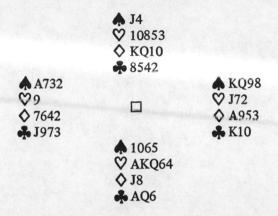

```
                    ♠ J4
                    ♡ 10853
                    ◇ KQ10
                    ♣ 8542
♠ A732                              ♠ KQ98
♡ 9                                 ♡ J72
◇ 7642          □                   ◇ A953
♣ J973                              ♣ K10
                    ♠ 1065
                    ♡ AKQ64
                    ◇ J8
                    ♣ AQ6
```

The only winning defense is to continue with the *spade King*, forcing declarer to take his spade ruff, which is his entry to dummy's third diamond, prematurely. You can hold up the diamond Ace once, and declarer will have to concede a club in the end, deprived of his vital diamond discard.*

Come to think of it, I guess this is really a kind of passive defense. But the idea of depriving declarer of one or more of his tricks as a defensive program is more often seen in the defense against notrump, which we will discuss next.

*The contract can still be made double-dummy.

PART TWO:
FOURTH-BEST
AND BEYOND

PRELIMINARIES

Chapter Two is twice as long as any of the others. But we are more than halfway through at this point, since the defenders have fewer options in their approach to the defense of a *notrump* contract. The absence of a trump suit eliminates some possible sources of tricks. There are really only three *PROGRAMS* (to stick to our same terminology) that may be considered, and we will look at each of them in turn.

You are no doubt familiar with the most common program, the *ACTIVE* attempt to establish *long cards*. Since the balance of the *high* cards is invariably held by the declaring side, this will usually be the defenders' best hope of tricks. They will therefore pound away at their longest suit at every opportunity, and they won't be tempted to switch to some other suit in the middle of the play unless there is a compelling reason to switch. Notrump defense can often boil down to a race between declarer and the defense, won by the side that gets its tricks established first. It's hard to win a race if you must start over after running the first lap.

The defense gets to make the opening lead, a head start in the race. But, as against that, they have some potential problems to worry about. The biggest one is this: *Even if the defense can get some long cards established, the hand that has them must be able to gain the lead.* Considering their inevitable shortness of high cards, the defenders may find entries as scarce as hens' teeth, and they must often *take care to preserve* an entry to the hand with some winners or potential winners.

Let's look at a hand or two that illustrate this important idea.

```
Dlr: South        ♠ Q1063
Vul: N–S          ♡ J6
                  ◇ 10863
                  ♣ KQ4
   ♠ A84                        ♠ 972
   ♡ K9852                      ♡ 1073
   ◇ J5          □             ◇ A42
   ♣ 952                        ♣ J1073
                  ♠ KJ5
                  ♡ AQ4
                  ◇ KQ97
                  ♣ A86
```

Bidding:	South	West	North	East
	1 ◇	Pass	1 ♠	Pass
	2NT	Pass	3NT	(All Pass)

West leads a heart. Declarer puts up dummy's Jack, which holds, and leads a low diamond. East should forget about "second-hand low" and dash up with his Ace to return partner's suit. The idea is that East should be happy to spend his entry early, hoping to establish the hearts while West retains *his* (hoped for) entry. On this deal, if declarer can steal an early diamond trick, he will shift over and knock out the spade Ace, for nine tricks. But note the outcome if East defends correctly.

Of course, East's play would also be necessary if his partner had AQxxx of hearts, and declarer needed a diamond for his ninth trick. On the hand above, substitute the AKx of spades and Kxx of hearts in South.

```
Dlr: South        ♠ 853
Vul: E-W          ♡ A5
                  ◇ K1095
                  ♣ A842
♠ J96                             ♠ Q102
♡ Q10873              □           ♡ J94
◇ A83                             ◇ J74
♣ 96                             ♣ J1073
                  ♠ AK74
                  ♡ K62
                  ◇ Q62
                  ♣ KQ5
```

N-S reached 3NT, and West led the seven of hearts. Declarer allowed East's Jack to hold the first trick, and won dummy's Ace on the next round. He led a diamond to his Queen, and West *ducked smoothly*, keeping in mind the principle of retaining his entry. This worked well, since declarer not unnaturally continued with another diamond, finessing dummy's ten. East won and returned his last heart, establishing West's suit while he still had the Ace of diamonds.

Of course, declarer could have had the diamond Jack as well as the Queen, in which case he would dislodge West's entry regardless; but West's duck could hardly cost him anything. As it was, if he had taken the diamond Ace immediately, declarer would have won the third heart lead and set up his ninth trick by ducking a second diamond safely to East.

The problems of getting a suit set up and cashed often force the defenders to worry about the *communication* between their two hands. Here is a simple example of how they may overcome problems of communication.

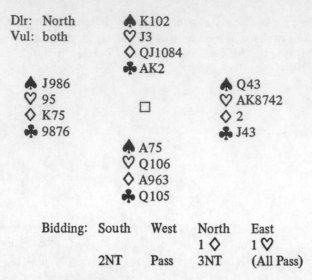

Dlr: North
Vul: both

♠ K102
♥ J3
◇ QJ1084
♣ AK2

♠ J986
♥ 95
◇ K75
♣ 9876

□

♠ Q43
♥ AK8742
◇ 2
♣ J43

♠ A75
♥ Q106
◇ A963
♣ Q105

Bidding:

	South	West	North	East
			1 ◇	1 ♥
	2NT	Pass	3NT	(All Pass)

West led the nine of hearts, and since East lacked a fast entry outside his suit, he played his *eight* to the first trick, letting declarer win his sure heart trick immediately. Declarer couldn't help losing a trick to the King of diamonds, and West then led his other heart, allowing East to run the rest of the suit, for down two.

Dlr: South
Vul: N-S

♠ 10
♥ K432
◇ Q64
♣ AQ1075

♠ Q9842
♥ 108
◇ J95
♣ 962

□

♠ AJ6
♥ Q975
◇ 10872
♣ K3

♠ K753
♥ AJ6
◇ AK3
♣ J84

South opened 1NT. North used Stayman and consigned the hand to 3NT when South responded in spades. West led a spade nevertheless. East took the Ace and returned the Jack. South ducked this and won the third spade.

He took a losing club finesse, and claimed the rest when East had no spade left to return.

This was weak defense by East. When he's looking at 10 HCP, declarer is much more likely to have the King of spades than the Queen. Say East plays his spade *Jack* at trick one. Declarer must win this—for all he knows, West could have AQ9xx of spades and the King of clubs, and ducking would lose a cold contract. Now when East wins the club King, he can continue with Ace and six of spades, and the whole suit will run.

The third-hand play of the spade Jack, which at worst might cost an undertrick here, prevents declarer from holding up his hypothetical King of spades. (This is an extension of the well-known play of the *Queen from AQx* by third hand, made for the same purpose.)

A *PASSIVE* program against notrump is relatively uncommon, but you can usually tell when such an approach is right. The circumstances will be the same as when you prefer a passive defense vs. a suit contract; that is, the dummy will be weak, and it will look as though declarer has no ready source of tricks and will have his work cut out. If you think the play will be a struggle for declarer, with every trick dearly bought, you may do best to try to exit *safely* each time you find yourself on lead, figuring that declarer may sooner or later run out of winners, especially if given no help by the defense.

In an active program, you must often give away a trick or two in the process of establishing your long suit. This may be a necessary and acceptable evil under some circumstances. But if declarer is starving for winners, the trick you give him could be the crucial one he needs (and can't get without a little assistance).

Consider this situation:

<pre>
              ♠ A94
              ♡ 975
              ◇ 10753
              ♣ K105
  ♠ Q85
  ♡ K10642   □
  ◇ Q6
  ♣ Q63
</pre>

South opened 1NT and all passed. You, West, led the four of hearts, and partner's eight lost to the Jack. Declarer then played a spade to the Ace and a spade back, finessing his Jack and losing to your Queen. This is in a match-point duplicate game, so overtricks are important. What would you do?

Probably, you should prefer to get out safely with your last spade. If you shift to either minor suit, you might give a trick away. For instance, a club play might find declarer with A9x. Now that dummy is almost out of values, you can afford to *wait* for your tricks, letting declarer lead from his hand, break new suits, guess his way along, and struggle with his weak dummy.

(In the next chapter, on opening leads, we will discuss the possibility of a passive program against notrump a little further.)

In winding up Part One of this chapter, we said that the idea of *making some of declarer's tricks inaccessible to him* is most often applied in notrump defense. Sometimes, you will see that if you can just *DEPRIVE DECLARER OF HIS BEST SOURCE OF TRICKS*, the contract will surely fail. So your emphasis can shift to an attack on declarer's entries or ruining his communication with dummy.

```
Dlr:  South        ♠ 84
Vul:  N–S          ♡ J64
                   ◇ KQ10943
                   ♣ A2

♠ Q7653                    ♠ 1092
♡ AQ          □            ♡ 10853
◇ 86                       ◇ AJ2
♣ 10954                    ♣ J86

                   ♠ AKJ
                   ♡ K972
                   ◇ 75
                   ♣ KQ73
```

In a rubber bridge game, South opened 1NT in the modern style, ignoring his weak doubleton. North leaped to 3NT, relying on his diamond suit. The opening lead was a spade, riding to the Jack. South led a diamond to the King, and East made the key play of *ducking*. The effect of this was that East remained with *two* diamond stoppers while South now had only *one* entry to dummy, and it was impossible for him to set up the diamonds. He returned to hand with a spade and tried another diamond, after which he had to guess well to go down just one.**

(**Incidentally, did you think declarer's line of play was OK? Decide if you would have played differently, and I'll let you know in a little while what I think.)

If East had taken the *first* diamond to return a spade, declarer would win and lead his other diamond to dummy's ten, setting up the suit with the club Ace as an entry. East's actual defense was based on the premise that, if declarer were unable to use his diamonds, he would surely find nine tricks impossible.

```
Dlr:  South        ♠ 94
Vul:  none         ♡ A4
                   ◇ QJ10874
                   ♣ 763
  ♠ J63                          ♠ Q10872
  ♡ 9873                         ♡ K106
  ◇ 6           □               ◇ A53
  ♣ QJ1084                       ♣ K9
                   ♠ AK5
                   ♡ QJ52
                   ◇ K92
                   ♣ A52
```

Bidding:	South	West	North	East
1NT	Pass	3◇ *	Pass
3NT	(All Pass)		

*By agreement, *invitational* to 3NT, if partner holds a fair hand and a good diamond fit.

West led the club Queen. East overtook with the King, and declarer was forced to duck. East knew that he could establish partner's suit with a club continuation; however, the bidding marked West with at most a Queen outside his club suit; therefore, no quick entry. So East decided to make his program killing *dummy's* suit instead. He switched to the *King of hearts*, removing the heart Ace as an entry to the diamonds. Subsequently, he held up the diamond Ace twice. Declarer never enjoyed his long diamonds and was held to two spades, three hearts, two diamonds, and one club, for down one.

(Oh, yes. Declarer's play on the previous hand. His first lead should have been a low diamond to the *ten*. Even if East can win the Jack, declarer will be able to lead his other diamond to knock out the Ace and set up the suit. More power to any East who can smoothly refuse the first diamond with AJx or Jx, perhaps setting the contract anyway.)

□   □   □

AT THE TABLE

One

One of the oldest strategies in bridge is the "psychic," a bid made on non-existent values, and intended as a bluff or a deception. Weak opponents may be intimidated by a "psych" and miss an easy game, and even an experienced pair might lose their way in the confusion once in a while.

There are several situations in which psychics may be employed, but in every case you run the same obvious risk: It may be your *partner* you fool. If you gaily open the bidding with QJxxx of spades and no other values, you might or might not talk the opponents out of a cold game, but if you happen to hit your *partner* with a good hand, you will surely get trampled in his rush to the five or six level. Some players rationalize this problem away, contending that the odds for success are favorable since there are two opponents at the table to fool and only one partner. Nevertheless, most of today's best-known experts are too partnership-oriented to psych frequently. A psychic, even if successful, can inevitably begin to erode a partnership's trust and confidence. Another drawback is that psychics can induce an unhealthy climate at the table. After your partner has seen you fool around a few times, he will know in what situations you are most likely to psych, and he'll always be on his toes for the possibility. This will give your pair a dishonest edge on your competition. In tournament bridge, where we adhere to a strict code of ethics, a good result "earned" because a player miraculously fielded a psychic by his partner is disallowed.

Of course, some psychs are more apt to turn the deal into a circus than others.

Dlr: South	♠ A6
Vul: none	♡ Q8763
IMPs	◇ 742
	♣ AQJ

		♠ J93
		♡ KJ105
□		◇ KJ5
		♣ 1087

Bidding:
	South	West	North	East
	1 ♣	Pass	1 ♡	Pass
	1NT	Pass	3NT	(All Pass)

West, your partner, leads the seven of spades. Dummy ducks, your Jack wins the trick, and declarer plays the two. You return a spade: five, four, Ace. At trick three, declarer leads a low diamond from dummy. Plan your defense.

□   □   □

The correct play (whether it works this time or not) is to put up the diamond *King*, hoping it will hold. The full deal, in fact, is:

                    ♠ A6
                    ♡ Q8763
                    ◇ 742
                    ♣ AQJ
    ♠ Q10874   ♠ J93
    ♡ 42   □   ♡ KJ105
    ◇ A3   ◇ KJ5
    ♣ 9643   ♣ 1087
                    ♠ K52
                    ♡ A9
                    ◇ Q10986
                    ♣ K52

This is a not-so-obvious case of *preserving partner's entry*. You hope he has the Ace of diamonds. If it's declarer who holds the Ace-Queen, he is about to take a winning finesse against you, so putting up your diamond King shouldn't cost you anything; and if the cards are distributed as above, this will be the only route to a set. (Your play could also gain if declarer's diamonds are A109x, and he wants to duck the first round to partner, dislodging his Queen.)

Notice the bidding again. Declarer seems to be one of those tricky individuals who like to bid what they don't have. He suppressed his five-card diamond suit in favor of a one club opening! This is a common and relatively harmless type of psych, intended to stop the defense from leading clubs against notrump.

□   □   □

Two

For my money, the most pleasant way to spend a bridge evening is playing in a cozy home team-of-four, preferably with lots of refreshments.

Over at a friend's for your regular Friday night get-together, you must cope with this deal:

Dlr: North   ♠ AK432
Vul: N–S   ♡ AK6
IMPs   ◇ KQ2
           ♣ 65

♠ 65
♡ QJ1073   □
◇ 765
♣ K72

Bidding:

South	West	North	East
		1 ♠	Pass
1NT	Pass	3NT	(All Pass)

You, West, lead the Queen of hearts, holding the first trick. Dummy wins the second heart, partner having followed with the five and nine, and declarer with the deuce and four. Declarer now plays a low club to his Queen. Plan your defense.

□   □   □

The full deal:

          ♠ AK432
          ♡ AK6
          ◇ KQ2
          ♣ 65

♠ 65   ♠ QJ10984
♡ QJ1073   □   ♡ 95
◇ 765   ◇ J1084
♣ K72   ♣ A4

          ♠ 7
          ♡ 842
          ◇ A93
          ♣ QJ109895

You can see that you must *duck the trick* to shut out declarer's suit. Ducking would also be the winner if declarer held AQ109x(x) of clubs and no Ace of diamonds. Even if your club holding were K2, it would still be correct to let declarer's Queen hold.

It's always harder to imagine you must keep declarer from establishing his best suit when it is concealed from sight (and concealed by the auction as well). Perhaps this deal will help you keep the possibility in mind in the future.

□   □   □

Three

In a six-session event like the Life Master Pairs, the whole game is managing to survive until the last day. There are massive cuts in the field after sessions two and four, and only sixty pairs qualify to compete in the two Final sets; so almost every pair in the Finals has a chance to finish high.

(There is a difference of opinion over what strategy this qualifying format should dictate. Some pairs believe a more conservative style in the early sessions helps their chance for qualification; they pull out all the stops only on the last day. Others like to play shoot-'em-up early, and shift to rock-solid type bridge against the tough opposition in the Finals.)

In the fourth session of the LMs, you have a chance to apply some book learning.

Dlr: South
Vul: both
Matchpoints

♠ K5
♡ K9742
♢ Q63
♣ A54

♠ QJ742
♡ AJ5
♢ J82
♣ 103

□

Bidding:	South	West	North	East
	1NT	Pass	2◇*	Pass
	2♡	Pass	3NT	(All Pass)

*A "transfer" response, which forces opener to bid two hearts.

You, West, lead the four of spades. Declarer plays low from dummy, and partner puts in the eight. Your heart sinks for a moment—but the eight holds! East returns the ten of spades to dummy's King. At trick three, dummy leads a heart. Partner plays the eight and declarer the Queen. Plan your defense.

This problem is based on a deal of Hugh Kelsey's. West must *duck* the first heart, a play that would heavily tax the instincts of most of us. The full deal is:

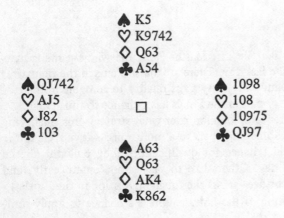

After his Queen of hearts holds, declarer will return the suit. When West's Jack appears, he will *duck* in dummy, playing East for the doubleton Ace-eight. West will be left on lead, and can clear the spades while he still holds the heart Ace! If West were to win the *first* heart, declarer would win the spade return and play a heart to the *nine*, establishing the suit while keeping West out of the lead.

Of course, West would have to duck his heart Ace *smoothly*. Any pause would give his holding away. But, as Kelsey points out, if he cherishes the necessity of *clinging to his entry* until his suit is established, he may be able to duck as though he had not a care in the world.

Four

You hear a lot about whether today's athletes are as good as those of bygone days. Was Hank Aaron the equal of Babe Ruth? Could Ali knock out Dempsey? Would Borg take Tilden, or Nicklaus defeat Bobby Jones?

Contract bridge has come a long way since its birth in 1925. In particular, ideas in constructive *bidding* have greatly evolved even since the heydey of Charles Goren's methods in the Fifties. The proliferation of new conventions and treatments in the past two decades has been amazing. The play, however, has not progressed so swiftly. Many of the standard techniques and abstruse coups in declarer's repertory were analyzed long, long ago; and today new wrinkles in play, such as in the scholarly presentations of Geza Ottlik, are greeted with much more than a passing interest. I think it would be fascinating to kibitz a match between the Aces, world champions of today, and a team made up of the Culbertsons and the Sims. Despite the clear edge the modernists would enjoy in the bidding, I think it might be a close match.

Many years ago, before everybody and his orchestra got to be a Life Master, there was a wonderful event, the Life Master Individual. This was definitely *not* one of those events that gave Individuals the frivolous reputation that burdens them now. It was a tough game, and a Title that was much sought after. I just wonder, if we put this deal into the LM Pairs of today and the LM Individual of forty years ago, which set of East players would handle it better?

```
Dlr: North        ♠ A5
Vul: N-S          ♡ AK1063
                  ◇ J54
                  ♣ QJ10
                            ♠ Q932
                  □         ♡ Q9
                            ◇ A63
                            ♣ K843
```

Bidding:	South	West	North	East
			1 ♡	Pass
	2 ◇	Pass	2 ♡	Pass
	2NT	Pass	3NT	(All Pass)

West, your partner, leads the six of spades. Declarer looks at the lead for some time, and then calls the five from dummy. Your Queen holds, as declarer plays the four. How do you continue?

□   □   □

Shift to the *King of clubs*. The club Ace is the only fast entry declarer could have to his diamond suit, so maybe you can beat him if you remove it. You can then hold up your diamond Ace twice, leaving the suit high and dry. The full deal:

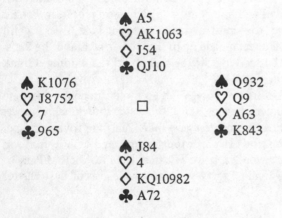

                    ♠ A5
                    ♡ AK1063
                    ◇ J54
                    ♣ QJ10
    ♠ K1076   ♠ Q932
    ♡ J8752   ♡ Q9
    ◇ 7   □   ◇ A63
    ♣ 965   ♣ K843
                    ♠ J84
                    ♡ 4
                    ◇ KQ10982
                    ♣ A72

If declarer wins the club Ace, he will make only three clubs, two diamonds, two hearts, and a spade. If he ducks, you will switch back to spades, and set him with three spade tricks, a club, and a diamond. Since spades were 4-4, declarer could have made the hand by winning the first trick, but it was hard for him to visualize what was about to happen to him.

Incidentally, the deliberate sacrifice of a high card to dislodge an entry is known as the "Merrimac Coup." During the Spanish-American War, the U.S. Navy scuttled the collier *Merrimac* (not the Civil War ironclad that fought the *Monitor*) in one of the Cuban harbor channels, neutralizing the Spanish ships in port. In the same manner, your play on this deal bottles up declarer's diamond suit. However, this Coup is more typically seen when there is the threat of a suit in *dummy*.

As its name suggests, this is an ancient strategem. I expect it was known in the days of auction bridge. Perhaps, then, the players of the mid-Forties might be more apt to see the right answer on this one!

☐   ☐   ☐

Five

Early in the first session of a Flighted Open Pairs, a couple of the perennial Little Old Ladies arrive at your table. Good, sweet, kind, gracious, friendly, wearers of those perpetually beatific expressions, and just as capable of handing you a zero as any of your other opponents, if you're not careful. Anybody can do you in, if you ease up on them.

One of the most memorable hands in my entire bridge-playing career arose in a club game about ten years ago. I sat down to play two LOLs, grist for my mill, and one of them promptly murmured, "Oh how nice, we get to play against the experts." I should have known, when I heard that, that disaster was on the way.

This was the fateful deal, as I saw it from the East chair.

```
Dlr: South        ♠ 952
Vul: none         ♡ AK
Matchpoints       ◇ KQ42
                  ♣ 10763
                              ♠ A3
                              ♡ J10873
                   ☐          ◇ J1086
                              ♣ A4
```

Bidding:	South	West	North	East
	1 ♣	Pass	1 ◇	Pass
	1NT	Pass	3NT	(All Pass)

West leads the six of spades. You win the Ace and return the suit, to declarer's Jack and partner's King. West now leads the eight of spades. Plan your defense.

You must *throw the club Ace* (!) On the bidding, there is barely room for partner to have a Queen remaining. But if declarer's clubs are KJxxx or perhaps KQxx, the discard of the club Ace will beat the hand by creating a club entry to partner's good spades!

I knew all about brilliancies like this, and I pitched my club Ace without hesitation. After all, the chance to make an immortal play like this one only comes around once every twenty years or so, so how could I pass up such a great opportunity? I'm sure you'd have done the same thing in my place.

Unfortunately, the full deal was:

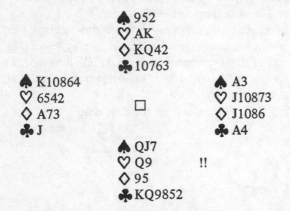

♠ 952
♡ AK
♢ KQ42
♣ 10763

♠ K10864
♡ 6542
♢ A73
♣ J

♠ A3
♡ J10873
♢ J1086
♣ A4

♠ QJ7
♡ Q9 !!
♢ 95
♣ KQ9852

I should have known better. Especially since I had seen South's style in the auction before. She always simply bid what she thought she could make and hoped for the best. After claiming nine tricks, with six clubs, a spade, and two hearts, declarer said that she had rebid 1NT only to limit her hand, and none of us, after a glance at the hand, could disagree with the logic of that. (Really, the spade eight should have saved me. See Chapter Four.)

The lessons here are three:

1. When you are defending notrump, trying to find an entry to your side's established long suit may require heroic measures.
2. There are more dead heroes than live ones.
3. Beware of Little Old Ladies.

But you *would* have done the same thing, right?

□ □ □

Six

Playing in a Men's Pairs against the top seed in your section, you managed a good result on the first board and would like another one on the second board.

```
Dlr:  North        ♠ A4
Vul:  E-W          ♡ AQ4
Matchpoints        ◇ K107652
                   ♣ J4
                              ♠ K105
              □              ♡ J9
                              ◇ AJ9
                              ♣ K9863
```

Bidding:	South	West	North	East
			1 ◇	Pass
	1 ♡	Pass	2 ◇	Pass
	3NT	(All Pass)		

West, your partner, leads the seven of spades. Plan your defense.

□ □ □

If declarer ducks in dummy, as he surely will, put in your spade *ten*. The full deal:

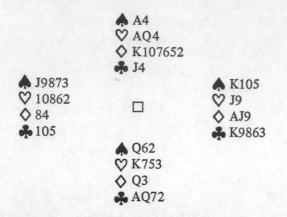

♠ A4
♡ AQ4
◇ K107652
♣ J4

♠ J9873   ♠ K105
♡ 10862   ♡ J9
◇ 84   ◇ AJ9
♣ 105   ♣ K9863

♠ Q62
♡ K753
◇ Q3
♣ AQ72

Dummy has 14 HCP, you have 12, and declarer should hold about 13 for his jump to game, so partner's spade honor is much more likely to be the *Jack*. If you allow declarer to win his spade Queen at trick one, you can lead your spade King later to force out the Ace, establish the suit, and preserve your link with partner's hand. This will be impossible if you win the first trick, though. If your spades had been *KJx*, the third-hand play of the *Jack* in this position would be a little more obvious.*

Partner made a good decision to lead a spade. With not a sign of an entry, many players would have tried a club from the West hand, hoping to hit *your* suit. This is a subject we'll talk about some more in the next chapter.

*Double-dummy, South could make 3NT by winning the spade Ace at trick one or by ducking your spade ten.

chapter three

INTELLIGENT
OPENING LEADS

PRELIMINARIES

This is a tough subject, and not one on which I or anybody else can be pontifical. Quite often, I make the opening lead, and even after the dummy comes down, I am uncertain whether my lead is going to turn out well or badly!

Clearly, the lead to the first trick might make or break the entire defense, but there are also the inevitable hands on which it doesn't matter what is led; and there will be hands on which the world's best opening leader, whoever he or she may be, might give away a trick (or the contract) with some ill-fated choice. The luck factor makes this a pretty confounding part of the game no matter who you are, but for that very reason, players find it especially gratifying to hit on an opening lead that is a real "killer."

Despite that, all anyone can realistically hope for is opening leads that are consistently above average. Consider what Bobby Jones wrote about playing golf: "Approximate squareness in striking the ball is all anyone can hope to attain." Bobby Jones was a pretty good bridge player, by the way.

Making effective opening leads requires imagination, visualization, experience, and luck. Basically, what an expert tries to do is picture what sort of values dummy will table, based on the bidding. The bidding may suggest that dummy will be weak or strong, balanced or unbalanced, with or without trump support, or with or without a side suit. The expert then tries to imagine in what direction the play is likely to go and how declarer will make use of his dummy. He may judge that declarer will face a tough fight for tricks, and make a safe, passive lead; or he may fear that declarer will have an easy time, with plenty of values available to make his contract in due time, and lead aggressively. Essentially, he is trying to put the right defensive *program* to work, hoping to counter declarer's plans, *before* he sees the dummy.

For this reason, it is of little value to base your choice of an opening lead on a *table* of attractive holdings, like those found in many bridge books. Our discussion here is intended to help you think in terms other than such a table. Instead of dealing in generalities, let's look at some hands and bidding sequences, and see if we can think the situation through and deduce the best lead. In each case, you are West.

Bidding:	North	South	
		1 ♥	♠ Q64
	1 ♠	2 ♥	♥ 763
	4 ♥		♦ KJ3
			♣ 10763

Lead the three of diamonds. Dummy will have a good hand, heart support, and probably a good spade suit which declarer can establish for discards. Your spade holding looks terrible. Any spade finesse declarer tries will work, and the suit is splitting pretty evenly, helpful to him if he wants to establish it with a ruff. You should make the most aggressive lead possible, hoping to set up or take tricks in a hurry, before it's too late.

Suppose, on the same auction, your hand were:

> ♠ KJ963
> ♥ 65
> ♦ KJ4
> ♣ 1097

Now dummy's spade suit is no threat, and you should prefer the pedestrian lead of the ten of clubs, which combines safety with mild aggression.

Bidding: North   South
                  1 ♡   ♠ J94
          1 ♠   2 ♡   ♡ K6
                             ◇ KJ3
                             ♣ Q10752

The dummy will have less than 10 HCP, perhaps as few as 6, so there is no reason to presume that the spade suit (or any suit) will furnish declarer with a lot of discards. The five of clubs would probably be the choice of most players, though a spade is possible. A diamond is out. When the dummy is known to be weak, there is no reason to panic and start looking for winners in a big hurry.

Notice that on the first deal, the opponents rolled easily into game. The defense has limited values and will be on lead infrequently, so they have to take advantage of the opening lead to try to establish some winners. If the contract is only two, though, the defenders rate to get in several times before the play is over. This means that, if it is right to lead diamonds against the two heart contract, you will get another chance before long.

Bidding: North   South
                  1 ◇   ♠ KQ104
          2 ◇   2NT   ♡ Q4
          3 ◇   ◇ 874
                            ♣ J1063

South made a game try after his partner's raise, and suggested 3NT. North's bidding meant he thinks there is no game, and he doesn't like notrump either. The dummy will be very weak in high cards, closer to 6 HCP, and distributional, since North apparently thinks his hand will be more useful at the suit contract. You should lead a trump. This is a particularly good example of how your thought processes should go when making the opening lead.

Bidding: South   West   North   East
                  Pass   Pass   1 ♠   ♠ K103
          2 ♣   2 ♠   3 ♣   4 ♠   ♡ J1074
          5 ♣   Dbl.   (All Pass)   ◇ K104
                                                 ♣ 763

Your side clearly has the balance of the high cards, judging from partner's leap to game. None of your top tricks are likely to go away, then, but declarer could make an extra trick or two by ruffing some of his losers in dummy. A trump lead is often called for when the opponents take a sacrifice. Lead a club.

Bidding: North   South
                 1 ♠   ♠ AQ97
       1NT   2 ◇   ♡ J104
                     ◇ 1043
                     ♣ K82

This is an automatic trump lead. Dummy will be weak in high cards, with tolerance for diamonds but probably a singleton spade. You can tell from your own hand that declarer has some losing spades, and he will surely want to ruff them, since dummy will be able to offer him little else in the way of tricks. If your hand were:

               ♠ 8764
               ♡ A4
               ◇ A8
               ♣ Q10974

a trump lead would be less attractive, since declarer's spades rate to be strong and he wouldn't need any ruffs. I'd try the club ten here, hoping for a forcing game.

Bidding: South   West   North   East
         1 ♣   Pass   Pass   Pass   ♠ K107
                                      ♡ J64
                                      ◇ J9653
                                      ♣ 64

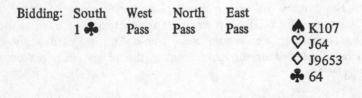

Your partner must have very strong clubs, since he failed to balance in a situation where he is marked with some values. Your best lead might be a club, perhaps preventing declarer from scoring his small trumps. Anyway, there is no attractive alternative.

Bidding: North   South
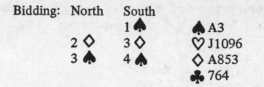

                           1 ♠   ♠ A3
      2 ◇   3 ◇   ♡ J1096
      3 ♠   4 ♠   ◇ A853
                           ♣ 764

No problem if you listen to the bidding. The opponents were prepared to play in diamonds, so they should have an eight or nine-card fit, marking partner with shortness. Lead the diamond Ace and continue the suit un-loss dummy is not at all what you expect. Actually, you might well have doubled this contract. You can visualize a two-trick set if partner has a trick somewhere.

Bidding: North   South
                           1 ♠   ♠ Q53
      2 ♣   2 ♡   ♡ J63
      4 ♠   4NT   ◇ 109642
      5 ♡   6 ♠   ♣ A4

Lead a diamond, not the club Ace. There are psychological considerations here. A diamond lead would be so normal on this auction that a good declarer would be suspicious if you gratuitously laid down the Ace of dummy's bid suit. He might decide you were motivated to cash out be- cause you were looking at the Queen of trumps, a possible setting trick. You would, of course, be happy to cash the *diamond* Ace, or even the heart Ace, if you could. The club Ace is unlikely to go away even if you don't take it immediately.

Bidding: North   South
                          1NT   ♠ Q9762
     4NT   6NT   ♡ A75
                          ◇ J109
                          ♣ 85

If the contract is *3NT*, the lead of a spade, hoping to establish long cards, would be routine. But you don't need long cards to beat *6NT*, just two tricks of any kind. Your partner is marked with nothing on the auction, so a spade lead would probably give away a trick, and it might be declarer's twelfth one. Prefer a safer diamond, perhaps a deceptive *ten*.

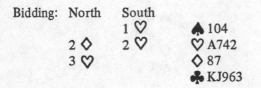

Bidding: North South
1NT ♠ 1064
3 ♥ 3NT ♥ 753
6NT ♦ A53
♣ K1072

This time North may have bid slam based on a long heart suit rather than a lot of high-card strength. Therefore, there is a case for an aggressive club lead, hoping to establish a club trick before they make the slam with lots of heart tricks and a few more in spades and diamonds.

Bidding: North South
1 ♥ ♠ 104
2 ♦ 2 ♥ ♥ A742
3 ♥ ♦ 87
♣ KJ963

With four trumps to the Ace, you should be thinking about a possible *forcing game*. If you can ruff declarer down a couple of times, he'll be out of control and won't be able to use dummy's diamonds. The suit declarer is most likely to have to ruff is the one in which you have length and strength, so you should lead the six of clubs.

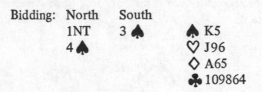

Bidding: North South
1NT 3 ♠ ♠ K5
4 ♠ ♥ J96
♦ A65
♣ 109864

Stay passive with the ten of clubs. North is known to have a balanced hand, so dummy is unlikely to provide declarer with a great many discards for his losers. I know some desperados who would try a low diamond, however!

Bidding: North South
1 ♠ ♠ J54
2 ♣ 2 ♥ ♥ 4
3 ♠ 4 ♠ ♦ KQ1043
♣ AQ65

King of diamonds. Resist the temptation to lead your singleton heart. When the opponents have had a strong auction to game and you have this many HCP, you're really living in a dream world if you think partner has the heart Ace. More likely, he has the heart Queen or Jack, and your lead will only help declarer bring in his second suit.

The practice of leading from shortness is much abused. Too often, your short suit will be declarer's long one, and you will lend him assistance by leading the suit for him. You should always be wary of a short-suit lead unless there is a real prospect of gain.

Avoid the lead of a singleton (or worthless doubleton) in several cases: when you have a trump holding like QJ10x, *certain trump tricks* in any case; when you have extra *length* in trumps and you judge that a forcing game will fare better (however, a rare exception to this occurs when you fear you might be *endplayed in trumps* unless you can shorten yourself by taking a ruff or two); or, *when the contract will be defeated anyway if partner can gain the lead.*

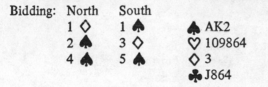

Bidding: North   South
          1 ◇   1 ♠   ♠ AK2
          2 ♠   3 ◇   ♡ 109864
          4 ♣   5 ♠   ◇ 3
                             ♣ J864

Ten of hearts. To lead your singleton diamond here would be awful. If partner has the diamond Ace (or the King behind dummy's Ace), the contract will always be set no matter what you do. But partner is surely more apt to have Qxx or J10xx, and a diamond lead would throw away your best chance for a set.

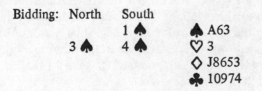

Bidding: North   South
                   1 ♠   ♠ A63
          3 ♠   4 ♠   ♡ 3
                             ◇ J8653
                             ♣ 10974

You could hardly construct a more suitable hand to lead your singleton heart. There are two key features. First, you have a poor hand, so partner must hold some values. Maybe he even has the heart Ace! In addition, you have control of the trump suit. They can't draw all the trumps without letting you back in for a second shot at your ruff, assuming you don't get it right away.

Once you have decided on a suit to lead, the card you choose from that suit is usually a matter of routine. But not always. "Always" is a dangerous word to use in bridge. There was a hand in the 1967 World Championship, where Alvin Roth, playing for the United States against Venezuela, was rewarded for using his imagination on opening lead.

Dlr: South   ♠ Q72
Vul: E-W   ♡ K1087
            ◇ 5
            ♣ 108764

♠ 8		♠ K1063
♡ AJ53	□	♡ 92
◇ AJ742		◇ K96
♣ K32		♣ AJ95

          ♠ AJ954
          ♡ Q64
          ◇ Q1083
          ♣ Q

	Root	Benaim	Roth	Vernon
Bidding:	South	West	North	East
	Pass	1 ◇	Pass	1 ♠
	Pass	2 ◇	Pass	3 ♣
	Pass	3NT	(All Pass)	

What motivated Roth's lead of the *spade Queen* is unknown. Perhaps he felt the heart suit wouldn't provide enough tricks to beat the contract, maybe he sensed that declarer was short in spades. Anyway, declarer assumed that North held the spade Jack as well, and as he wanted to avoid an early heart play through his AJ53, he ducked the first trick. But the defenders now picked up the whole spade suit, and added a couple of hearts and a diamond, for three down. 3NT was made in the other room (it was played from the other side of the table), and the U.S. gained 14 IMPs.

The other end of the spectrum:

Bidding:	North	South	
		1 ◇	♠ 76
	1 ♠	1NT	♡ A76
	3NT		◇ QJ1042
			♣ K75

If you beat this contract, it should be with your diamonds. But declarer bid the suit, and your partner is probably short. Perhaps your best chance is to find him with the singleton or doubleton King, or the doubleton nine. In either case, you might need to lead *low*, letting your partner's intermediate do its work. The diamond situation could be:

$$\diamondsuit\ 76$$
$$\diamondsuit\ QJ1042 \qquad \square \qquad \diamondsuit\ 95$$
$$\diamondsuit\ AK83$$

You'll get tangled up if you start with the *Queen*.

Bidding:	North	South
	1 ♣	3 ♠
	4 ♠	

♠ 1054
♡ K6
♢ J952
♣ J1094

Speculate with the King of hearts. Desperation measures may be needed to beat this.

Bidding:	North	South
	3 ♢	3NT

♠ KJ4
♡ J10
♢ 753
♣ J9652

A spade. I would tend to make as active a lead as possible in this situation, especially when my diamond holding suggests that declarer will have seven running tricks available as soon as he gets in. Many players would disagree and lead a stodgy club or heart. If you do prefer a spade lead, you might need to start the King or Jack to overcome a blockage in the suit.

Bidding:	North	South
		1NT
	3NT	

♠ J10
♡ 964
♢ 875
♣ J9652

Try the Jack of spades. Since you lack entries, a club lead looks futile. But partner surely has an entry or two, and he should hold some spade length.

Note that few full deals have accompanied our problems. It would be simple enough for me to construct deals that would make my suggestions look good, and just as easy to arrange the cards so that my recommended lead would be the only one to let the contract make! So I have done neither. Our objective in this discussion has been to select the lead that would turn out best *in the long run*; and to learn some *principles* that guide a good player in making his opening leads.

Remember, then, that your opening lead goal should be *consistency*. If one of your picks goes badly wrong, do as I do and shrug it off as an unfortunate fluke.

□   □   □

AT THE TABLE

In the North American Swiss Teams, you need to win your last match of the day to qualify for the Finals tomorrow. The matches in this National Championship are of nine boards. Three of the nine in your match turn out to be flat: An easy slam is bid at both tables; both teams go down in a good game, on bad splits; and there is a part-score deal on which you are +100 and your teammates are −110, for no swing.

There is more life in the rest of the boards, though. On each one of them, the opponents buy the contract, and you find yourself on opening lead. So, you may well be in charge of your own fate in this match.

Board 1

Dlr: South
Vul: N–S

Bidding:	South	West	North	East
	1♣	Pass	1♠	Pass
	1NT	Pass	2NT	(All Pass)

You, West, hold: ♠104
                   ♡952
                   ◇Q1072
                   ♣KJ94

☐   ☐   ☐

Board 3

Dlr: East
Vul: none

Bidding:	South	West	North	East
				Pass
	1♠	Pass	2♡	Pass
	2♣	Pass	3♠	Pass
	4♣	(All Pass)		

You, West, hold: ♠65
                   ♡862
                   ◇J10863
                   ♣K103

☐   ☐   ☐

Board 4

Dlr: East
Vul: both

Bidding:	South	West	North	East
				1♠
	Pass	2♣	Dbl.	3♠
	4♡	(All Pass)		

You, West, hold: ♠K9762
                   ♡52
                   ◇J93
                   ♣862

☐   ☐   ☐

Board 6

Dlr: South
Vul: N-S

Bidding:	South	West	North	East
	1 ◇	Pass	1 ♡	1 ♠
	1NT	Pass	2 ◇	(All Pass)

You, West, hold:

♠ 104
♡ Q1097
◇ 852
♣ KJ97

☐　　☐　　☐

Board 8

Dlr: South
Vul: both

Bidding:	South	West	North	East
	1 ◇	Pass	1 ♡	Pass
	1NT	Pass	2NT	Pass
	3NT	(All Pass)		

You, West, hold:

♠ 1083
♡ 10854
◇ A742
♣ 104

☐　　☐　　☐

Board 9

Dlr: North
Vul: N–S

Bidding:	South	West	North	East
			1 ◇	Pass
	1 ♡	Pass	3 ◇	Pass
	3 ♡	Pass	3 ♠	Pass
	3NT	(All Pass)		

You, West, hold:

♠ K103
♡ K986
◇ 4
♣ 97642

□   □   □

THE COMPARISON

(If you wish, refer to the Glossary for the IMP scale.)

Board 1

Lead the *ten of spades*. This might be a good time to depart from the normal "fourth from your longest and strongest" approach in favor of a passive program. The opponents will have no high card strength to spare on this bidding, and you can tell that declarer may find the going rough in the play. You have his club suit under control, and partner is marked with at least four spades behind dummy, so that suit may not be very productive for declarer either. The point is, you may not need to establish diamonds to beat this—the contract may die of natural causes, when declarer finds eight winners are too hard to come by.

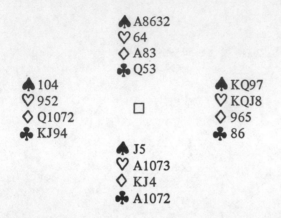

♠ A8632
♡ 64
◇ A83
♣ Q53

♠ 104　　　　　　　♠ KQ97
♡ 952　　　　　　　♡ KQJ8
◇ Q1072　　□　　　◇ 965
♣ KJ94　　　　　　　♣ 86

♠ J5
♡ A1073
◇ KJ4
♣ A1072

Declarer passed your spade ten to partner's Queen. The King and Jack of hearts won the next two tricks, and East switched to the nine of diamonds. Declarer ducked in hand and won dummy's Ace. He tried a club to the Ace and a club back. You won the King and led your other spade. Declarer ducked again, to partner's King. On the diamond return, he finessed his Jack unsuccessfully, and wound up making only six tricks, +200 to you.

At the other table, the bidding was identical, but they led a diamond. Your teammate in the South then played double-dummy to make his contract. He won the diamond Jack, and led a low club, won by West's King. Another diamond was taken by the Ace, and declarer led a low spade. East put up his Queen, and led high hearts, declarer winning the second. He cashed the Queen and Ace of clubs and the diamond King, arriving at:

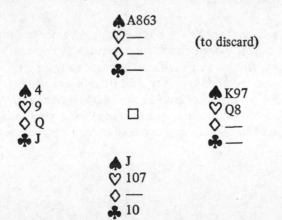

♠ A863
♡ —　　　　　(to discard)
◇ —
♣ —

♠ 4　　　　　　　　♠ K97
♡ 9　　　　　　　　♡ Q8
◇ Q　　　　□　　　◇ —
♣ J　　　　　　　　♣ —

♠ J
♡ 107
◇ —
♣ 10

There was nothing East could do. If he threw a spade, he would be thrown in with Ace and another spade, and forced to give declarer his ten of hearts in the end. And when he actually threw a heart, declarer exited with a heart. He ducked the spade King return, and East had to lead from his 97 of spades into dummy's A8 at trick twelve.

8 IMPs to you if you found the best lead of a spade. They'd probably go one down on a heart lead, and you'd gain 6 IMPs. On a diamond or club lead, the deal is a tie.

Board 3

The dummy will have five or more good hearts, and your heart holding is not encouraging. Better get busy. A club is your most aggressive lead.

♠ KJ
♡ AQ10743
◇ 92
♣ J75

♠ 65   ♠ Q93
♡ 862   ♡ KJ5
◇ J10863   ◇ A74
♣ K103   ♣ Q964

♠ A108742
♡ 9
◇ KQ5
♣ A82

Your lead of the club three was covered by dummy's five. Partner correctly put his nine in, and the Ace won. Declarer took a heart finesse in desperation, but that only resulted in down two; you cashed your clubs and the Ace of diamonds, and declarer misguessed trumps later.

In the replay, they led a "safe" Jack of diamonds to East's Ace. Declarer ducked the club return and won his club Ace on the next round. He played his high diamonds, discarding dummy's last club, ruffed a club with the spade Jack, and cashed the spade King. He ruffed a heart to get back to his hand, laid down the trump Ace, and claimed four, losing one trump trick.

11 IMPs to you if you chose a club lead. They're a favorite to tie the board on any other lead.

☐ ☐ ☐

Board 4

This is probably the only time you'll be on lead for the duration of the play. Therefore, in the interests of flexibility, lead the spade *King*. This may allow your side to decide where the first trick is won. For example, partner might like it if you could lead something *through* dummy at trick two.

```
              ♠8
              ♡KQ84
              ◇K82
              ♣AJ973
♠K9762                      ♠AQ1053
♡52              ☐          ♡10
◇J93                        ◇AQ104
♣862                        ♣Q54
              ♠J4
              ♡AJ9763
              ◇765
              ♣K10
```

Partner dropped his spade *Queen* on your King, as a suit preference signal (see Chapter Four), and you had no trouble finding the good shift to the Jack of diamonds, putting declarer down before he could get started. +100 to you.

In the other room, the heart game was also bid, but E–W saved at four spades. Your teammates had to find their club ruff to beat this one trick, but they were +200 all right.

You gain 7 IMPs if you justified your decision not to save against four hearts by holding the first trick with the spade King. (You'd also win four tricks on a diamond lead, but only if partner bravely underled his spade honors to put you in again.) They make it on any other defense, and you lose 9 IMPs.

Board 6

A trump lead is clearly indicated, despite the fact your partner overcalled. North ran from notrump, so he must have a distributional hand. Declarer will surely be ruffing some of his spades in dummy. It is certain that he won't make extra tricks from any *other* source, since you have a robust holding in both hearts and clubs.

```
                 ♠ 5
                 ♡ K642
                 ◇ J974
                 ♣ Q864
   ♠ 104                        ♠ AQ9832
   ♡ Q1097                      ♡ 85
   ◇ 852           □            ◇ A6
   ♣ KJ97                       ♣ A53
                 ♠ KJ76
                 ♡ AJ3
                 ◇ KQ103
                 ♣ 102
```

On your trump lead, partner won the Ace and played a second round. Declarer won in dummy and led a low spade. Partner took his Ace, and shifted to the heart eight. Declarer won the Ace, cashed his spade King and ruffed a spade, but he couldn't get off dummy, and had to let you in to play your third trump. His fourth spade was a loser in the end. He also lost two clubs, a heart, and the diamond and spade Aces, for down one, and +100 to you.

When the board was replayed, East competed to two spades, and all passed. Understandably, your South led the King of diamonds instead of looking for a ruff with the club ten, and declarer just got home with the contract by getting in the trumps and establishing a heart trick.

The board is a tie if you led a trump against two diamonds, otherwise you lose a double part-score swing and 5 IMPs.

☐   ☐   ☐

Board 8

The question here is which black suit your partner is more likely to have length in. He holds about 11 HCP, and might have overcalled if he could have done so at the *one* level. But he might consider a *two*-level entry too risky, especially at IMPs. Prefer to lead the ten of clubs.

```
                    ♠ K642
                    ♡ AK73
                    ◊ J3
                    ♣ 863
    ♠ 1083                        ♠ AJ5
    ♡ 10854                       ♡ J9
    ◊ A742        ☐              ◊ 986
    ♣ 104                         ♣ KQ972
                    ♠ Q97
                    ♡ Q62
                    ◊ KQ105
                    ♣ AJ5
```

When you started the club ten, partner made the fine play of ducking, forcing declarer to win one of his two club tricks immediately with the Jack. Declarer could still have made by playing a spade at trick two, but he couldn't see all four hands. He led a diamond instead. You jumped in with the diamond Ace, preserving partner's entry, and returned your other club. A one-trick defeat was now inevitable. +100 to you.

At the other table, East must not have trusted his partner to produce the best lead without some help, for he threw in the two club overcall that your partner passed up. Your teammates were happy to take the cash by doubling this, but they dropped a trick on defense and only got it for 500.

A club lead gains you 12 IMPs, therefore, and you only lose 3 IMPs if you led something else and they scored up the notrump game.

☐   ☐   ☐

Board 9

Nothing looks really attractive. Your club intermediates certainly don't seem too promising. Perhaps your best hope is to get out the shotgun by leading the *King of spades*. Partner did not double three spades, so you can't expect him to have QJ98x. But maybe he has a diamond stopper, and you might knock the spade Ace out of dummy so declarer can't use it as an entry to the diamonds.

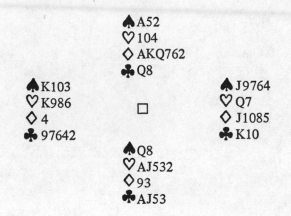

```
              ♠ A52
              ♡ 104
              ◇ AKQ762
              ♣ Q8
♠ K103                        ♠ J9764
♡ K986          □             ♡ Q7
◇ 4                           ◇ J1085
♣ 97642                       ♣ K10
              ♠ Q8
              ♡ AJ532
              ◇ 93
              ♣ AJ53
```

Declarer won your spade King lead and had visions of making twelve tricks for a possible small gain. He unwisely took two top diamonds, neglecting the safety play of *ducking* the first round, and the 4-1 split meant that even nine tricks were suddenly out of his reach.

At the other table, the opening lead against 3NT was a club, covered by the Queen, King, and Ace. With the spade Ace still in dummy, South needed no safety plays. He also played diamonds from the top, but he ended with nine tricks.

You gain 12 IMPs if you got your fingers on the spade King. Otherwise, the board is tied.

Well, did you live to play another day?

chapter four

GETTING YOUR
SIGNALS STRAIGHT

PRELIMINARIES

This is a fairly broad subject, and compressing everything you need to know into one chapter isn't going to be easy. But I'll give it a try.

The defenders are handicapped by not being able to see each other's hands. To help overcome this, they normally adhere to certain conventional practices in defensive carding, such as leading the top card from a sequence of honors, playing the cheapest card of equals as third hand, and so forth. But the most important means they have of communicating their holdings is through defensive signalling. You probably know something about the three types of defensive signals, but just to make sure all bets arc covered, I'll review the basic ideas behind them for you briefly.

1. *ATTITUDE*, the signal that suggests *like or dislike* for the suit in which the signal is given, and helps the defense decide what suits they should and should not attack. A defender may be able to show ATTITUDE in a suit when his partner leads the suit; or as he discards in the suit. The play of a *high* spot is used to show interest, while a *low* spot suggests disinterest, and in some cases may demand that the suit not be led again.

2. *COUNT*, the signal that indicates *how many* cards are held in a suit. This information may aid the defenders in the important task of reconstructing declarer's hand; or help them decide whether it is safe to hold off winning a high card. With one or two rare exceptions, this signal is used as the defenders follow to a trick *declarer* has led to. A *high-low* sequence of play indicates an *even* number of cards in the suit led, while a *low-high* sequence shows an *odd* number.

3. *SUIT PREFERENCE*, the rarely-used signal with which you may show interest in a specific suit *other than the one being led*. Under the right circumstances, the play of an *unusually high card* in one suit can be used to suggest strength in another, *high-ranking* suit. An *unusually low card* may show interest in another, *low-ranking* suit.

That's it in a nutshell. In our discussion, we will concentrate on some common misconceptions many players seem to have about signalling, and how good judgment must accompany your use of the signals, if they are to be effective.

ATTITUDE

This is the most important kind of signal and the most frequently used. And, since knowing what suits to lead or not to lead is the biggest problem the defenders face, the use of the ATTITUDE signal generally precedes that of any other signal. Here are some important points to remember about showing ATTITUDE.

The purpose of any ATTITUDE signal is not to confirm or deny the possession of specific high cards, but to suggest to partner a possible line of defense.

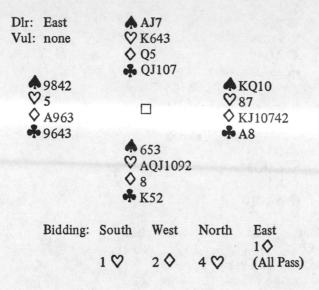

Dlr: East
Vul: none

♠ AJ7
♥ K643
♦ Q5
♣ QJ107

♠ 9842
♥ 5
♦ A963
♣ 9643

□

♠ KQ10
♥ 87
♦ KJ10742
♣ A8

♠ 653
♥ AQJ1092
♦ 8
♣ K52

Bidding:

South	West	North	East
			1♦
1♥	2♦	4♥	(All Pass)

West leads the Ace of diamonds. Look at East's hand and decide how he should signal. He should play the *two* in spite of his good diamonds, telling partner he thinks it is best to lead something else. West should look at the dummy and try to judge what other suit his partner could be interested in. In this case, he should shift to a spade, the suit in which East may have values behind dummy. The defense will set up two spade tricks before declarer can establish a discard in clubs.

There are two salient points in this example. First, East is known to have a choice of several diamonds with which to signal at trick one. When he plays the two in such a situation, West is practically *compelled* to shift, especially since a switch to spades is particularly attractive and the defense will surely need some black-suit tricks to prevail. (As we will see later, not every low card need have such an unequivocal meaning.) Second, the diamond *two* does not direct a shift to any particular suit; West must use his judgment and decide what shift East would most logically be interested in. As in most cases, that is not difficult here.

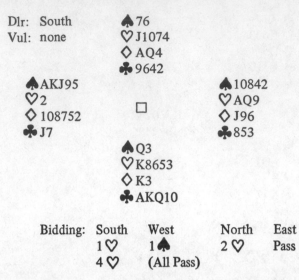

Dlr: South   ♠ 76
Vul: none   ♡ J1074
             ♢ AQ4
             ♣ 9642

♠ AKJ95   ♠ 10842
♡ 2   ♡ AQ9
♢ 108752   ☐   ♢ J96
♣ J7   ♣ 853

             ♠ Q3
             ♡ K8653
             ♢ K3
             ♣ AKQ10

Bidding: | South | West | North | East |
|---|---|---|---|
| 1 ♡ | 1 ♠ | 2 ♡ | Pass |
| 4 ♡ | (All Pass) | | |

West leads the Ace of spades (suggesting possession of the King as well). East can tell that he has the contract down if West will only cash his other spade trick. He should therefore play his spade *ten*. Without this encouragement, West might decide to shift to a diamond through dummy.

Dlr: West   ♠ KQ5
Vul: none   ♡ K53
             ♢ J964
             ♣ 1064

                   ♠ J842
                   ♡ J84
      ☐   ♢ 1073
                   ♣ A53

Bidding: | South | West | North | East |
|---|---|---|---|
| | 1 ♢ | Pass | 1 ♠ |
| 2 ♣ | Pass | 3 ♣ | (All Pass) |

West leads the Ace of spades. This lead doesn't look too dynamic, but East should play the *eight* nevertheless, asking for a continuation. Otherwise, partner may shift to a heart away from the Queen or lay down the diamond

Ace, costing the defense a trick. If East can't stand a red-suit shift, he'd do better to encourage spades.

While the good tidings of a *high* spot are seldom disobeyed, a *low* spot can convey a more ambiguous message. On the very first hand we gave, East's signal, the two of diamonds, gave West virtually no choice but to shift suits. But a low card can be a noncommittal kind of signal, which only suggests apathy or uncertainty about a suit.

Dlr: South ♠Q84
Vul: both   ♥K94
     ♦853
     ♣Q963

♠K5
♥J63   □
♦AK962
♣1072

South opened one spade, and North's raise to two spades was passed out. West leads the Ace of diamonds: three, seven, four. He should continue with the diamond King. Even though East has played his lowest diamond, he hasn't demanded a switch. For one thing, no switch is particularly attractive. And, since the contract is only *two*, no switch may be desperately needed. In a case like this, West would interpret partner's diamond seven to mean, "I have no particular desire for you to continue diamonds." But West may use his judgment. Here, there is no lie of the cards on which a second diamond would cost him.

Do you begin to see what I mean about using your *judgment* in conjunction with the signals?

There is no such thing as "seven or higher encourages, six or lower discourages." What nonsense! The size of the spots has to be relative, not absolute. If you have AK52, the *five* is the highest encouraging spot you can come up with. If you have to discourage with 1098, the *eight* is the best you can do. When your partner signals, you must look at your own spots, the ones in dummy, and the one declarer plays, and try to *interpret* the message your partner is trying to send.

Incidentally, once you decide *how* you should signal, *play the highest or lowest spot you can afford*. Don't be finicky. If partner leads the Ace of diamonds and you want to show interest with KQ973, play the *nine*.

Don't compromise with the seven, which might somehow be unclear. A good partner will watch the spots like a hawk, and might draw some mistaken inference if he notices that the nine is missing.

Don't signal if your information might prove of more use to declarer than to your partner. *Ideally, your signalling should be kept to the minimum.* You would prefer to signal only when you are afraid partner can't judge what to do without a signal to help him. This is another instance when good judgment, born of experience at the table, is essential.

In discarding, you must not signal with a high card that you might need later as a winner! Instead, throw away *low* cards in the other suits, trusting partner to act on the negative inference available from your play.

You may signal from a *sequence* of equals by playing the *top* card, just as if you were leading to the trick. This idea can be useful, as the following deal shows:

```
Dlr:  West        ♠ 87
Vul:  E–W         ♡ A83
                  ♢ AKQ732
                  ♣ 106
      ♠ AK962                  ♠ QJ5
      ♡ 92              □       ♡ J6
      ♢ 64                     ♢ J1098
      ♣ AQ43                   ♣ 9872
                  ♠ 1043
                  ♡ KQ10754
                  ♢ 5
                  ♣ KJ5
```

Bidding: South   West   North   East
                   1 ♠   2 ♢   Pass
          2 ♡   Pass   3 ♡   Pass
          4 ♡   (All Pass)

West leads the Ace of spades, and East drops his *Queen*. West can now underlead in spades to East's known Jack, and the club return will beat the contract.

COUNT

Each of our three types of signals is intended to handle a separate kind of defensive problem. When your partner leads a suit, you may be obliged to help him by signalling your ATTITUDE. But when a suit is led by *declarer*, the defenders can usually assume that this is a suit they aren't too interested in. Therefore, showing ATTITUDE is no longer so important, and the defense may wish to signal COUNT instead. Bear in mind that the ATTITUDE signal has priority over COUNT. That is, if you think your partner has signalled you, treat his play as ATTITUDE unless his attitude is somehow already known to you, or is patently obvious to everyone.

Here are some important points to remember about showing COUNT.

I repeat: You can't show COUNT when your ATTITUDE is ambiguous. I see defenses like this one perpetrated quite often:

```
Dlr: West        ♠Q875
Vul: both        ♡A53
                 ◇K94
                 ♣KQ5
♠AK106                      ♠J942
♡K986            □          ♡QJ72
◇A85                        ◇10732
♣97                         ♣8
                 ♠3
                 ♡104
                 ◇QJ6
                 ♣AJ106432
```

Bidding:	South	West	North	East
		1◇	Pass	Pass
	2♣	Pass	2NT	Pass
	4♣	Pass	5♣	(All Pass)

West led the spade Ace. East thought he could show COUNT and ATTITUDE all at once by playing the four. However, West decided that his partner had the doubleton four-deuce, and he continued with the spade Ace. Declarer ruffed this, and obtained a discard for his losing heart.

Of course, if East had his priorities straight, he would have played his spade *two* to the first trick. He should have been anxious to show ATTITUDE first and foremost (especially when he would have looked so favorably on a heart switch).

As when showing attitude, play the highest or lowest spot you can afford. Avoid wishy-washy spots, which might make your message unclear.

Not every card you play is a signal. You should show COUNT only when you deem it safe to do so, and when you judge that partner may need distributional information to defend correctly. Your partner, in turn, should interpret your play as COUNT only if he thinks you would judge that the situation requires you to signal. On an auction like this, for example:

Bidding:

South	West	North	East
1NT	Pass	2♣	Pass
2♠	Pass	3NT	Pass
4♡	(All Pass)		

you need not show COUNT in spades when declarer gets around to leading that suit, since partner can tell from the bidding how many spades you have. If you signal here, the information might be put to use by declarer, thus:

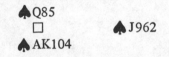

♠Q85
♠73   □   ♠J962
♠AK104

Declarer plays the spade Ace and a spade to the Queen. If both defenders busily high-low, showing an even number, declarer might decide to believe them and lead to his ten on the third round.

You can see that a lot of partnership trust and cooperation is required here! Matter of fact, the proper use of the COUNT signal may require more judgment and experience than any of the others.

You can't signal your length exactly, only within a *two-card range*. But the bidding may help resolve the times when there is ambiguity.

We said that the COUNT signal is employed when *declarer* leads a suit, but there are rare exceptions, mostly in cash-out situations. Say you are defending six hearts, and you are on lead with the AK1074 of spades. You choose to lay down your spade King, and dummy hits with Q83. Partner should *show COUNT* here, since that is the critical piece of information you need. If he follows with the spade two (showing an odd number) and declarer fails to ruff, your other high spade should cash.

A special procedure is used to show COUNT in the *trump* suit. The order of play is *inverted* here because, with a doubleton trump, you may not be willing to release your higher one on the first round to show a doubleton. A high spot in trumps could be too valuable a card to waste. Therefore, you may suggest an *odd* number of trumps (three, almost always) by playing your *middle* trump at your first turn, then your lowest. To show an *even* number, play your *lowest* trump first.

This scheme has some potential benefits. For example, you can tell when it is still possible to give partner a ruff. Many players, in fact, feel that an *echo* in trumps (a high-low sequence) implies a powerful interest in taking a ruff. Others prefer to give partner the COUNT in trumps *whenever* it is safe to do so, to help him in working out declarer's distribution.

SUIT PREFERENCE

Finally, the last signal! It's also the most beautiful, the most abused, and the most troublesome. We have seen that ATTITUDE and COUNT signals are significant in relation to the same suit in which they are played. But a SUIT PREFERENCE signal is a little more complicated because it directs attention to some *other* suit. The classic example of SUIT PREFERENCE is seen on a hand like this:

```
Dlr: West        ♠ AQ64
Vul: none        ♡ Q1074
                 ◇ K
                 ♣ KJ105
                            ♠ 5
                            ♡ A952
              □             ◇ Q863
                            ♣ 8762
```

Bidding:	South	West	North	East
		3 ◇	Dbl.	5 ◇
	6 ♠	(All Pass)		

West leads the Ace of diamonds. East should shock partner by throwing his diamond *Queen*. On the bidding, this can't be a singleton. What else could such an *unusually high* spade be but a SUIT PREFERENCE signal, showing interest in hearts, the *high-ranking* of the other suits (excluding trumps)? This is a typical SUIT PREFERENCE signal, a play of *unmistakable* significance that cannot possibly be interpreted as any other type of signal.

The SUIT PREFERENCE signal has many applications. Two of the most common are seen below.

Dlr: South
Vul: E-W

```
                    ♠ J53
                    ♡ 84
                    ◇ AQJ84
                    ♣ J43
   ♠ A6                              ♠ Q9742
   ♡ Q10753                          ♡ KJ9
   ◇ 953            □                ◇ K2
   ♣ 1065                            ♣ 987
                    ♠ K108
                    ♡ A62
                    ◇ 1076
                    ♣ AKQ2
```

N-S reach 3NT and West leads a heart. Declarer ducks the King and Jack, winning on the third round. On this trick, West should dump his heart *Queen* under the Ace. At this point, all his hearts are winners, so the one he plays can be used to indicate the location of his side entry. Without SUIT PREFERENCE, East would probably return a club on winning the diamond King. A spade return away from his Queen would look very dangerous to him.

Dlr: South
Vul: none

```
                    ♠ Q5
                    ♡ J75
                    ◇ Q1065
                    ♣ K1076
   ♠ K9642                           ♠ AJ3
   ♡ 2                               ♡ KQ964
   ◇ J73            □                ◇ K8
   ♣ 9843                            ♣ J52
                    ♠ 1087
                    ♡ A1083
                    ◇ A942
                    ♣ AQ
```

Bidding:

	South	West	North	East
	1 ◇	Pass	2 ◇	2 ♡
	Pass	Pass	3 ◇	(All Pass)

West leads the two of hearts, to the five, Queen, and Ace. Declarer quickly plays Ace and a diamond. West is careful to echo with the seven and three, showing his three trumps. When East wins the diamond King, he will continue with the King of hearts and another, giving partner his ruff. His third heart lead will be the *nine*, a SUIT PREFERENCE signal for spades, anticipating that West will want to know what suit to lead after taking his ruff. What other significance could the nine of hearts have? Without some help from partner here, West might be reluctant to lead away from his spade King. (True, East could simply cash his spade Ace before giving the ruff, but this is a discussion on signals.)

The situations we have seen so far are pretty straightforward and don't seem to be too troublesome, do they? Well, the *trouble* with SUIT PREFERENCE starts when players abuse it by trying to apply the caviar of SUIT PREFERENCE in situations when the meat and potatoes of ATTITUDE would do the job very well. The confusion can be terrible to behold. For example:

Dlr: West
Vul: none

```
            ♠ K853
            ♡ K4
            ◇ 863
            ♣ AKJ10
                              ♠ 74
                              ♡ J952
        □                     ◇ AQ5
                              ♣ 9863
```

Bidding:

	South	West	North	East
		1 ♡	Dbl.	2 ♡
	3 ♠	Pass	4 ♠	(All Pass)

West leads the Ace of hearts, and the question is: what should East play to trick one? The answer is based on the *priorities* with which the three types of signals are used. ATTITUDE, we said, is most important, therefore it always takes precedence. COUNT is next. And, I'm here to tell you, SUIT PREFERENCE is *last*.

You must adhere to the following principles, otherwise you may be headed for trouble: The basic signal is ATTITUDE, and any signal must be so interpreted as long as ATTITUDE is a conceivable message the signaller might want to send. A signal may be interpreted as SUIT PREFERENCE only if there is no other possible message (such as attitude or count). Signaller's play can have no significance in relation to its own suit. A typical SUIT PREFERENCE signal is an *unusual* play that makes you sit up and take notice.

If East applies these principles to our problem, he will simply play the heart *two* on West's Ace, which says, "Please shift." When West looks at dummy, the right shift will be apparent.

Now, there are some players who are so obsessed with SUIT PREFERENCE that they would shift to a *club* when East played his lowest heart. But this is contrary to our signalling principles; and besides, what East would want a club shift with dummy so strong in clubs? Perhaps a similar example will make all this clearer.

Dlr: West   ♠ K853
Vul: none   ♡ K4
             ◇ 863
             ♣ AKJ10

                            ♠ A4
            □   ♡ J952
                            ◇ 952
                            ♣ 9863

Bidding: South   West   North   East
                  1♡   Dbl.   2♡
          3♠   Pass   4♠   (All Pass)

Same bidding, same dummy, and West leads the heart Ace again. This time, East should play the *nine*. Once again, this is plain old ATTITUDE, suggesting that partner lead more hearts. Even though dummy can win, there is no reason why a passive heart continuation can't be right. From East's point of view, a switch to either minor could be costly.

Note that, once again, there is no need for any fancy signals. Most of the time, ATTITUDE alone will handle your signalling problems just fine.

How about this hand?

Dlr: South   ♠ Q93
Vul: N–S   ♡ Q97
            ◊ K872
            ♣ Q97

♠ 62   ♠ 75
♡ K64   ♡ AJ102
◊ AJ1065   □   ◊ Q94
♣ K64   ♣ 10852

            ♠ AKJ1084
            ♡ 853
            ◊ 3
            ♣ AJ3

Bidding:	South	West	North	East
	1♠	2◊	2♠	3◊
	3♠	(All Pass)		

West leads the Ace of diamonds, and here, East should play his diamond *Queen*. This *is* a time when a SUIT PREFERENCE signal is required. West should feel like shifting, since declarer is now in position to take a (possibly vital) discard on the diamond King; but from West's chair, there is no *obvious* switch, so ATTITUDE alone won't do the job. If East could only signal "Switch," West would have to guess which suit to lead. Note that the *Queen* of diamonds is the kind of sit-up-and-take-notice play that West will surely interpret as SUIT PREFERENCE.

Let's look again at a hand we discussed in the section on COUNT.

Dlr: West   ♠ Q875
Vul: both   ♡ A53
            ◊ K94
            ♣ KQ5

♠ AK106   ♠ J942
♡ K986   ♡ QJ72
◊ A85   □   ◊ 10732
♣ 97   ♣ 8

            ♠ 3
            ♡ 104
            ◊ QJ6
            ♣ AJ106432

Bidding:	South	West	North	East
		1◇	Pass	Pass
	2♣	Pass	2NT	Pass
	4♣	Pass	5♣	(All Pass)

Before, we saw that West led the Ace of spades against the five club contract, and East misguidedly played the four, leading to misdefense. Now suppose that West's opening bid had been *one spade*, East had raised to two spades, and N-S reached five clubs again. On the same Ace of spades lead, East would play his spade *Jack*.

Does this play hold up according to our principles? Yes, it does. East's ATTITUDE is known. He cannot want a spade continuation, which would set up dummy's Queen, when he is known to have length in the suit for his raise. His play of a high spade might be interpreted as showing COUNT, an even number of cards in the suit; and his *unusually* high spade should be SUIT PREFERENCE, for hearts.

Always keep in mind the signalling priorities we emphasized. ATTITUDE, COUNT, and SUIT PREFERENCE, *in that order*. Not nearly as many problems that way.

□   □   □

AT THE TABLE

One

The long-suffering average player always finds it heartwarming when an expert slips up and produces a ludicrous result. On this hand, from the 1982 Grand National Teams semifinals in Albuquerque, Atlanta vs. Michigan, neither team gave what you'd call a polished performance

Dlr: North   ♠ AK10953
Vul: E-W   ♡ 104
IMPs   ◇ K5
            ♣ Q86

♠ Q4
♡ 6   □
◇ A10942
♣ K10753

Bidding:

	South	West	North	East
			1 ♠	Pass
	2♡*	Pass	2 ♠	Pass
	3♡	Pass	4 ♡	Pass
	5 ♣	Pass	5 ◊	Pass
	6 ♡	(All Pass)		

*forcing to game in N–S's bidding system.

You are West, and you lead the Ace of diamonds. This draws the five, six, and three. How do you continue?

□   □ . □

The full deal was:

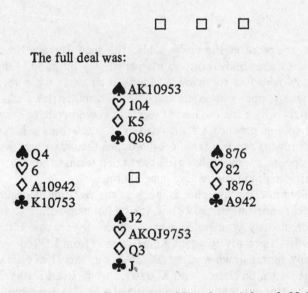

♠ AK10953
♡ 104
◊ K5
♣ Q86

♠ Q4
♡ 6
◊ A10942
♣ K10753

♠ 876
♡ 82
◊ J876
♣ A942

♠ J2
♡ AKQJ9753
◊ Q3
♣ J

The board looked flat at one table, where Atlanta's N–S pair managed to put the brakes on at five hearts and made that contract exactly. But when the Michigan players held the N–S cards in the other room, they bid as shown above. Since South's suit happened to be hearts, the auction got somewhat crowded. Both North and South had to cue-bid a *second*-round control at the five level as their first slam try, and an undignified slam resulted. Looking back, perhaps South should have settled for five hearts over five diamonds, trusting his partner to bid six with the right hand.

All sins in the auction were washed clean, however. After laying down the Ace of diamonds, the Atlanta West played another diamond! Apparently, he was intent on the idea of knocking the diamond King out of dummy before South could use it as an entry to the spade suit. As it was, declarer scampered off with his slam, and Michigan gained heavily.

West overlooked the fact that he had a partner at the table. An expert East would surely have played a higher diamond on the opening lead to encourage a diamond continuation, *unless he held the club Ace*. West should have interpreted the six of diamonds for what it was, a simple message that said, "Shift!" Even an expert can find himself operating in the dark if he ignores the simplicity of the basic signals.

□   □   □

Two

Everybody has a pet peeve at the bridge table. The great Terence Reese doesn't like it when somebody borrows his pencil. My bugaboo is unschooled opponents who like to viciously thumb their cards when they play them. I've seen people who could cash the third undertrick against my doubled contract with a snap so loud it seemed to reverberate to every corner of the room and produce a faint echo. You know how a Major League pitcher's throwing arm is often more developed than his other one? One lady I often oppose, I'll swear, has a right wrist that seems to be slightly bigger than her left. No doubt it's just my imagination.

I don't really mind the snapping as much as the fact that it occurs only on some tricks, not on others. I guess it's just human nature to be subconsciously affected by your holding to a certain degree. One Little Old Lady I know leads a relatively serene King of hearts from KQ964; the card will practically flutter down to the tabletop like a falling leaf wafted in the breeze. But let her be blessed with KQJ109, and the heart King will hit the table with a thump that can be heard in the bar. And the bar is three doors down from the bridge club.

I know very well that players don't deliberately intend anything improper by this. To them, signalling loud and soft as well as high and low is just part of the game. But it still bothers me. Of course, in an expert game, where the standard of ethics is very high, such shenanigans are unheard of. Everybody carefully observes the Proprieties (the section of the Laws of Contract Bridge that deals with conduct and etiquette), which caution that cards should be played without emphasis.

This hand, which had an amusing outcome, came up in a cut-around rubber bridge game. South, North, and West were experts, while East was a doubtful aspirant to expert status.

Dlr: South   ♠ A4
Vul: N–S   ♡ Q9852
          ◇ J63
          ♣ Q84

♠ 63
♡ 74   □
◇ K842
♣ AKJ95

Bidding: South   West   North   East
           1 ♡   2 ♣   3 ♡   5 ♣
           5 ♡   (All Pass)

You, West, lead the Ace of clubs, and you hold the trick as partner plays
the seven and declarer the three. How do you continue?

Partner's attitude and count in clubs are obvious to both of you, so
his play to trick one should be a suit preference signal. His club holding
must have been 10762. He would have played the *ten* with strong spades
and the *two* with strong diamonds, so the *seven* must show a tolerance for
the lead of *either* suit. (It is also possible East is trying to warn you *against*
a switch to either side suit—his only honor might be in trumps—but that is
unlikely on this bidding.) Since he is asking you to use your judgment, you
should shift to the *two of diamonds*. The full deal:

          ♠ A4
          ♡ Q9852
          ◇ J63
          ♣ Q84

♠ 63   ♠ K10872
♡ 74   □   ♡ 6
◇ K842   ◇ Q107
♣ AKJ95   ♣ 10762

          ♠ QJ95
          ♡ AKJ103
          ◇ A95
          ♣ 3

As you can see, the diamond shift is probably necessary to beat five hearts.

East's seven of clubs was a thoughtful play. Suppose the East hand and dummy were the same, but the full deal had been:

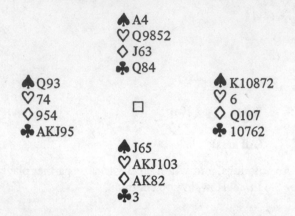

```
                    ♠ A4
                    ♡ Q9852
                    ◊ J63
                    ♣ Q84
♠ Q93                              ♠ K10872
♡ 74                               ♡ 6
◊ 954          □                   ◊ Q107
♣ AKJ95                            ♣ 10762
                    ♠ J65
                    ♡ AKJ103
                    ◊ AK82
                    ♣ 3
```

Now West must shift to a *spade* if the defense is to win three tricks. East's signal, which implied something in both spades and diamonds, allowed West to make an informed decision.

What happened when the hand was actually played? East went into a huddle at trick one and came to the conclusion that there was no need to let partner exercise his judgment. He therefore placed the club ten on the table with a vicious smack, and looked at West expectantly. North and South glared at this performance menacingly, and West sighed. With a sharp word to his partner about his unethical behavior, he shifted to a defiant *diamond*! So justice was served after all.

Maybe it really does pay to be honest.

Three

I may have created some mistaken impressions on the last hand. We have plenty of snappers in the tournament bridge world, but outright cheaters are few and far between. Most tournament players are basically true-blue honest, intelligent people, and premeditated cheating is exceedingly rare.

It's a shame that the infrequent *cause célèbre* is invariably splashed all over the media, creating a rather different impression. I was writing a manual for bridge teachers a while back, and in the interests of research, I deviously passed myself off as an intermediate student at one of the local Community School classes. Halfway through the evening, something led the instructor to digress about "serious" bridge players and what she knew of the tournament scene. She offered the opinion that most duplicate players had a little "edge" going for them. Is this really the perception the average person has of organized bridge?

The abhorrence of cheating among good players is not motivated entirely by altruism or fear of the consequences of being caught. If you've played bridge for very long, you know how sensitive most players are, and what an ego trip the game can be. Well, most people who play in tournament competition normally have a big enough ego that they figure they don't *need* to cheat to beat anybody they want!

The fact is, it's almost impossible to cheat over an extended period in high-level competition and get away with it. The game has a built-in protection factor. It's so difficult to win consistently at the national level, against the best players in North America, that anybody who does will invariably find himself scrutinized. In a way, the tournament world could be likened to a great big *National Enquirer*. If you and your partner start getting off to a few too many strange but devastating opening leads; if you always bid those laydown grand slams when the field doesn't even reach six; if your competitive bidding decisions are miraculously right on target time after time, the remarkable pattern of your results will begat talk, and the talk will feed on itself. You'll be under an unofficial microscope from then on, and God help you if you're fooling around.

I'll bet that, even today, there are people, maybe like that local bridge teacher I met, who would think that some of our sophisticated signalling methods are a little bit on the shady side. Take the following deal:

Dlr: South   ♠ K73
Vul: both   ♡ Q9
IMPs   ◇ KJ1064
          ♣ Q42

♠ J10954
♡ 432   □
◇ A87
♣ 106

Bidding:	South	West	North	East
	1NT	Pass	3NT	(All Pass)

You, West, lead the Jack of spades. Partner plays the two, and declarer's Ace wins. At trick two, declarer tosses out the Queen of diamonds. You duck, and partner plays the three. The two of diamonds is led next. You win your Ace this time, and partner contributes the nine. What do you lead now?

This is routine. You shift to a heart. The missing hands are:

```
                              ♠ 82
                              ♡ AKJ10
              □               ♦ 953
                              ♣ 9873
        ♠ AQ6
        ♡ 8765
        ♦ Q2
        ♣ AKJ5
```

Let's examine East's carding. His *two* of spades at trick one was attitude, showing no interest in your suit. When declarer led the Queen of diamonds, attitude was no consideration; his first responsibility was to show count, which he did with the diamond *three*. On the next diamond, there was nothing left for him to do but make a suit preference play. His *nine* of diamonds suggested he had better hearts than clubs (an understatement this time). With good clubs, he would play his *middle* diamond on the second round.

The *card you play* is a perfectly legitimate way of signalling your partner. It would, of course, be wrong to kick him under the table. Or, as would be more appropriate on this deal, to cough and beat your chest as he thought about what to lead after winning his Ace of diamonds.

Four

Playing in a Sectional Mixed Pairs, you sit down against the notorious Mike (Machine Gun) Kelly, the quickest draw in town.

The inordinately fast player is most dangerous when he is declarer and can best control the pace of the play. Let him get his hands on the dummy, and he'll have the whole hand sized up and the best line of play determined in less than a split second after the opening lead is made. Then ensues the famed Stampede, with declarer slapping down his cards at a terrifying rate of speed, as if the object of the game were to finish in the shortest possible time.

Such speed demons are common, and the defenders must be careful not to fall victim to a silly mistake because they let themselves get caught up in declarer's tempo. However, there are times when this may be easier said than done.

Dlr: South
Vul: N-S
Matchpoints

♠ AJ94
♡ K104
♦ 753
♣ Q73

♠ KQ83
♡ A8652
♦ 102
♣ J6

□

Bidding:	(MGK) South	(You) West	North	East
	1 ♦	Pass	1 ♠	Pass
	3 ♣	Pass	3 ♦	Pass
	5 ♦	Pass	6 ♦	(All Pass)

You lead the King of spades against Mike's slam. Dummy's Ace wins, partner plays the spade seven, and declarer the six. Hardly pausing for thought, declarer leads a diamond to his Ace and, in the same motion, tables the three of hearts. What do you do? (Quick!)

□ □ □

Whatever your decision, I hope you made it without a flicker. As it happens, the full deal is:

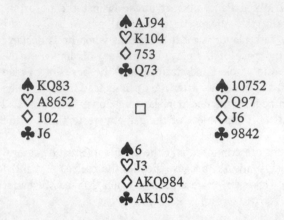

♠ AJ94
♡ K104
◇ 753
♣ Q73

♠ KQ83   ♠ 10752
♡ A8652   ♡ Q97
◇ 102   ◇ J6
♣ J6   ♣ 9842

♠ 6
♡ J3
◇ AKQ984
♣ AK105

Note that partner gave you *count* on the opening lead. He wanted to try to tell you whether the Queen of spades would cash. This is the rare occasion when showing attitude on partner's lead is secondary, a situation where the defense needs just *two* tricks to beat a slam. Almost surely, East's seven of spades suggests *four* cards. If he had a *doubleton* spade, declarer would have three, and would have showed his spade tolerance over three diamonds in case North had a five-card spade suit.

Since the dummy is fairly strong, and West knows declarer has no spade loser, he should duck the heart. Winning two heart tricks should be his best hope.

It was a good psychological stroke for Mike to go on and lead a heart at trick two. (He gave up on the technical play of trying to ruff out the spade Queen, which also requires a 2–2 trump break.) You might have jumped up with the heart Ace and tried to cash a spade, had you not trusted your partner's seven of spades. You'd really have to be on the ball to see your partner's signal, interpret it correctly, and play low to the second trick smoothly, all when declarer is determined to give you so little time for thought.

□   □   □

Five

Playing in a Pair game, but with scoring at IMPs, you and partner must handle this deal correctly:

Dlr: West ♠ Q98
Vul: both ♡ K96
           ◇ J85
           ♣ Q1052

                        ♠ A4
              □   ♡ AQ104
                        ◇ K9742
                        ♣ 87

Bidding:	South	West	North	East
		Pass	Pass	1 ◇
	1 ♠	Pass	2 ♠	Pass
	4 ♠	(All Pass)		

West, your partner, leads the three of diamonds. Dummy's Jack, your King, and declarer's Ace make up the first trick. Declarer then leads the two of spades to the six, Queen, and your Ace. What do you return?

□   □   □

The nine of diamonds. If partner happens to ruff this trick, you would like him to lead a heart next.

Partner obliges by ruffing with the spade five, and he obediently returns the three of hearts. Declarer puts up dummy's King, losing to your Ace. What do you lead next?

□   □   □

The seven of diamonds. Partner played high-low in trumps, so he had three, and can ruff another diamond. Your Queen of hearts may not cash. The full deal:

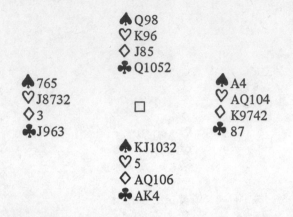

♠ Q98
♡ K96
◇ J85
♣ Q1052

♠ 765
♡ J8732
◇ 3
♣ J963

♠ A4
♡ AQ104
◇ K9742
♣ 87

♠ KJ1032
♡ 5
◇ AQ106
♣ AK4

If partner had failed to echo in trumps, you would be forced to try to cash a second heart.

☐   ☐   ☐

Six

Pairs composed of two blood relatives have always killed me, and it's gotten to the point that playing against them gives me a vague feeling of unease. Identical twins are the worst. I'm convinced a scientific study would show they don't need conventional defensive signals. Their common genes must provide a link, a special sort of super-partnership rapport, something close to ESP. Mother-son combinations are next. And even most husbands and wives operate against me as though they have all four hands in plain view. They must talk over their methods constantly: over breakfast, in bed, everywhere. No doubt before my bridge-playing days are over, I'll face a team-of-four made up of a set of quadruplets and get totally blown out. Too bad I was an only child.

In a Mens' Swiss, you must play against a brother-brother act. Luckily, you and partner wind up defending most of the hands, including:

Dlr: North   ♠ K94
Vul: N-S   ♡ 10
IMPs   ◇ K10642
            ♣ AQ84

♠ 3
♡ AKJ842   □
◇ A95
♣ 952

Bidding:	South	West	North	East
			1 ◇	Pass
	1 ♠	2 ♡	2 ♠	4 ♡*
	4 ♠	5 ♡	Pass	Pass
	5 ♠	(All Pass)		

     *Strictly preemptive; partner could have a terrible hand. He would start with a *cue-bid* if he held lots of high cards.

You, West, lead the heart Ace. Partner plays the seven, declarer the six. Plan your defense from here.

Lead the heart King. Partner has offered you a normally high heart, so his play should be considered as attitude, suggesting a heart continuation. Even though dummy will ruff, partner may judge that this is your best defense. Maybe he can see no good shift, and wants you to defend passively. As it is, he has a very good reason for desiring a further heart lead. The full deal is:

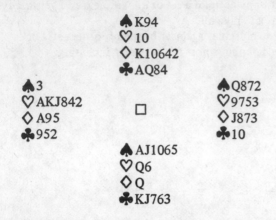

♠K94
♥10
♦K10642
♣AQ84

♠3
♥AKJ842
♦A95
♣952

♠Q872
♥9753
♦J873
♣10

♠AJ1065
♥Q6
♦Q
♣KJ763

If you force dummy, declarer will be unable to pick up partner's Queen of trumps, and will have to concede a spade trick as well as the diamond Ace, for down one. This hand is a good illustration of our principle that a high card should be *attitude*, asking for a continuation of the suit, if such an interpretation is at all conceivable.

By the way, are you and your partner related?

chapter five

MAKE COUNTING
A HABIT

PRELIMINARIES

If you've read a good book on declarer play, you know that declarer can occasionally use various techniques of *counting* to advantage. A judicious count of sure winners and potential losers can be of benefit in planning his play; a reconstruction of the defenders' distribution, or a count of the high-card points they show in the play might help him place the location of some crucial missing cards. However, declarer need not attempt to count the opponents' shape or high cards on *every* hand he plays; many problems in declarer play can be dealt with by relying on some of the purely technical weapons in his arsenal, such as a knowledge of card combinations or percentage play.

But for the defenders, who operate in the dark, often without adequate knowledge of each other's holdings, trying to figure out declarer's hand is a vital task—there are few times when they won't find it helpful (or mandatory) to *count*. I can promise you that unless you are willing to make counting a number one priority on every hand you defend, you're in for a lot of grief. Consistently tight defense will be impossible.

There are several applications of counting on defense, each one of which can be crucial. Nothing has changed since Chapter One, in which we saw that the defenders can count their potential tricks just as declarer counts his. In addition, reconstructing declarer's hand demands that you count his *distribution* and high-card *points*. Finally, it may help to try counting declarer's available *tricks*. As we saw in Chapter Two, this will help you decide whether you must hurry up and win some tricks for yourself, or whether you can play a safe, passive defense and *wait* for your tricks.

Suppose we look at how the various kinds of counting can help the defenders.

```
Dlr:  South        ♠ A5
Vul:  none         ♡ 32
                   ◇ Q1064
                   ♣ A8643
   ♠ J976                      ♠ K832
   ♡ J975                      ♡ 108
   ◇ 87         □              ◇ A52
   ♣ 1052                      ♣ KJ97
                   ♠ Q104
                   ♡ AKQ64
                   ◇ KJ93
                   ♣ Q
```

Bidding:
	South	West	North	East
	1 ♡	Pass	2 ♣	Pass
	2 ◇	Pass	3 ◇	Pass
	3NT	(All Pass)		

West leads the six of spades. Declarer ducks this, since West could have a five-card spade suit to the King-Jack, and East the diamond Ace. When East wins the spade King (declarer follows low, neglecting to falsecard with his ten), he should try to figure out declarer's distribution before proceeding. Declarer is known to have at least nine cards in the red suits (he would open one diamond with four hearts and four diamonds), but probably no more than nine (he would rebid any six-card heart suit at some point and would perhaps have preferred the diamond game to 3NT with five hearts and five diamonds). He has at least three spades, from West's opening lead. So, declarer should have at most one club. East can confidently bang down his *club King* (in case South's singleton club is the Queen), setting up five tricks for certain. This is the only sure-fire defense. Note the result if East returns partner's spade lead without stopping to do his counting. Declarer is a favorite to hold the spade Queen—his bid of 3NT would be a little strange otherwise. But even if West has that card, a spade return cannot possibly set up enough tricks to beat the contract.

```
Dlr:  South        ♠Q962
Vul:  none         ♡104
                   ◇J10753
                   ♣AQ
   ♠K4                        ♠75
   ♡AQ5                       ♡8762
   ◇K82        □              ◇96
   ♣J10853                    ♣K9742
                   ♠AJ1083
                   ♡KJ93
                   ◇AQ4
                   ♣6
```

South opened one spade, and when West doubled for takeout, North jumped to 2NT, which conventionally showed a spade raise with game-invitational values. East tried three clubs but South bid four spades. West judged correctly to let this play, but, unfortunately, his defense was less sharp than his bidding judgment. He led a club, which declarer won with dummy's Ace. A trump finesse lost, and declarer ruffed a club continuation. After drawing another trump, South sneakily played Ace of diamonds and a low diamond toward dummy. West ducked smoothly, hoping his partner could win and play a heart through, but dummy's ten held, and declarer exited with a diamond. West found himself stuck on lead, and he had to give up a heart trick or a ruff-and-discard.

A count of declarer's tricks would have saved West. He knew that declarer had one trick in clubs and only four in spades, so even if declarer took four diamond tricks, he would still be a trick short of his contract. West should therefore have gone up with his King of diamonds and gotten out with his last diamond, knowing that he would be sure to make two heart tricks eventually.

Dlr: South   ♠ A842
Vul: none   ♡ J93
              ◇ AJ42
              ♣ J7

```
♠ 75                              ♠ J1093
♡ A852            □              ♡ Q764
◇ 105                             ◇ 983
♣ K9642                           ♣ A3
```

              ♠ KQ6
              ♡ K10
              ◇ KQ76
              ♣ Q1085

Bidding:	South	West	North	East
	1 ◇	Pass	1 ♠	Pass
	2 ♠	Pass	3 ◇	Pass
	3NT	(All Pass)		

West leads the club four, and East wins. He knows that West has at most five clubs, so declarer has at least four. South opened one diamond and should have four or more cards in that suit. He raised spades, probably with only three-card support (since he bid game in notrump). Therefore, declarer should hold at most two hearts.

A heart switch looks more productive than a club continuation when declarer has four clubs (especially when West did not have a club sequence to lead from). West wins the heart Ace and returns a heart. East ducks, of course, and South has to win his King. The defense will be able to cash two more hearts (based on a deal of Alfred Sheinwold), for down one, when declarer has to knock out the other high club.

Dlr: North   ♠ AK6
Vul: none   ♡ Q94
              ◇ 1064
              ♣ A1043

```
♠ QJ4                             ♠ 109752
♡ K63             □              ♡ 105
◇ AJ52                            ◇ K97
♣ QJ5                             ♣ 987
```

              ♠ 83
              ♡ AJ872
              ◇ Q83
              ♣ K62

Bidding:

South	West	North	East
		1♣	Pass
1♡	Pass	2♡	Pass
Pass	Dbl.	Pass	2♠
3♡	(All Pass)		

West leads the spade Queen, won in dummy. Declarer passes the Queen of hearts to West's King, and wins the spade return. He draws the rest of the trumps, cashes the club King, and plays another club, ducking West's Jack. West knows that declarer had eight HCP in clubs and hearts. With the King of diamonds as well, he would have been strong enough to try for game once his partner raised hearts. West can safely underlead his diamond honors, and when East wins the diamond King and returns the nine (suggesting that he originally had only three), West will know where to cash the setting trick.

Dlr: West
Vul: N-S

♠KQ63
♡A4
◊Q10964
♣J4

♠A8
♡K10973
◊K73
♣A95

□

♠94
♡Q8652
◊852
♣Q107

♠J10752
♡J
◊AJ
♣K8632

Bidding:

South	West	North	East
		1♡	
		Dbl.	3♡
4♠	(All Pass)		

The opening lead is the ten of hearts. Declarer wins in dummy and leads a trump. West wins and leads a heart, ruffed. Declarer draws another round of trumps and plays Ace and Jack of diamonds to West's King. The key here is for West to count declarer's tricks. He can count four in diamonds, the heart Ace, and no more than four in trumps. Since declarer cannot make his contract without a trick in clubs, West can afford to exit safely with his last diamond. Declarer can throw away three clubs (really, he's discarding *winners*, since these are cards that he could ruff in dummy just as easily), but he must make a club play sooner or later, losing two tricks there.

Another way for West to look at the situation is that declarer is known to have at most six major-suit cards, so he has no fewer than seven cards in clubs and diamonds. After he plays five rounds of diamonds, there will still be two clubs left in his hand; so there is no hurry for West to lay down his club Ace. Any club tricks he has coming cannot go away.

□　　□　　□

AT THE TABLE

One

"Boy, Marvin, I made one terrible play tonight," you wailed as you pulled a stool up to the bar. "I can't believe that," Marvin replied generously. You know all about Marvin. He's the bartender at the little place down the street from the bridge club. He's never played bridge in his life, as far as we know. Nevertheless, we treat him as an equal because of the vast amount of bridge knowledge he's absorbed by osmosis, merely from listening to a thousand post-mortems in the bar. He's always ready to lend a sympathetic ear to the bridge players' woes and always agrees with them amiably (he gets bigger tips that way). Indeed, certain of our players have almost conferred *expert* status on Marvin. Their rationale is simple: They figure that anybody who agrees with them as often as he does just has to be a great bridge player.

"What happened?" Marvin asked, beginning to construct a strawberry daiquiri. You hastened to put the problem on paper; the nearest thing handy was a cocktail napkin.

Dlr: South　♠ K53
Vul: none　♥ Q7
Matchpoints　♦ QJ1064
　　　　　　♣ 1053

♠ A8
♥ J10963
♦ 95　　　□
♣ AJ72

"They bid 1NT–2NT–3NT," you said. "I led the Jack of hearts." Marvin nodded. "The Queen held in dummy, and declarer led a spade to his Queen. I won, and . . ."

☐　　☐　　☐

Marvin looked at the napkin and frowned. "Don't tell me you continued hearts." "I'm afraid I did just that," you said sheepishly. "Well," said Marvin in a disturbing tone, "I'll have to admit that was questionable." "Questionable?" you said. "Very good, Marvin. Very tactful. It was questionable, all right." "Yeah," Marvin said. "You knew declarer had the Ace-King of hearts and the spade Queen. That's nine HCP. He had to have the diamond Ace-King, else why did he not set up his diamonds first thing? If his diamond holding were Kx or Axx, he'd make a diamond play immediately. And he'd never win the first trick in dummy and take out what might be the only entry to the diamond suit unless he could see the suit was ready to run. So that's sixteen of his HCP you could account for. He couldn't have the club King. That would give him nineteen HCP, too many to open 1NT. A low club switch is completely safe." "Not only safe," you finished, "it was mandatory. I could count at least nine tricks for declarer at this point, so the only chance to beat him was to run four clubs." "What was the full deal?" Marvin asked. You scribbled in the other hands.

```
                    ♠ K53
                    ♥ Q7
                    ♦ QJ1064
                    ♣ 1053
♠ A8                                    ♠ J976
♥ J10963                                ♥ 852
♦ 95              ☐                     ♦ 832
♣ AJ72                                   ♣ K96
                    ♠ Q1042
                    ♥ AK4
                    ♦ AK7
                    ♣ Q84
```

"Even if you shift, your partner might have returned a heart instead of a club," Marvin said solicitously. "Not if I lead the *deuce* of clubs," you said grimly. "I'd lead a higher club spot if I was still interested in the suit I led to begin with. The deuce of clubs should say 'return clubs.'" Marvin set the daiquiri on the bar, along with a long straw, and shrugged. "You won't make another error like that for awhile, I'll bet." "Hopefully not," you said. "By the way, Marvin, how'd you like to play sometime? I think your talents are being wasted in here."

□ □ □

Two

Playing against capable opposition in a Regional Open Pairs final, you pick up:

Dlr: South   ♠Q4
Vul: E-W   ♡J964
Matchpoints   ◊J63
             ♣Q1072

The opponents have a simple auction to game: one spade-three spades-four spades. For no very excellent reason, you decide to lead a club, and this dummy hits:

            ♠A952
            ♡A83
            ◊K1072
            ♣J5

♠Q4
♡J964
◊J63   □
♣Q1072

Dummy plays low at trick one, partner puts up the King, and declarer's Ace wins. He leads a spade to the Ace and a spade back to his King, partner's Jack and your Queen crashing. Next, declarer plays the heart King, heart Ace, and ruffs a heart in hand. Finally, he exits with a club to your Queen. Your play.

□ □ □

A club return has to be right. If declarer has a club or two left in hand, you only give him a ruff that he can take anyway. But even if he's out of clubs and he gets the dreaded ruff-and-discard, it won't help him. Declarer had five spades and two hearts; if he has only two clubs, then he has *four* diamonds, and he must still lose at least one diamond trick unless he has both the Ace and Queen.

A diamond play would be very dangerous, since declarer is marked on the bidding with at least one honor. And a heart return would give him a ruff-sluff he *could* use if his distribution were 5-2-3-3. The full deal:

```
                    ♠ A952
                    ♡ A83
                    ◇ K1072
                    ♣ J5
      ♠ Q4                        ♠ J8
      ♡ J964          □           ♡ Q1072
      ◇ J63                       ◇ Q85
      ♣ Q1072                     ♣ K843
                    ♠ K10763
                    ♡ K5
                    ◇ A94
                    ♣ A96
```

The best you can do is hold this hand to five, but that should worth a fair matchpoint score. In a Regional Open Pairs final, you'd get a zero if they made six.

□   □   □

Three

A Men's Board-a-Match Teams is about as tough an event as they come. Unfortunately, there are very few of them to play in, since Board-a-Match has been relegated to backseat status in favor of the popular Swiss format. However, there is a four-session National Championship at the Spring Nationals, scored this way. A valued prize to win.

Battling to place in the men's B-a-M, you hold, as West:

Dlr: South   ♠ K53
Vul: N–S   ♡ 10642
            ◊ 9
            ♣ AJ953

Bidding:	South	West	North	East
	1♠	Pass	2♡	Pass
	2♠	Pass	3♠	(All Pass)

With a mediocre hand plus trump control, you lead your singleton diamond. You see:

            ♠ Q1064
            ♡ AKQ3
            ◊ 1064
            ♣ 86
♠ K53
♡ 10642   □
◊ 9
♣ AJ953

Your diamond nine rides to declarer's Queen; partner contributes an encouraging eight. Declarer then plays off dummy's three top hearts, pitching the seven of clubs, and leads the spade Queen. Partner follows low, and declarer finesses to your King. How do you defend?

Declarer has the diamond Ace-Queen and spade Ace-Jack; that's 11 HCP. The club King would make 14, and with such a nice minimum, he would have accepted the try for game. You can *underlead* your club Ace to partner, ruff the high diamond return, and your side should score a fourth trick with partner's diamond intermediates. The full deal:

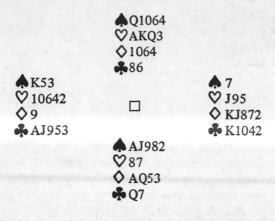

♠Q1064
♡AKQ3
◊1064
♣86

♠K53
♡10642
◊9
♣AJ953

♠7
♡J95
◊KJ872
♣K1042

♠AJ982
♡87
◊AQ53
♣Q7

Declarer could have made four by leading dummy's last heart and discarding his club Queen on it, ruining your communication with partner's hand (a "Scissors Coup"!), but he couldn't tell who had the last heart, and he hated to give up the trump finesse anyway. Note that if declarer's clubs were Kx, he would be less anxious to take a fast discard, as he did.

At the other table, your teammates reached three spades also, but West led the club Ace and continued a club to the King. East, however, shifted to a *low* diamond instead of the Jack, a horrendous play that deserved to lose the board. Your declarer happily passed this to dummy's ten and wound up with ten tricks, one more than they should have made against you.

□ □ □

Four

I never like to eat a big meal between sessions of a two-session event. If I pig out, all the blood heads for my stomach instead of servicing my brain, and I invariably make a lot of empty-headed mistakes in the evening.

Out for a quick bite between sessions of the Sunday Swiss, you settle for the salad bar. This gives one of your gourmet friends plenty of room to write down a defensive problem on one half of your placemat. "This was from our first match," he says. "If you get it right, you win the match."

Dlr: West   ♠ QJ65
Vul: both   ♡ 7
IMPs   ◇ QJ102
           ♣ AK86

♠ A8
♡ J10952   □
◇ AK75
♣ J4

Your friend furnished the auction. "You opened one heart as dealer. North doubled, your partner preempted with three hearts, and South jumped to four spades. You have too much defense to save and you're vulnerable anyway, so four spades is passed out. Say you lead the diamond Ace: two, three, four. What's your plan from here?"

□   □   □

The solution proved to be easy, if not altogether obvious, because you've always had the habit of estimating your possible defensive tricks against game and slam contracts. Your analysis went like this: "If declarer has a four spade bid, partner is marked with at most a Queen in addition to his likely heart honor. The heart Queen would be of no use to the defense but the club Queen might. To protect my possible club trick, though, I have to keep declarer from discarding his club losers on dummy's diamonds. So I continue with King and another diamond." "Partner follows and declarer sheds a club," your friend says through a mouthful of baked potato. "Now declarer comes to the heart Ace to lead a trump." "I fly with the Ace and play a fourth diamond. If partner is able to ruff dummy's winner, declarer may be stranded with a little club." "Very nice," said your inquisitor. The full deal had been:

           ♠ QJ65
           ♡ 7
           ◇ QJ102
           ♣ AK86

♠ A8   ♠ 32
♡ J10952   □   ♡ Q8643
◇ AK75   ◇ 983
♣ J4   ♣ Q103

           ♠ K10974
           ♡ AK
           ◇ 64
           ♣ 9752

This hand could just as well have gone in Chapter One.

"So what happened at your table?" you asked. But your friend hastily turned his attention to an overflowing plate of ribs, and seemed too busy to reply.

☐　　☐　　☐

Five

The ACBL's Master Point plan is designed to recognize experience and expertise at tournament bridge. The plan was simple enough at its inception (decades ago). Winning a National Championship back then might get you only a full master point or two(!). Today, tournament bridge has become big business. There are master points to be won in thousands of tournament events yearly, events of all kinds. Figuring out just how many points are awarded for placing fourth in a 15-table section in a 251-table game restricted to players with less than 750 master points using only Class A conventions has become a pretty complicated affair. Inevitably, there will be inequities in so complex a system.

In 1981, my partner and I played our buns off to finish ninth in the Life Master Pairs, a six-session National Championship with brutal cuts in the field after the second and fourth sessions. Apparently, the League doesn't think much of people who finish ninth. For finishing ahead of 539 pairs of Life Masters, we got about as many master points as three section tops in the weaker, Regionally-rated pair games (which ran concurrently) would have brought.

The Knockout events are an occasional source of complaints along the same line. To win a Knockout (an event in which teams-of-four play a long head-to-head match; the winner moves on to the next round; the loser is eliminated), several tough sessions of play are required. This is the most demanding event on the typical tournament schedule. But, it is argued, the master point award is often incompatible with the amount of time (and skill) involved in winning. Worse, the KO is often run concurrently with some of the two-session pair events, so that players can effectively be penalized master point-wise for preferring to slug it out in the KOs.

I won't get myself in trouble by speculating on why the Men's and Womens' Pairs have the same awards when the record clearly indicates that most of the better players are men. But there are some other problems that come to mind . . .

This hand comes from a Regional Open Pairs, run concurrently with the first day of the Knockout event. Since almost all the better players are over in the KOs, this Open figures to be a complete turkey-shoot. Since you know and appreciate the value of master points, you're to be found in the pair game. Pretty soon:

```
Dlr:  South        ♠ KJ4
Vul:  none         ♡ K953
Matchpoints        ◇ J6
                   ♣ AJ105
                              ♠ 8532
                              ♡ A7
            □                 ◇ Q105
                              ♣ KQ92
```

Bidding:	South	West	North	East
	1♡	Pass	3♡	Pass
	4♡	(All Pass)		

Partner leads the ten of spades, won by dummy's King. Declarer calls for a low trump. Would you win immediately or duck?

□   □   □

It's best to win, to avoid the possibility of being endplayed with the trump Ace later. Suppose you return a passive trump. Declarer wins and partner follows low (not with the Queen, thank goodness). Declarer now cashes his Ace and Queen of spades, partner following, and leads a low club to the ten and your King. With declarer gazing confidently in your direction, what do you return?

□   □   □

Count declarer's tricks. Three in spades, four in hearts. If he has Axx of diamonds, ten tricks are certain. But if partner holds the diamond Ace (and declarer has, say, Kxx) you can always set the hand with a *club* return. Declarer will get two club tricks (that's nine in all), but he'll never make a trick in diamonds unless you break the suit for him. A spade return, of course, would give away a trick. The full deal:

                    ♠ KJ4
                    ♡ K953
                    ◇ J6
                    ♣ AJ105
    ♠ 1097   ♠ 8532
    ♡ 86   ♡ A7
    ◇ A8732   □   ◇ Q105
    ♣ 864   ♣ KQ92
                    ♠ AQ6
                    ♡ QJ1042
                    ◇ K94
                    ♣ 73

Note that declarer cannot have Ax in diamonds. He could always make then, simply by exiting with Ace and a diamond. The defense would have to help him by breaking the club suit.

It's too bad that they don't dish out some large number of master points on the spot for defending a hand so well!

□   □   □

Six

Speaking of bigger and better tournaments and the chance for more master points, a morning Knockout event is now offered at the National Tournaments. For a long time, there were only pair games in the A.M., but a KO was added recently, perhaps on the theory that if somebody was willing to get up at the ungodly hour of 8:30, it might as well be for a worthwhile reason. If you think you can play bridge on less sleep than the other guy, this could be your event. I'm afraid I'd have mixed emotions about winning a match. If you get beat, you can at least sleep late the next morning.

Trying to capture the Fishbein Trophy (awarded for most master points won at the Summer Nationals), you enter everything in sight, including the morning KO. Having swallowed mass quantities of black coffee, you should be ready to defend this hand:

Dlr: East   ♠ K106
Vul: both   ♡ K7
IMPs   ◊ AJ5
          ♣ K10863

♠ Q52
♡ J10963   □
◊ 942
♣ A7

Bidding:

South	West	North	East
			Pass
Pass	Pass	1♣	Pass
1NT	(All Pass)		

You start your heart Jack. Declarer puts up dummy's King, losing to partner's Ace. The eight of hearts comes back, declarer plays low, and you
overtake to continue the suit. Declarer wins his Queen and partner follows.
A diamond to the Ace wins, and when the diamond Jack is led next, partner's Queen comes up. Declarer wins the King, pauses for a moment (and
you should be thinking at this point as well), and then leads the club Jack.
How should you defend? (Quick!)

□   □   □

I recommend you duck. Declarer appears to have five diamond tricks
and a heart. So partner will need to have the spade Ace. He rates to have
the club Queen, too; declarer wouldn't try an immediate diamond finesse
if he had the Queen and Jack of clubs. If you duck this trick, declarer will
have a chance to misguess, allowing the defense to take four hearts, two
clubs, and the spade Ace. Of course, you could rise with the club Ace, cash
your hearts, and lead a spade, hoping declarer might be more apt to guess
wrong in spades. However, any reasonable declarer will probably go right—he
might simply play for the black Aces to be in different hands; or he might
expect you would have balanced with five decent hearts and two Aces.

Did someone say, why not win the club Ace, cash hearts, and hope
for partner to have the spade Ace-Jack? You need to order another pot of
coffee. Partner had the heart Ace, and the minor-suit Queens. The Ace and
Jack of spades would give him 13 HCP, and he would have opened the
bidding.

Maybe you should take a quick nap the next time you're the dummy.

chapter six

THE LOGIC
OF DEFENSE

PRELIMINARIES

To play this game well, you must be willing to think hard. A session of play amounts to a long string of little problem situations. The winners are usually the players who solve (or guess the answers to) most of the problems. Some of the problems can be handled adequately by adherence to a set of rules, but the answers to others must be *deduced*. Bridge is a logical game, a game for thinking. (I've always believed that the brooding sculpted figure of Rodin's "The Thinker" must be hunched over an invisible card table, pondering whether to return a club or a diamond.) If you like to solve enigmatic mathematical puzzles, murder mysteries such as the complex edifices of Ellery Queen, or problems that demand intuitively good reasoning, you'd make a good bridge player. Computer programmers are often skilled at the game.

One of the techniques we discussed in the preceding chapter was *counting* the opponents' high-card points. You may be able to arrive at some helpful conclusions, based on the logical interpretation of this evidence. For example, if player A passed as dealer, he should have less than 13 HCP, so if he shows up with two Aces, a King, and a Jack, you can safely assume he will have no more high cards. This is called drawing an *inference*. In contract bridge, the techniques of counting and inference complement each other.

The inferences that are frequently drawn from what happens (or doesn't happen) in the bidding are usually simple and obvious, but there are many other, more subtle, sources of information. In this chapter, we will deal primarily with inferences drawn from the way declarer handles his dummy. If declarer is known to be a capable player and can be relied on to play logically and correctly, the defenders may gain some information. It can, in a way, be easier to play against strong opposition whose play you can trust implicitly.

Inferences from declarer's play may be drawn from his plan of play as a whole, but even the way he attacks individual suits can be revealing. Say you are defending a heart contract. Declarer has drawn trumps, leaving a couple remaining in dummy, and now he makes a play in the spade suit:

♠ A73   ♠ KJ94

He leads a low spade to dummy's nine, losing to partner's ten. What's going on? Well, partner must have the spade Queen. And declarer has at least two more spades in hand. If he started with a doubleton spade, he would have played the King or Jack of spades on the first lead, trying for just one loser in this suit. Therefore, when he leads a second spade toward dummy, you should be prepared to duck again, and declarer will have a chance to misguess a second time.

 ♠ QJ73   ♠64

Declarer leads the four of spades to his nine, losing to your Jack. Partner would have hastened to win the trick if he had both the Ace and King of spades, so declarer is marked with one honor. He must have something like A9xx; with K9xx he would have put up his King, hoping it would hold.

♠ AJ73   ♠64

Declarer leads dummy's four of spades to his ten, losing to your Jack. Partner would have split his honors to insure one trick if he had King-Queen, so declarer holds one honor. As before, he would have been willing to play the King if he had it, hoping for just one loser; so his holding might be Q10xx.

Similar situations arise when the play is at notrump. Say your opening lead vs. 1NT is the spade five from K10752. Dummy produces AQ6. Declarer finesses the Queen successfully, but your partner is marked with the Jack, declarer having failed to duck your lead to his hand. You can safely press the attack on this suit when you regain the lead. Or, suppose partner leads the spade deuce, and you sit behind dummy's KJ6 with A85. If declarer calls for the Jack, you may infer he does not hold 10xx. The purpose of this type of mental exercise, of course, is to help the defenders build up a picture of declarer's high cards and distribution. This, we have seen, may be an essential step toward producing the best defense.

<pre>
                  ♠ QJ1064
                  ♡ Q10
                  ♢ A853
                  ♣ 75
  ♠ A5   ♠ 9873
  ♡ 74   ♡ 65
  ♢ K10962   □   ♢ Q4
  ♣ AJ83   ♣ Q9642
                  ♠ K2
                  ♡ AKJ9832
                  ♢ J7
                  ♣ K10
</pre>

Bidding: | South | West | North | East |
|---|---|---|---|
| | 1♢ | 1♠ | Pass |
| 3♡ | Pass | 4♡ | (All Pass) |

Figuring that if they're good enough to bid, they're good enough to lead, West starts with the ten of diamonds. Dummy's Ace wins, East playing the four and declarer the seven. Declarer cashes the heart Queen and leads a spade to his King and West's Ace. West can infer his partner has the Queen of diamonds, else declarer would have ducked the opening lead to his hand. He can underlead the diamond King again (he might try a suit-preference *deuce*), and East's club return will set the contract.

Now that we have sharpened up our card sense by considering some suits in isolation, we can move on and see some simple examples of drawing

inferences from declarer's approach to the hand as a whole. Inference, for
instance, may help you choose your defensive *program*.

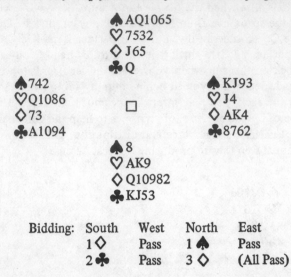

Bidding:

	South	West	North	East
	1♦	Pass	1♠	Pass
	2♣	Pass	3♦	(All Pass)

Favoring the unbid suit, West leads the six of hearts, which goes to the
Jack and Ace. When declarer plays a club next, West should shift to trumps
after winning. Some players might look at dummy's imposing spade suit
and, afraid that declarer will get discards, continue hearts. However, declarer's interest in preparing club ruffs in dummy makes it unlikely he has
the spade King. He's rather more likely to have a *singleton*. On a trump
switch, East will play off three rounds, and N–S will take a minus score for
getting carried away in the bidding.

♠764
♡J932
♦J865
♣75

♠Q1052
♡64
♦KQ43
♣Q103

♠AK3
♡10
♦972
♣J98642

♠J98
♡AKQ875
♦A10
♣AK

South reaches four hearts after opening with two clubs (strong and arti-
ficial). West finds a low spade lead, and the defenders cash out their book.
West then shifts to the King of diamonds. Declarer wins and runs six heart
tricks and the top clubs, forcing West to decide what his final discard
should be. Clearly, he should hang on to the diamond Queen. Declarer's
hand cannot be:

♠ J98
♡ AKQ875
◇ A
♣ AKJ

since he could have easily ruffed his losing club before taking out all of
dummy's trumps.

```
                    ♠ AKQ1075
                    ♡ Q105
                    ◇ 103
                    ♣ 104
♠ 82                                    ♠ 963
♡ K6                                    ♡ AJ92
◇ J765              □                   ◇ A82
♣ J8752                                 ♣ K93
                    ♠ J4
                    ♡ 8743
                    ◇ KQ94
                    ♣ AQ6
```

Bidding:

	South	West	North	East
			1 ♠	Dbl.
	Redbl.	2 ♣	2 ♠	Pass
	3NT	(All Pass)		

West leads the five of clubs. Declarer puts up dummy's ten, and wins East's
King with the Ace. He goes to dummy with a spade and leads the ten of
diamonds, trying to sneak the ninth trick through. East should place declarer with the Ace and Queen of clubs. With Axx, he would have *held up*
his Ace, and with AJx, he would have insured a second stopper by playing
a low club from dummy on the opening lead. Declarer is surely about to
play the King of diamonds if he has it (he will not misguess, on the bidding,

if he holds KJx). East should hop up with his diamond Ace and return a low heart as the only chance for a set.

Note that East can't play declarer for the heart King and the Queen-Jack of diamonds. He could then have set up his ninth trick with an immediate heart play.

```
                    ♠ KJ1084
                    ♡ AQJ
                    ◇ J105
                    ♣ Q5
   ♠ A62                          ♠ Q953
   ♡ 10875                        ♡ K3
   ◇ K6            □              ◇ 8732
   ♣ A1063                        ♣ 874
                    ♠ 7
                    ♡ 9642
                    ◇ AQ94
                    ♣ KJ92
```

Bidding:	South	West	North	East
			1 ♠	Pass
	2 ◇	Pass	2 ♠	Pass
	2NT	Pass	3NT	(All Pass)

Trapped by the odd two diamond response, West tries an opening club lead, which goes to declarer's nine. Declarer plays a heart to the Jack, losing to the King. East returns the eight of clubs, and West takes his Ace. He should lead a low spade now, expecting his partner to have the Queen. If declarer held the Queen of spades, it is very likely his first play would have been a spade to dislodge the Ace.

On the actual layout, the defense must set up a second spade trick, else declarer has time to establish his diamonds and make his ninth trick with a good guess in spades.

□   □   □

AT THE TABLE

One

It is often said that learning bridge will improve one's memory, or that persons with good memories are more apt to excel at the game. In truth, long-term memory plays little part in success or failure, except insofar as memory and the ability to learn from experience are related. There is a little irony here, considering how well constant bridge players remember the hands they play. Go out to dinner with a group between sessions of an Open Pairs and everybody knows and can discuss all 26 hands from that afternoon. Riding home, you can bring up a hand from early in the tournament, played perhaps three days before, and somebody will invariably say, "Oh yes, I remember that hand," and he'll proceed to tell you what happened when it came to his table. Non-bridge players and many social players find all this quite remarkable.

Not long ago, I came across a musty set of hand records from a session I played at the Summer Nationals in Miami in 1975. Some of the deals looked totally unfamiliar, but on a few, a memory stirred. Some feature of the hand flicked a rusty switch and the result of the deal came back to me after nine years. Not that I have an especially good memory—I just play a lot of bridge. Of course, remembering the hands can be an affliction. There are certain hands I'd love to forget, if they'd only go away.

Why should bridge players remember the hands so well? Partly, it may simply be born of a strong desire to remember, or because session after session of bridge makes remembering routine. A good analogy would be a Major League pitcher in *his* element; after a game, he can tell the sportswriters about every pitch he threw, in their precise order, whether they were balls or strikes, and so on. Similarly, a Grandmaster at chess can replay in his mind many games from throughout his career.

This is a hand I defended in a Regional Masters' Pairs in 1976. It's unusual for me to recall a hand like this because the only hands I usually remember from so far back are the ones on which I did something ghastly.

Dlr: North
Vul: both
Matcnpoints

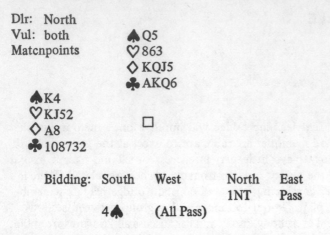

♠ Q5
♡ 863
◇ KQJ5
♣ AKQ6

♠ K4
♡ KJ52
◇ A8
♣ 108732

☐

Bidding:

South	West	North	East
		1NT	Pass
4♠	(All Pass)		

For reasons that now escape me, I led an aggressive low heart. Perhaps I was afraid dummy would have a good diamond suit, for discards. Partner produced the heart Queen and declarer won the Ace. Declarer now led a club to dummy and finessed the spade Queen to my King. How would you defend from here?

☐   ☐   ☐

The memories are especially sweet because this was a good thinking hand, a sheep-from-the-goats type hand. And for once I passed the test. I returned a club. Declarer couldn't have a heart loser unless he also had three clubs. This was a matchpoint event, remember, and he couldn't forego his best play for an overtrick in what was surely a normal contract. How would *you* play at matchpoints if you were looking at a heart loser and only one or two clubs? Right. You'd try to get rid of your loser before taking what might be a losing trump finesse.

As it happened, partner ruffed the club, put me back in with the diamond Ace, and ruffed another club, for down one and a cold top to us.

The full deal was:

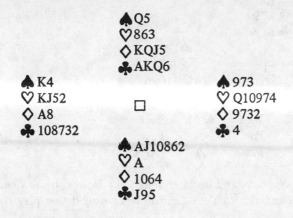

♠Q5
♡863
◇KQJ5
♣AKQ6

♠K4
♡KJ52
◇A8
♣108732

♠973
♡Q10974
◇9732
♣4

♠AJ10862
♡A
◇1064
♣J95

Ah, sweet memories!

□   □   □

Two

Playing in the second session of a Flighted Open Pairs, you are having an excellent game. You've made few errors and none that were costly. You've gotten the most out of your own hands and the opposition has fallen down on some of theirs. No nice old ladies have come along and saddled you with some horrible fix. Since you had a fair score in the first session, you figure you're in fine position to take this event, if you don't miss any obvious opportunities from here on. This is the first board of the next-to-last round, vs. a seeded pair.

Dlr: South   ♠ KJ87
Vul: N–S   ♡ K6
Matchpoints   ♦ 875
              ♣ KQ95

                         ♠ Q53
                         ♡ J873
           □   ♦ J1096
                         ♣ A2

Bidding:	South	West	North	East
	1NT	Pass	2♣	Pass
	2♠	Pass	4♠	(All Pass)

Partner leads the heart deuce, and declarer wins your Jack with the Ace. The spade ten is led and run to your Queen. What should you play to trick three?

    There is a strong temptation to switch to diamonds, but it's the "automatic" plays that should be most carefully examined. How would declarer play the trump suit with A109x opposite dummy's KJ87? If he feared a diamond shift through his hand, he would take his finesse the other way. But no matter which way he chose to finesse, he would *cash a high honor* in one hand before finessing. Partner should have the Ace of spades! If he does, he can have no other high cards, so a diamond play is futile. However, you may set the contract by playing Ace and another club now. Perhaps partner can give you a ruff when he gets in. The full deal was:

             ♠ KJ87
             ♡ K6
             ♦ 875
             ♣ KQ95
♠ A2   ♠ Q53
♡ 10952   ♡ J873
♦ 432   □   ♦ J1096
♣ 8763   ♣ A2
             ♠ 10964
             ♡ AQ4
             ♦ AKQ
             ♣ J104

You were headed for a good matchpoint result when they arrived in spades instead of 3NT, but a set and a plus score should earn a top and might sew up the event for you.

□   □   □

Three

In a Swiss Team-of-Four, the teams play each other in a series of short matches (usually eight or nine of them). Pairings are determined by matching teams with similar won-lost records (like a Swiss format in a chess tournament, hence the name). The team that wins the most matches captures the event. If there are eight matches, the most crucial (beside the last one, which usually determines the final outcome, and the first one, which sets the tone for the whole day) can be number Three. It is at this point that the stronger teams, who have usually won their first two matches (against unseeded opposition) without difficulty, start to knock heads. If you have winning aspirations, you're apt to find out right here if there is any hope for your team, or whether you can resign yourself to another mundane 5-and-3 day.

You are 2-and-0, and so are they. The exchanges seem to be very close at your table. They bid a good slam, but you got them for 500 in a phantom save. What might be going on at the other table, you can't imagine, but you know this part-score hand could make the difference in the match.

Dlr: North
Vul: both
IMPs

♠ 1075
♡ J1075
◊ 86
♣ A652

♠ A83
♡ 9642
◊ A5
♣ KQ108

□

Bidding:	South	West	North	East
			Pass	1 ♣
	1 ◊	1 ♠	Pass	2 ♠
	3 ◊	(All Pass)		

Partner leads the King of hearts. Declarer wins the Ace and pushes out the King of diamonds, which you take. What should you return?

□　□　□

If partner got out the shotgun by leading the heart King from Kx, your chances of winning five tricks are zero. However, if he does hold the heart Queen, he almost surely began with King-Queen *doubleton*. Suppose, instead, that declarer's heart holding were *Ax*. He would return a heart at trick two, setting up a quick discard for a black-suit loser. (It is practically certain that if declarer had only two hearts and at most three spades, he would have a club loser.) He would not concede a tempo by leading a trump to you.

Therefore, you should return a heart to (hopefully) partner. He can put you back in with the spade Ace, you give him a heart ruff, and his club shift may establish the setting trick in time. The full deal:

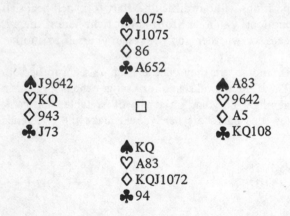

```
              ♠ 1075
              ♡ J1075
              ◇ 86
              ♣ A652
♠ J9642                      ♠ A83
♡ KQ                         ♡ 9642
◇ 943          □            ◇ A5
♣ J73                        ♣ KQ108
              ♠ KQ
              ♡ A83
              ◇ KQJ1072
              ♣ 94
```

At the other table, your opponents took a questionable push to three spades on the E-W cards. Declarer was able to ruff his losing diamond in dummy, but when he played Ace and another trump to South, a further diamond lead promoted the ten of spades for the setting trick, and your teammates scored up +100. They had only a fair set otherwise, though, and you needed to beat three diamonds at your table, for a combined result of +200 and a gain of 5 IMPs, to pull this match out and keep your chances of taking the event alive.

□　□　□

Four

Judging by the many letters to the editor that appear in the ACBL *Bulletin*, play-for-play is a rather controversial subject. Many experts, of course, hire themselves out as partners and teammates for ACBL events. Some people think this is a practice in the great American capitalistic tradition, while others see it as patently odious and unfair. The idea of paying some expert to help you win master points that you would find hard to come by on your own skills does seem a little repugnant (even to me, and I play professionally all the time), and the players who hire a pro strictly for this purpose have to live with the results they obtain.

However, there are more constructive reasons for retaining a professional. I admire anyone who views a professional date as primarily a *learning* experience. To me, this seems no different from taking a playing lesson from a tennis pro, and there is no stigma attached to *that*. Then there are other players who simply appreciate the beauties of the game, love to see it played well, and are willing to pay for a good partner and a good partnership. Who could criticize such an altruistic attitude? If professionalism in bridge is banned (and now and then, there are rumblings to that effect), both the good and bad facets will disappear. Personally, I think the practice is too well entrenched. If anything, the advent of the League-approved professional organizations is giving it more legitimacy and impetus.

Playing with a client in a Regional pair event (for your usual 44 cents a card), you hold, as West:

♠ 93
♡ K1062
♦ Q104
♣ K752

Nobody is vulnerable, and there are three passes to partner, who opens one heart. South overcalls one spade, you raise to two hearts, and North lifts to two spades. Your partner jumps to four hearts, and South bids four spades of course, giving you one of those awkward problems that playing with a customer can pose.

The opponents have clearly taken a sacrifice against the value of your game. You have a sound raise, four trumps, and no waste in spades, so technically you can and should encourage partner to bid five hearts by *passing* around to him. That would be the correct action with a trustworthy partner, but a client may not realize what is going on. He may think, since you passed, that he's supposed to pass as well, and the opponents will get to play undoubled in their save! Your options under the circumstances are: Do what you know is right and, if necessary, explain to partner after the session how he should have known to take some action; or try to guess the winning action yourself. Being a pragmatist, you double, and all pass.

Having read Chapter Three, you lead the King of hearts, reserving the chance to switch at trick two. The table hits with:

        ♠ A10752
        ♡ Q75
        ◇ 75
        ♣ Q106

♠ 93
♡ K1062   □
◇ Q104
♣ K752

Your heart King holds, partner playing the nine, so you continue hearts, and declarer ruffs. He plays a spade to the Ace, partner dropping the Queen, and leads a diamond: two, nine, ten. What do you lead now?

        □   □   □

What do you think the diamond situation is? Declarer is marked with one honor (partner would not have ducked with both Ace and King), and he should hold the *Ace*. He would have played the King if that were his honor, hoping for just one diamond loser. If declarer has the spade King, spade Jack, diamond Ace (and perhaps the diamond Jack), he can't have the Ace of clubs. A club lead (preferably the King) is safe, and may be badly needed. The full deal, in fact, is:

        ♠ A10752
        ♡ Q75
        ◇ 75
        ♣ Q106

♠ 93   ♠ Q
♡ K1062   □   ♡ AJ983
◇ Q104   ◇ K62
♣ K752   ♣ AJ94

        ♠ KJ864
        ♡ 4
        ◇ AJ983
        ♣ 83

If you fail to cash out, declarer can establish his diamonds with one ruff and pitch two clubs from dummy, making his contract and embarrassing you in front of your client, which wouldn't do at all. Partner could have made five hearts by guessing everything in sight, but you surely made the best practical decision in doubling four spades. You did beat them, didn't you?

□   □   □

Five

At an Atlanta tournament, the great Bob Hamman walked by while I was talking to a couple of prospective clients. I grabbed the chance for introductions. "Ladies," I announced with a flourish, "I want you to meet one of the best players in the country." Hamman laughed, bowed, and then told this story on himself.

It seemed that he had wandered into the Los Angeles Bridge Club one afternoon while Eddie Kantar was teaching a lesson to a class of intermediates. There was a hand on the blackboard, which Hamman recognized, from his vantage point in the back of the room, as one of his own. Sure enough, Kantar began to detail the play, noting how Hamman, the declarer, had brought home a shaky contract with a little astute card reading. "And that," Kantar finished up, "is why many people consider Bob Hamman one of the best tournament bridge players in the country." Everyone seemed impressed and Hamman allowed his chest a tiny swell of pride. Kantar then looked at the class, shook his head sadly, and said, "Unfortunately for Bob, most bridge tournaments are held in the *city*."

Jousting at IMPs against one of the best players in the country (not Hamman; this is a guy who farms soybeans somewhere south of Montgomery), you are dealt a good hand. Such hands can cause headaches on defense, as this occasion will show.

♠ A3
♡ A8
◊ K942
♣ KJ983

Of course, the opponents promptly bid a vulnerable game.

		(You)		
Bidding:	South	West	North	East
	1NT*	Pass	2◇**	Pass
	2♡	Pass	2NT	Pass
	4♡	(All Pass)		

*15–17 HCP
**A "transfer," which forces opener to bid two hearts.

What is your opening lead?

☐   ☐   ☐

South's decision to play in hearts indicates ruffing potential in his hand. Since you hold so much high-card strength, declarer is likely to try for the extra tricks he needs in trumps. You should be anxious to protect your high cards by leading the trump Ace (and probably another trump when you see dummy).

The table has:

```
                 ♠ J75
                 ♡ Q10653
                 ◇ AJ5
                 ♣ 75
 ♠ A3
 ♡ A8                    ☐
 ◇ K942
 ♣ KJ983
```

Declarer wins the second trump, shrugs, and draws a third round. Partner follows and you pitch a low club. (No point in signalling high; partner will never be in to lead a club.) A spade is led to declarer's King, and you win and get out with a spade. Declarer cashes the Jack and Queen of spades, and ruffs his fourth spade in dummy. Partner's spades were 109xx. You shed a club and a diamond. Now the five of clubs is led: six, ten, Jack. You're in, in this position:

What should you return?

In practice, West led back a disastrous club. The full deal:

```
              ♠ J75
              ♡ Q10653
              ◇ AJ5
              ♣ 75
♠ A3                      ♠ 10986
♡ A8                      ♡ 742
◇ K942        □           ◇ Q1083
♣ KJ983                   ♣ 62
              ♠ KQ42
              ♡ KJ9
              ◇ 76
              ♣ AQ104
```

A careful analysis shows that a diamond return is correct.

East must have a minor-suit Queen for the defense to have a chance. Now, declarer is known to hold four spades and three hearts, and his minor-suit distribution is surely 4-2. With 4-3-3-3 pattern, he would have no reason to prefer the suit game (and, on the assumption that East has a Queen, declarer has only 15 HCP, and couldn't bid game without a little shape). Suppose declarer has four diamonds and two clubs. His play of the hand would be illogical. He would be leading diamonds, trying to set up some tricks in that suit, not clubs. But if declarer has four clubs and two diamonds, he cannot have the diamond Queen. If he did, he would have taken the diamond finesse at trick two, intending to ruff dummy's low diamond if it worked. So, declarer is a favorite to hold his actual hand.

This is a complicated piece of reasoning, but that's part of what it takes to play tight defense. If you worked it all out, take my word, you too may be one of the best players in the country.

□   □   □

Six

Declarer is playing a contract of 1NT. Dummy holds Q5 of hearts, and declarer leads a low heart from his hand. If you sit in front of dummy with KJ94, it can hardly cost a trick for you to go on and win your King. But if your holding is K1084, it may well be costly for you to go up, and you should consider ducking.

What we refer to as "card sense" is a real attribute, and one that all good bridge players seem to possess, but it is hard to describe. It involves the ability to visualize matrices of cards and imagine what will happen as they are played, but that is an incomplete definition. It is certain, however, that card sense, or at least card *skill*, can be learned to a certain extent.

Much of what I know about bridge, I have absorbed from reading and study. Of course, there is no substitute for actual play as a learning experience, since this is a judgment game and one must develop his judgment by making and learning from a few thousand poor decisions. But if you want to improve to expert status, do not minimize the importance of reading and rereading every text and periodical you can find. There are many more books on bridge (over 15,000, I think) than on any other card game, as well as several entertaining and instructive magazines. (Of course, the fact that you're reading *this* book shows hope—some would probably say a particularly high degree of tenacity!)

A few assorted aches and pains obliged you to make an appointment with an orthopedist. But the good doctor was delayed in surgery, forcing you to cool your heels in his waiting room for a couple of hours. Luckily, he was a bridge player, and the place was well stocked with back issues of *Bridge World*. As you leafed through one idly, this problem caught your eye:

Dlr: South   ♠ 63
Vul: E–W   ♡ Q1074
IMPs   ◇ KJ94
       ♣ A95

                      ♠ Q1052
                      ♡ 32
           □   ◇ A853
                      ♣ J82

Bidding:	South	West	North	East
	1NT	Pass	2♣	Pass
	2♠	Pass	3NT	Pass
	4♡	(All Pass)		

West, your partner, leads the ten of diamonds, covered by dummy's Jack. How should you defend?

□   □   □

     The ten of diamonds cannot be a singleton, since declarer would then have four diamonds in addition to his four hearts and four spades, a very strange 1NT opening. West should have a doubleton diamond, and since the diamond Ace is your only fast entry, you must duck this trick. Having led from shortness, partner may well have trump control. When he gets back in with his trump trick, he can return his other diamond, and now you can win and give him the ruff he seeks.

                ♠ 63
                ♡ Q1074
                ◇ KJ94
                ♣ A95

♠ K97   ♠ Q1052
♡ K96   ♡ 32
◇ 102   □   ◇ A853
♣ 107643   ♣ J82

                ♠ AJ84
                ♡ AJ85
                ◇ Q76
                ♣ KQ

Don't forget to signal with your diamond *eight*. (If you carelessly play your three, *especially after some consideration*, an ethical West would feel pressured to shift to a club instead of leading another diamond.)

INTERLUDE: THE INFERENTIAL COUNT

PRELIMINARIES

As you can gather from the discussion in the last two chapters, the techniques of *counting* and *inference* are often used together. The most striking instance of this marriage of techniques will be discussed here.

We have seen that the defenders' job of reconstructing declarer's hand begins with the bidding, which will usually provide at least a general indication of his pattern. Further information may come from the opening lead; and as the play proceeds, various suits are led, and players begin to show out, it will often be possible for the defense to complete their picture of the entire hand. Very simple, in principle. The only potential snag is that you may have a crucial decision to make *very early* in the play or, at least, before you have enough information about declarer's distribution to be sure of what to do. In that case, your only chance will be to *infer* his pattern, based on what has happened in the bidding and play so far.

Look at this situation. The opponents have bid 1NT–3NT, your partner (West) has led the two of spades, and you see these cards from the East chair:

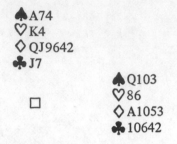

♠A74
♡K4
◇QJ9642
♣J7

☐

♠Q103
♡86
◇A1053
♣10642

At trick one, you should be able to figure out the distribution of all four hands! Let's try. Partner's two of spades indicates he led from a four-card suit, so declarer has THREE SPADES. But partner would surely have preferred to lead from a five-card heart suit on this auction, so declarer should have FIVE HEARTS. Likewise, partner would have started a club with as many as five cards in that suit, so declarer must have at least THREE CLUBS. But declarer can hold no less than TWO DIAMONDS for his 1NT opening. Put it all together, and you can see declarer's pattern must be 3-5-2-3!

How much help this information will be to you in the defense of this particular deal, I couldn't say. But you can see from this example something of how an inferential count may be obtained.

Suppose your opponents' bidding is:

OPENER   RESPONDER
1♣   1♠
3♠   4♠
Pass

What should opener's hand look like? His sequence shows extra values, perhaps 15-17 HCP. But with a balanced hand in this range, he would have opened 1NT, so you can expect an unbalanced dummy. Perhaps 4-2-2-5 or 4-3-1-5 pattern, maybe 4-4-1-4. Not 4-1-4-4, since most players would open one diamond with that shape. You would probably choose an aggressive red-suit lead against this auction, since dummy may well have length and strength in clubs.

How about this auction?

OPENER	RESPONDER
1 ◊	1 ♡
1NT	

Opener failed to raise hearts or rebid one spade, so he must have at least four diamonds. In fact, he should have a five-card diamond suit unless his pattern is exactly 3-3-4-3. The only other balanced pattern containing four diamonds is 2-3-4-4 (3-2-4-4), and most players would usually open the lower-ranking of the two four-card minors.

The final hand in Chapter Six is an easy inferential counting hand. The auction, you remember, was:

OPENER	RESPONDER
1NT	2 ♣
2 ♠	3NT
4 ♡	Pass

Your partner led a high diamond spot, and you had to decide whether it was a singleton, in which case you needed to win your Ace right away and return the suit, or the top of a doubleton, where you needed to duck to keep communications. The diamond situation was:

◊ KJ94

◊ 10 led   □   ◊ A853

You figured out that the ten of diamonds couldn't be a singleton, since that would give declarer four diamonds in addition to his four hearts and four spades, and he wouldn't have opened 1NT.

Each of the situations above allows you to get an inferential count from the bidding. Here is a further, less obvious, case.

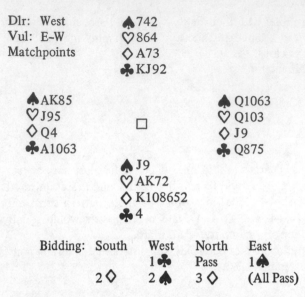

Dlr: West
Vul: E–W
Matchpoints

♠742
♡864
◇A73
♣KJ92

♠AK85
♡J95
◇Q4
♣A1063

□

♠Q1063
♡Q103
◇J9
♣Q875

♠J9
♡AK72
◇K108652
♣4

Bidding:

	South	West	North	East
		1♣	Pass	1♠
	2◇	2♠	3◇	(All Pass)

West cashed the Ace and King of spades, and led a third spade, ruffed. De-clarer played the Ace and King of trumps, crashing the Queen and Jack. Next, he led his club, and put up the King when West ducked smoothly. He conceded a heart and claimed an overtrick. E–W didn't score a bottom for their –130, since a few pairs unwisely pushed on to three spades and went for –200, but –110 would have been an excellent matchpoint result.

West missed a subtle inference. East was known to have only four spades, and with four hearts as well, he would have responded "up-the-line" with one heart. So declarer was marked with four hearts in addition to his two spades and six diamonds, and the club lead could hardly be anything other than a singleton.

An inferential count can be based on declarer's *play of the hand*, perhaps even more often than when the bidding provides a clue. The fol-lowing deal is based on one from Marshall Miles' *All 52 Cards*, one of the best books ever written on the subject of drawing inferences at bridge.

```
Dlr:              ♠ K5
Vul: West         ♡ K52
IMPs N-S          ◇ J762
                  ♣ J432
  ♠ J82                        ♠ 9
  ♡ 1096                       ♡ Q8743
  ◇ A985          □            ◇ Q103
  ♣ A106                       ♣ Q985
                  ♠ AQ107643
                  ♡ AJ
                  ◇ K4
                  ♣ K7
```

After he heard three passes, South thought it best to open four spades and be done with it. West led the ten of hearts, won by declarer's Jack. The spade and heart Aces were cashed, and South crossed to the spade King and discarded a diamond ᴄn the heart King. Next, he tried a club to the King, losing to West's Ace. The ten of clubs was returned and ducked in dummy, but East, after a momentary pause, overtook with the Queen and played a heart. Declarer pitched his King of diamonds here, but West threw his last club. A club lead then promoted the spade Jack for the setting trick.

East's defense was based on an inferential count of declarer's hand. He "knew" that declarer had seven spades (at any rate, the contract was impregnable if South owned an eight-card suit) and two hearts. If his minor-suit distribution were 3-1 or 1-3, he would surely have *discarded his worthless singleton* on the heart King before attacking the other minor. But declarer was marked with the diamond King since West would have laid down a high diamond if he had held both top honors. So East placed declarer with 7-2-2-2 pattern, and tried for his successful trump promotion.

□   □   □

AT THE TABLE

Having given up a football Sunday to play in a Sectional Swiss Teams fifty miles up the road, you find yourself in contention for the whole cookie jar going into the last match. Little do you know what's in store for you. All six boards will require you to get a count inferentially to produce the best defense.

Board 1

Dlr: North
Vul: none

♠ 75
♡ A954
◇ Q75
♣ KQ104

♠ K1062
♡ 76
◇ KJ94
♣ A87

□

Bidding:	South	West	North	East
	1 ♡	Dbl.	Redbl.	Pass
	Pass	1 ♠	2 ♡	Pass
	3 ♡	Pass	4 ♡	(All Pass)

You, West, choose a trump lead. Declarer wins and draws another round, partner following with the two and ten. Declarer then produces the Jack of clubs, ducked by you, and another club, which you win. Partner has contributed the six and deuce of clubs. What do you lead at trick five?

Board 2

Dlr: East
Vul: N-S

♠ 1094
♡ KJ94
◇ AK108
♣ 76

□

♠ 53
♡ A732
◇ Q743
♣ J85

Bidding:

South	West	North	East
			Pass
1 ♠	Pass	2 ◇	Pass
2NT*	Pass	3 ♠	Pass
4 ♠	(All Pass)		

*Does not promise extra values

West, your partner, leads the ten of hearts, covered by dummy's Jack. **Plan the defense.** (I know you've played musical chairs since the first board—the directions are changed for convenience.)

Board 3

Dlr: South
Vul: none

♠ AQ
♡ J943
◇ KQ3
♣ Q753

♠ 65
♡ K5
◇ 7654
♣ J10942

Bidding:

South	West	North	East
1 ♣	Pass	2NT	Pass
3 ♡	Pass	4 ♡	Pass
4NT	Pass	5 ◇	Pass
6 ♡	(All Pass)		

You, West, lead the Jack of clubs against South's slam: Queen, King, Ace. Declarer then goes to the spade Ace and passes the Jack of hearts to your King. What should you lead now?

Board 4

Dlr: West
Vul: both

♠52
♡KQ43
◇1073
♣A1062

♠A93
♡65
◇K9864
♣Q94

☐

Bidding:

	South	West	North	East
		Pass	Pass	Pass
	1NT*	Pass	2♣	Pass
	2♠	Pass	2NT	Pass
	3NT	(All Pass)		

*16–18 HCP

You, West, lead the six of diamonds, to the three, Jack, and Queen. Declarer begins by cashing the Ace, King, and Queen of hearts. Partner and declarer follow suit, and you pitch a low spade on the third heart. Next, declarer cashes the club Ace and continues a club to his Jack, partner playing the three and eight. After winning the club Queen, what should you return?

Board 5

Dlr: North
Vul: N–S

♠J1065
♡K75
◇K8
♣AK85

♠32
♡A10842
◇753
♣J109

☐

Bidding:	South	West	North	East
			1 ♣	Pass
	1 ♠	Pass	2 ♠	Pass
	2NT	Pass	4 ♠	(All Pass)

You, West, lead the Jack of clubs. Dummy's King wins, partner plays the two, and declarer the six. A spade is led from dummy, and partner's King holds. He shifts to the nine of hearts, declarer playing the three. Plan your defense.

Board 6

Dlr: East
Vul: E–W

♠ A95
♡ A86
◇ KJ86
♣ AKJ

☐

♠ 4
♡ KJ942
◇ A10954
♣ 75

Bidding:	South	West	North	East
				Pass
	Pass	Pass	1 ◇	1 ♡
	1 ♠	Pass	2 ♡	Pass
	3 ♣	Pass	4 ♠	Pass
	6 ♠	(All Pass)		

West, your partner (fruitbasket-turnover again), leads the seven of hearts, won by dummy's Ace. At trick two, declarer calls for the six of diamonds. Plan your defense.

☐   ☐   ☐

THE COMPARISON

(If you wish, refer to the IMP table in the Glossary.)

Board 1

The point here is that, knowing your takeout double strongly suggests support for the other major, partner would have been happy to bid one spade over North's redouble with as many as four cards in the suit. So you can assume that South has four spades. In that case, there is no hurry to cash spade tricks, since two discards on the clubs will still leave declarer with two spades. If partner holds the diamond Ace, though, you must get your diamond tricks right now. Note that a diamond switch cannot cost even if declarer holds the Ace; he would throw his small diamond on the clubs anyway. Your best play is the diamond King, followed by the Jack in case declarer has 10x.

```
                   ♠ 75
                   ♡ A954
                   ◇ Q75
                   ♣ KQ104
  ♠ K1062                        ♠ 983
  ♡ 76                           ♡ 102
  ◇ KJ94          □              ◇ A832
  ♣ A87                          ♣ 9632
                   ♠ AQJ4
                   ♡ KQJ83
                   ◇ 106
                   ♣ J5
```

The same contract was reached at the other table, but there West found a diamond lead. When East switched to a spade, declarer never had a chance.

So you needed to find the shift to the diamond King or Jack at your table to tie the board. Any other defense loses 11 IMPs.

□   □   □

Board 2

You should duck the heart, signalling with the seven. Declarer cannot have four hearts, since with that he would have rebid two hearts, not 2NT. Perhaps partner has a doubleton heart and a trump entry, and can take a later ruff if you preserve a link with his hand.

```
                  ♠ 1094
                  ♡ KJ94
                  ◇ AK108
                  ♣ 76
♠ K82                            ♠ 53
♡ 105                            ♡ A732
◇ 965          □                ◇ Q743
♣ A9432                          ♣ J85
                  ♠ AQJ76
                  ♡ Q86
                  ◇ J2
                  ♣ KQ10
```

In replay, they reached 3NT. Your teammate in the South won the club lead, went to dummy with a diamond, and led a low heart. East fell from grace by ducking, so declarer swiftly shifted over to spades and established that suit. Eventually he made four spades, one heart, two diamonds, and two clubs. If you beat the four spade contract, therefore, you gain 12 IMPs.

□   □   □

Board 3

Declarer is known to have at least nine major-suit cards, probably more. What you must realize is that, if he has a losing club, he must also lack the diamond Ace. Otherwise, he would immediately play diamonds and dispatch his club loser. Your proper play is a diamond.

$$
\begin{array}{c}
\spadesuit \text{ AQ} \\
\heartsuit \text{ J943} \\
\diamondsuit \text{ KQ3} \\
\clubsuit \text{ Q753}
\end{array}
$$

♠ 65		♠ 943
♡ K5	☐	♡ 86
◇ 7654		◇ AJ1098
♣ J10942		♣ K86

$$
\begin{array}{c}
\spadesuit \text{ KJ10872} \\
\heartsuit \text{ AQ1072} \\
\diamondsuit \text{ 2} \\
\clubsuit \text{ A}
\end{array}
$$

It might cross your mind that declarer could have a diamond *void*, but no good player would use the Blackwood convention in such circumstances. Notice that declarer made a good play at trick one, when he covered the Jack of clubs with dummy's Queen in spite of his singleton Ace! He aimed to create the impression that he did in fact have a club loser in hand, and induce you to try to cash a club if you won a trump trick.

　　　Your teammates managed to stop in five hearts in the replay and they made twelve tricks, so you gained 11 IMPs or lost 11 depending on whether you beat the slam.

☐　　☐　　☐

Board 4

Declarer's method of handling the club suit suggests that he has four cards in the suit. If he is now down to the bare club King, he has left a winner stranded in dummy. (Partner would not necessarily give count on the club plays.) South is known to have three hearts (but cannot have more, since he would have taken out 3NT to four hearts), and he showed four cards in spades. So declarer should have only a doubleton diamond, and it is safe for you to lead that suit again.

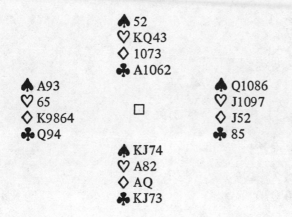

```
                    ♠ 52
                    ♡ KQ43
                    ◇ 1073
                    ♣ A1062
  ♠ A93                          ♠ Q1086
  ♡ 65             □             ♡ J1097
  ◇ K9864                        ◇ J52
  ♣ Q94                          ♣ 85
                    ♠ KJ74
                    ♡ A82
                    ◇ AQ
                    ♣ KJ73
```

Your diamond continuation will assure the defense of five tricks.

The contract and lead were the same at the other table, but declarer began with a heart to dummy and a spade to his Jack. Unsure of the position at this point, West returned a spade, and declarer made nine tricks even though he also misguessed the club Queen. You'd gain 12 IMPs if you set up your diamond suit; otherwise, the board is a tie.

□ □ □

Board 5

South's bidding suggests invitational values (about 11 HCP), with flat distribution and poor spades. Assuming declarer has only a four-card spade suit, partner's heart cannot be a singleton. With four spades and four hearts, declarer would have responded one heart to one club, showing his major suits "up the line." So, you should play your ten of hearts on partner's nine. When he wins the spade Ace, he can lead his other heart, and now you can give him the ruff he seeks.

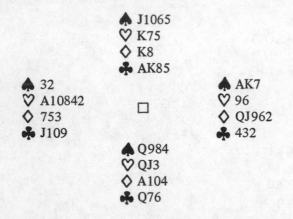

Your allies at the other table did well to reach 3NT, and when West led an uninspired heart, the contract was made with an overtrick. If you ducked the first heart lead, you gain 12 IMPs. The board is tied otherwise.

□   □   □

Board 6

I hope you ducked the diamond, because the full deal is:

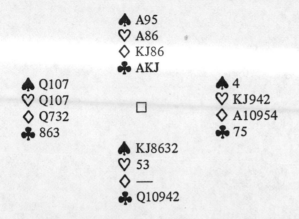

♠ A95
♥ A86
♦ KJ86
♣ AKJ

♠ Q107
♥ Q107
♦ Q732
♣ 863

♠ 4
♥ KJ942
♦ A10954
♣ 75

♠ KJ8632
♥ 53
♦ —
♣ Q10942

On the bidding, declarer just has to have a diamond void; else why did he not stop off to check on controls with Blackwood?

In the other room, your pair had an accident, stopping in 6NT. After the lead of the diamond Ace and a heart shift, this contract went three down. So you had to beat six spades to hold the loss to just 3 IMPs. If you went up with the diamond Ace, they made it, discarding the heart loser on the King of diamonds, and you lose 14 IMPs.

The Swiss is over, and you and your teammates are headed out the door for the drive home. Do you exit as champions or also-rans?

chapter seven

ODDS AND ENDS

PRELIMINARIES

In the last chapter, we had something to say about the elusive quality of "card sense." Some lucky people, born under the right star, enjoy a natural flair for card games; but most of us must acquire our skills the hard way, through assiduous study and practice. It is especially important to cultivate a feel for the cards on *defense*, when partner's and declarer's hands are both concealed, and visualization and inference are so necessary. In this chapter, we'll look at a few miscellaneous points of play, all of which involve the correct handling of some combination of cards by the defenders. So a well-developed card sense, whether it be innate or learned, will be helpful.

When we discussed defensive approaches at notrump (Chapter Two), we saw that *communications* (quite often, *preserving an entry* to potential long card tricks) was a problem implicit in most attempts to establish a long suit. To preserve their communications, the defenders may have to take unusual measures.

```
Dlr: North        ♠ 874
Vul: N–S          ♡ KJ1085
                  ◇ AQ5
                  ♣ A8
   ♠Q                        ♠ K109652
   ♡732                      ♡ AQ6
   ◇J964          □          ◇ 108
   ♣J9532                    ♣ 107
                  ♠ AJ3
                  ♡ 94
                  ◇ K732
                  ♣ KQ64
```

North opens one heart, East overcalls one spade, and South jumps to 3NT. (A 2NT response would be only an *invitational* action over East's interference.)

West leads his Queen of spades. If East is content to signal with a middle spade, declarer will duck. When West must shift, declarer has time to establish hearts and make an overtrick. On the bidding, East should expect declarer to have AJx of spades, so it cannot cost to "signal" with the spade *King* at trick one. Declarer will be forced to spend one of his spade stoppers while East still has two entries in hearts, and eight tricks will be his limit.

Knowing when to shelve your preconceived ideas on leading to a trick can occasionally prove useful.

```
Dlr: East         ♠Q952
Vul: none         ♡A86
                  ◇1083
                  ♣A108
   ♠104                      ♠ 76
   ♡J943                     ♡ Q1052
   ◇QJ92          □          ◇ 765
   ♣Q94                      ♣ J632
                  ♠ AKJ83
                  ♡ K7
                  ◇ AK4
                  ♣ K75
```

West leads the Queen of diamonds against N-S's six spades. Declarer wins, picks up the trumps, eliminates hearts with a ruff, and exits to West with the third round of diamonds. Forced to open up the club suit, West should lead his *Queen*, and declarer has no countermove. Notice the likely outcome if West leads any other club.

The lead of the Queen would still be right if the defense lacked the nine of clubs; declarer would be left to guess who had the missing Jack. Since West holds the club nine, best defense will always set the contract.

A somewhat similar situation lends itself to what is often called a "surrounding" play. Positions like the one below are fascinating.

```
Dlr: South        ♠K53
Vul: both         ♡AQ1075
                  ◇J5
                  ♣964
     ♠94                        ♠10862
     ♡8432           □          ♡K6
     ◇Q973                      ◇A42
     ♣Q75                       ♣K1083
                  ♠AQJ7
                  ♡J9
                  ◇K1086
                  ♣AJ2
```

Bidding: South   West   North East
           1NT   Pass   3♡   Pass
           3NT   (All Pass)

West leads the three of diamonds, won by the Ace. East knows that declarer has four diamonds, probably including a couple of honors, so he decides to shift to clubs. If the *three* is led, declarer may duck, and he retains his AJ tenace when West has to win the club Queen. But suppose East leads the club *ten*. No matter what declarer does, he is held to one club trick, and the defense will end up with three clubs, a diamond, and a heart.

Similarly, if you must attack diamonds in this position:

```
                  ◇Q75
     ◇ KJ8          □
```

Be sure to lead the *Jack,* in case declarer holds 10xx and partner A9xx.

Situations like these are common. To handle them correctly, you *imagine that your holding is sequential* and lead the appropriate card. In the full deal above, for instance, East would pretend his clubs were *K1093.*

The examples we have given so far are not too difficult, but there are other positions that are more obscure.

	Q72	
AJ53	□	1086
	K94	

If the defense must break this suit, the lead of the *eight* by East will save a trick under every circumstance.

There are other card combinations that are similar, but not quite in the same vein. Here is one, noted by Terence Reese. Suppose West must attack this suit at notrump, and East is known to have a weak hand, without a side entry:

	105	
AJ84	□	Q62
	K973	

If he leads the *four*, East will have to put the Queen up, and declarer can win his King and still have the makings of a second stopper. If West suspects the position, he might be able to lead the *Jack* effectively.

In the same manner, the lead of the *Queen* would gain in this layout, provided declarer grabbed his Ace right away:

	J5	
Q1084	□	K72
	A963	

These odd positions are something of unexplored territory in the bridge world.

This might be a good place to talk about the Rule of Eleven, a little device of which you may have heard. This is one Rule I can cheerfully endorse the use of, because it may *help you make judgments* in the play. The Rule may be applied when the lead to a trick is known to be a player's fourth-highest card. By subtracting leader's spot from eleven, you learn the number of higher-ranking cards held by the other players. The usual illustration is something like:

♠K63

♠7 (led)   □   ♠ AQ102

Partner leads the spade seven against a notrump contract, and declarer plays the three from dummy. Assuming that the seven is fourth best, you may apply the Rule of Eleven. Subtract seven, partner's spot, from eleven. The remainder, four, gives the number of higher cards held by dummy, you, and declarer. Since you can see all four of these, it follows that declarer cannot beat the seven. You can therefore play your two, leaving partner on lead to come through dummy's King again.

Here is the Rule of Eleven illustrated in a full deal:

Dlr: South   ♠K106
Vul: N–S   ♥1076
        ♦ AJ7
        ♣ 10864

♠72   ♠98
♥KJ92   □   ♥ Q854
♦ Q1086   ♦ K954
♣ Q92   ♣ KJ7

        ♠ AQJ543
        ♥ A3
        ♦ 32
        ♣A53

N–S overreach to four spades, missing the cold 3NT. West leads the six of diamonds, and declarer puts in dummy's seven. East should get out the Rule of Eleven. Six from eleven is five. Five outstanding higher cards this time, and again, they are all in plain sight. So East can safely play his *nine*, knowing it will win the trick. If he were to play a careless *King*, declarer would finesse the diamond Jack later for a crucial discard.

Handy gadget, isn't this? The Rule of Eleven won't tell you your partner's exact holding on every lead he makes, but on many hands, using it will be the key to a successful defense.

Blocked suits and other entanglements can pose a special hazard for the defenders, who cannot see each other's hands as declarer can see his dummy. No doubt you've met situations like this one:

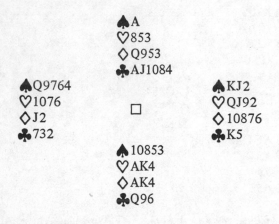

104

KJ653   □   Q972

A8

West leads this suit vs. notrump, and East's Queen forces the Ace. Later, West gains entry and starts to run his suit. East unblocks his seven and nine on the King and Jack, and the whole suit can be cashed without a possibly troublesome interruption.

This hand illustrates another situation of the same type:

♠A
♡853
◇Q953
♣AJ1084

♠Q9764   ♠KJ2
♡1076   ♡QJ92
◇J2   □   ◇10876
♣732   ♣K5

♠10853
♡AK4
◇AK4
♣Q96

N–S reach a routine 3NT. When West leads the six of spades to dummy's bare Ace, East should definitely get his Jack out of the way. The Rule of Eleven indicates that declarer has two spades higher than the six. If he holds 109xx (the *only* case in which the unblock would seem to cost a trick), the contract is unbeatable anyway, since there aren't enough missing HCP for West to have the spade Queen plus a fast entry. As it is, the unblock allows E–W to win all their tricks the next time they get in.

A rare kind of unblocking maneuver came up in the 1969 World Championship, with the United States team opposing the perennial winners, the Italians. (The hand was analyzed in *Bridge World* magazine.)

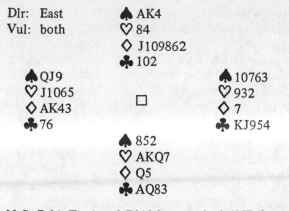

Dlr: East   ♠ AK4
Vul: both   ♡ 84
                ◇ J109862
                ♣ 102

  ♠ QJ9   ♠ 10763
  ♡ J1065   ♡ 932
  ◇ AK43   □   ◇ 7
  ♣ 76   ♣ KJ954

           ♠ 852
           ♡ AKQ7
           ◇ Q5
           ♣ AQ83

N–S, Pabis Ticci and D'Alelio, reached 3NT for Italy. West for the U.S. was Sidney Lazard of New Orleans, one of the world's great players. He led the Queen of spades, holding the first trick, and continued the suit. Declarer led a diamond to the Queen. Lazard won and led a third spade, killing dummy. At this point, declarer took a winning club finesse and led his other diamond. West won and got out with his last club, to declarer's Ace. Now declarer cashed his three top hearts. He intended to put West in with the fourth heart, forcing him to lead to dummy's good diamonds. But Lazard saw this coming; he threw his Jack and ten of hearts away on the Ace and King!

    At trick eleven, declarer found that his seven of hearts was good, but, still in his hand and forced to lead a club, he had to lose the last two tricks to East, for down one.

    The next deal illustrates another kind of unblocking play that is not at all uncommon.

Dlr: South   ♠ K932
Vul: both   ♡ A65
               ◇ A64
               ♣ AQ5

  ♠ J6   ♠ 74
  ♡ Q1083   ♡ K7
  ◇ QJ107   □   ◇ 9832
  ♣ 984   ♣ J10732

           ♠ AQ1085
           ♡ J942
           ◇ K5
           ♣ K6

South opened one spade, and although he made no encouraging noises after that, North drove to six spades. West led the Queen of diamonds. Declarer won the King, drew trumps, and played a heart to the Ace. East, however, could infer that his partner held at least one heart honor, since declarer had failed to take a simple heart finesse; so he alertly dumped his King of hearts under the Ace! Declarer was finished by this play—he had to lose two heart tricks to West. If East had held on to his heart King, declarer would have eliminated the minor suits and exited with a heart, forcing East to yield a ruff-and-discard and the contract.

To wind up this discussion, we can watch Edgar Kaplan and Norman Kay, one of the world's top pairs, defend a hand with a couple of crucial card combinations. This well-known hand is from the 1966 Reisinger Board-a-Match Teams, near the beginning of their partnership.

```
Dlr:  South        ♠ Q1063
Vul:  both         ♡ A763
                   ◇ K7
                   ♣ 875
      ♠ KJ                       ♠ 4
      ♡ QJ5                      ♡ K1082
      ◇ AQJ43        □          ◇ 10982
      ♣ Q104                     ♣ 9632
                   ♠ A98752
                   ♡ 94
                   ◇ 65
                   ♣ AKJ
```

		Kaplan		Kay
Bidding:	South	West	North	East
	1 ♠	1NT	Dbl.	Pass
	Pass	2 ◇	2 ♠	Pass
	4 ♠	(All Pass)		

Kaplan led the heart Queen. Declarer ducked this, and Kay grabbed what looked like his only chance to gain the lead by overtaking with the *King*. Declarer won a club shift and immediately led a diamond. Kaplan played his *Jack* to this trick. Dummy's King won, but Kay subsequently found himself on lead with the diamond ten. Another club lead from East took Kaplan off the impending club endplay, and the defense ended with one trick in each suit. The same contract was made at the other table, after less precise defense.

Kaplan knew that it was safe to duck the first diamond lead since declarer could not hold a singleton. Kay was almost certain to have only one spade, so with a five-card diamond suit, he would surely have removed 1NT doubled to two diamonds.

□   □   □

AT THE TABLE

One

Contract bridge was invented in the Twenties. Before that, *auction* bridge was the rage. In auction, it wasn't necessary to bid game to score a bonus, so long as the necessary tricks were made; so it's no wonder that contract, with its emphasis on accuracy in the bidding, rapidly took over and auction bridge has become extinct.

There were, to be sure, simple trick-taking games before auction bridge. People played *whist* and *bid whist*. Many of our popular defensive cliches, like "cover an honor with an honor," date from these elder days. That whist was once as popular a pastime as bridge is today can be deduced from the fact that there used to be well-known whist-playing figures, just as Charles Goren and Alfred Sheinwold are modern-day bridge authorities. One of these personalities was a Frenchman named Guillaume le Breton Deschapelles (1780-1847). Which brings us to the following hand.

In a Men's Swiss, you hold, as dealer and vulnerable:

♠ Q864
♡ AQ3
◇ J1042
♣ Q10

After three passes, your RHO opens one heart. You decide to back in with a double now, LHO bids 1NT, and everyone passes. Partner's opening lead is the club five, and this dummy hits.

♠A10
♡KJ1084
◇AQ8
♣762

♠Q864
♡AQ3
◇J1042
♣Q10

Declarer ducks your club Queen at trick one. He wins the Ace when you continue the suit, and partner follows with the four. Now the nine of hearts is led and passed to your Queen, partner playing the deuce. How should you defend from here?

□   □   □

Partner's clubs are probably good now (and there is no hope for a set otherwise); but you'll have to invent a way to get him in to cash them, and the only fast entry he could have is the spade King. To make sure of creating the entry partner needs, lead your spade *Queen*. The full deal:

♠A10
♡KJ1084
◇AQ8
♣762

♠K95
♡762
◇95
♣KJ954

♠Q864
♡AQ3
◇J1042
♣Q10

♠J732
♡95
◇K763
♣A83

The lead of a low spade wouldn't do the job, you can see. Declarer would be safe whether or not partner put up his spade King. (Incidentally, note that declarer, a passed hand, avoided a [now non-forcing] one spade response on his poor suit, in favor of the more descriptive 1NT response.)

As for West, he might have indicated his entry by playing a suit preference *King* on the second round of clubs. He chose to give you the count instead, assuming that you could hardly lead anything other than a spade if you got in.

The deliberate sacrifice of a high card to promote an entry to partner's hand is a beautiful gambit, not as uncommon as you might imagine. And, as the legends would have us believe, this play was invented back in the days of whist by . . . Guillaume le Breton Deschapelles. Perhaps there is some truth to the legends, because this type of play is known even today as the Deschapelles Coup.

□   □   □

Two

Playing in the Unmixed Pairs at a Sectional tournament close to home, you and partner find yourselves outnumbered 4 to 2 at an early table. Your opponents are two charming but very pregnant young ladies. After the obligatory smiles and comments (Partner: "Well, I can see you girls haven't been spending *all* your time playing bridge"), you can get on with the first board.

Dlr: South   ♠ J973
Vul: none   ♡ AQ
Matchpoints   ◊ QJ1084
            ♣ K5

♠ K102
♡ J9743   □
◊ K9
♣ 973

Bidding:	South	West	North	East
	1♣	Pass	1♠	Pass
	1NT	Pass	3NT	(All Pass)

You, West, lead a heart, and upon viewing dummy, you see that North evidently belongs to the school that takes no chances on missing a major suit fit. Dummy's heart Ace wins the first trick, with East playing the two, and declarer runs the Queen of diamonds, losing to your King. What should you lead at this point?

It is clear to switch to spades, but you must be careful to lead your *ten*, a play that is unlikely to cost and may unblock the suit. The full deal is:

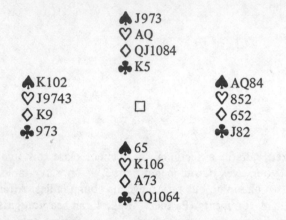

♠ J973
♥ AQ
♦ QJ1084
♣ K5

♠ K102
♥ J9743
♦ K9
♣ 973

♠ AQ84
♥ 852
♦ 652
♣ J82

♠ 65
♥ K106
♦ A73
♣ AQ1064

Partner will win his spade Ace and return a low one to the King. Now your low spade will go through dummy's 9-7 to partner's Q-8, for down one. Declarer could have made the contract by cashing nine fast tricks, but at matchpoints, she couldn't ignore the chance for overtricks via the diamond finesse. You can't blame her for playing as she did, especially since she would still have made 3NT against most defenders.

Three

It is well established that there are many more unlucky bridge players than lucky ones. If you are an unlucky player, your dummy always hits with the wrong cards, and you can't remember the last time a finesse worked when you really needed it. Your opponents consistently play like machines, while partner operates in a pea-soup fog. If you draw trumps, you get stuck with some losers you could have ruffed; if you don't draw them, the opponents promptly play one, with great relish, on one of your side-suit Aces. I know, friend, I know.

My friend Jack LaNoue, of New Orleans, is an unlucky player. But like so many unlucky players, Jack is in no way a loser. He's a consistent winner, a professional player whose skills are highly respected. It's just that he always seems to be at the table when Nemesis gets into a sour mood and decides to put in a personal appearance. In his long career, Jack has had first-hand experience with every kind of awful fix known to bridgedom. Be very optimistic in the auction when you sit down against him. If you bid a 2 percent slam, it'll be sure to come home, probably with an overtrick.

The 1983 Summer National tournament was held in New Orleans, and the tournament program contained an article profiling some of the host city's best players. My friend was included—there was an "everything-happens-to-Jack" write-up. Nevertheless, he advanced to the Spingold Knockout Teams, the premier event on the tournament slate, with confidence, even when his six-man New Orleans squad was scheduled to meet the powerful Rosenkranz team, one of the top seeds in the event. The plan was for Jack and partner to play the first quarter of the match, rest for the middle two, and return to the lineup for the final stanza. The opening 16 boards went well, and when Jack passed the torch to his teammates, the locals led by a healthy 36 IMPs. So Jack's optimism remained intact when he returned some time later for his second tour of duty; that is, until he learned the third-quarter score, which was . . . Rosenkranz up by 63 . . .

One of the unluckiest incidents I ever heard of happened on the hand below. First, look at this defensive problem:

```
Dlr: South      ♠ Q532
Vul: N-S        ♡ J1086
Matchpoints     ◇ KQ2
                ♣ J6
                              ♠ K8
                              ♡ 972
                 □            ◇ 10987
                              ♣ Q874
```

Bidding: South   West   North   East
          1NT   Pass   2♣   Pass
          2◇   Pass   2NT   Pass
          3NT   (All Pass)

West leads the spade Jack. Plan the defense.

□   □   □

If you're going to beat this with the spade suit, West must hold either AJ10xx plus an entry, or J109xx plus *two* entries. In either case, if dummy plays low at trick one, East must put up his *King*. Look at the full deal:

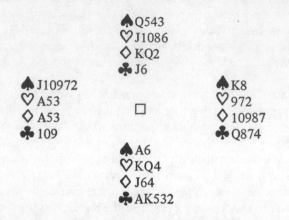

♠Q543
♥J1086
◇KQ2
♣J6

♠J10972
♥A53
◇A53
♣109

♠K8
♥972
◇10987
♣Q874

♠A6
♥KQ4
◇J64
♣AK532

If East plays low on the opening lead, declarer wins and establishes hearts. West continues spades, and declarer ducks again, this time to the bare King. He now has time to knock out the diamond Ace, making nine tricks. You can see the difference if East unblocks his spade King at trick one, gaining a tempo for the defenders.

A different friend of mine lost a Regional event on this hand (or one almost exactly like it). Playing against two slightly deaf old ladies, he reached 3NT like everybody else, and called for dummy's three on the opening spade lead. East promptly put up the King and the contract was duly defeated. After the play had ended, declarer couldn't stand it. "That was some play you made," he said to his right-hand opponent with acid mixed with admiration. "Well, I know enough to cover an honor," the old lady snapped.

It turned out that she thought she had heard him call the spade *Queen* from dummy at trick one. As if being saddled with a complete zero wasn't enough, my friend had to listen to his LHO berate her brilliant partner for not paying attention, and his RHO proffer sincere-sounding apologies for not beating the contract *two*!

□   □   □

Four

It would be nice if you could save your best bids and plays for the more important events. The World Championships, for example, are heavily covered by the Press and brilliancies are widely publicized (though not in my city, where, sadly, the local media seem to have decided that competitive bridge is not a newsworthy item). Every year, the ACBL puts out a World Championship book, in which most of the important hands are analyzed in detail. Knowing that his performance will be thoroughly dissected, each player fervently hopes he'll be able to give the analysts lots of good things to write about, and very few "accidents."

Playing for the U.S. in the Olympiad Open Teams, you have an opportunity to bring honor on your house.

Dlr: South
Vul: E-W
IMPs

♠ 76
♡ J94
◇ Q1085
♣ KQ85

□

♠ 932
♡ AK32
◇ K962
♣ 104

South opens one heart, North raises to two hearts, and South leaps to the heart game. West, your partner, leads the spade Jack, won by declarer's Queen. A trump is led to the nine, partner following low. Do you win this trick?

It can't cost to duck, and it may help. If you wait to win one of your high hearts, partner may be able to give a helpful signal on the next heart lead. Declarer continues with a trump, you win this time, and partner shows out as expected, pitching the two of clubs. How should you defend?

You must play partner for the diamond Ace, but if declarer has a singleton diamond, your only chance is to force him to ruff diamonds *twice* so that he'll lose control. Note that it won't do to start with a low diamond to partner's Ace. Declarer will insert dummy's ten on the diamond return, forcing your King and establishing a diamond winner that he can use to avoid your force.

Instead, you must lead your *King* of diamonds and continue with a low one. If declarer ruffs, you can force him again when you win your other trump trick, and you will then have one more trump than he does. If declarer discards on the second diamond, partner's diamond Ace will score the setting trick.

The full deal:

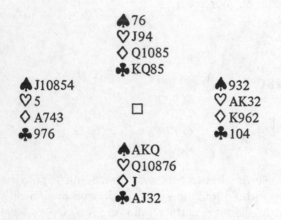

```
                    ♠ 76
                    ♡ J94
                    ◇ Q1085
                    ♣ KQ85
♠ J10854                              ♠ 932
♡ 5                    □              ♡ AK32
◇ A743                               ◇ K962
♣ 976                                ♣ 104
                    ♠ AKQ
                    ♡ Q10876
                    ◇ J
                    ♣ AJ32
```

If there's any justice, you'll make the front page.

□   □   □

Five

Three or four times a year, the League runs a special nationwide tournament game to raise a little extra cash for some worthy cause, like the ACBL Charity Foundation. The same hands are played in clubs across the country, and after the game is over, the participants are provided with a printed record of the deals, including an analysis of the proper bidding and play on each one. Quite often, any resemblance between the events at my table and the predictions found on the analysis sheet has been purely coincidental, but every once in a while, there will be a textbook point of play in one of the hands, which the analyst is no doubt relieved and delighted to see.

Playing in a Continent-Wide Olympiad Fund game, you have a chance to earn a Continent-Wide top.

Dlr: South   ♠ J107
Vul: none   ♡ K5
Matchpoints   ◇ J74
       ♣ AQ1075

♠ K5
♡ 10984   □
◇ Q1083
♣ 983

Bidding:
	South	West	North	East
	1♠	Pass	2♣	Pass
	2NT	Pass	3♠	Pass
	4♠	(All Pass)		

You, West, lead the ten of hearts. The King wins in dummy, and declarer runs the spade Jack to your King. How do you continue?

□   □   □

No doubt you switched to diamonds, but did you remember to lead your *ten*? The full deal is:

         ♠ J107
         ♡ K5
         ◇ J74
         ♣ AQ1075

♠ K5   ♠ 863
♡ 10984   □   ♡ QJ32
◇ Q1083   ◇ K65
♣ 983   ♣ K62

         ♠ AQ942
         ♡ A76
         ◇ A92
         ♣ J4

The ten of diamonds will be covered by the Jack and King, and when partner gets in with the King of clubs, the diamond return will go through declarer's nine to your Queen-eight. If you led a misguided diamond *three*, declarer ducks, and the defense can no longer take the two diamond tricks they need.

If you got this hand right, how'd you like some work analyzing other hands for the *next* Continent-Wide game?

□   □   □

Six

Bridge is a game of errors. Because of human frailties and imperfections, errors are inevitable. Even the best players make, on the average, a couple of errors a session; if they can hold it down to maybe one clear error in technique and a couple of minor slips in the judgment department per 30 boards, that's an acceptable performance. Bridge is a game of errors. Errors are inevitable . . .

That was the conversation you kept having with yourself on the long drive home. The tournament was over, the night was clear and cold as your car bore on its way, the stars flickered peacefully above and ahead of you. Inside your brain, there was little peace. Too many hands from the day's play running up and down the long corridors. This was a blessing in a way, since you were fatigued, and a card-by-card replay of the day's two sessions eliminated any chance of your dozing off and waking up in a cornfield.

There were many triumphs to recall, but frustrating, disturbing deals as well. One in particular, the hand on which you lost 6 IMPs and second place in the Swiss, returned again and again . . .

Dlr: South   ♠ K94
Vul: none   ♡ K852
IMPs   ◇ 53
          ♣ KJ62

                 ♠ AQJ2
          □   ♡ J1074
                 ◇ 962
                 ♣ Q3

Bidding: South   West   North   East
            1NT   Pass   2♣   Pass
            2♠   Pass   3NT   (All Pass)

West, your partner, led the five of clubs. You won the Queen when dummy played low, and declarer dropped the seven. What should you lead at trick two?

□   □   □

You returned a diamond up to dummy's weakness without thinking about it too much, being careful to lead the nine to deny club strength. Maybe partner would produce a ten of spades when he got in. Declarer won the diamond Queen, considered, and led the club ten to partner's Ace. And after a pause, partner produced . . . the *nine* of spades. Really, the ten was too much to ask of him. The deal was:

```
                    ♠ K94
                    ♡ K852
                    ◇ 53
                    ♣ KJ62
      ♠ 83                       ♠ AQJ2
      ♡ 96                       ♡ J1074
      ◇ 10874         □          ◇ 962
      ♣ A9854                    ♣ Q3
                    ♠ 65
                    ♡ AQ3
                    ◇ AKQJ
                    ♣ 107
```

When dummy ducked, the best you could do was cash two spades; declarer then took his nine tricks. Not too good, especially when your teammates had a foul-up in the bidding and failed to reach game at the other table.

It was a small consolation that you didn't see the right answer until long after the match. With partner marked with the club Ace, for an entry, you could always beat it by returning your *low spade* at trick two. You would be assured of three spade tricks and two clubs.

The charm of contract bridge is that perfect play is a beckoning but unattainable goal. If the game offered an endless range of peaks and no valleys, players would swiftly retire to some other, more confounding, game. Luckily, it's the nature of men and women to try and fail, and so we expect there will always be errors and there will always be a bridge game.

There were no mountaintops this time around, but another tournament waits next weekend, and if you've a mind to, you can give it your best shot one more time.

chapter eight

BAITING THE TRAP

PRELIMINARIES

The chance to play an effective falsecard or indulge in some sneaky deceptive play is one that all defenders look forward to. It is most gratifying to invent a way to deflect declarer from making a contract that looks cast-iron at first glance. The area of falsecards and deception by the defense is very broad. There are many positions that have been studied and have become more or less standard in the defenders' repertory, but new and unstudied opportunities for deceptive play pop up all the time. This is one of the areas in card play that remains fertile ground for innovation. In this chapter we will look at some of the better known deceptive themes as well as a few that aren't so familiar.

A *falsecard* is one that offers declarer a losing option in the play. There are various types of falsecards. Some are called *obligatory*; that is, the defender *must* falsecard or declarer is certain to go right. The best known of all obligatory falsecards is seen in this position:

```
              KJx
Q10x          □              xxx
              A9xx
```

Needing four tricks, declarer plays low to the Jack, winning, and continues with the King. West *must* drop his *Queen* on this trick. If he does not, declarer will lead low to his Ace next, knowing that the Queen remains on his left. But if declarer sees the Queen fall on the *second* round, he may play to his *nine* next, expecting East to have 10xxx!

There is a falsecarding principle seen in this example that extends to many other positions. West might gain by *playing the card declarer already knows he has*. Quite often, a good falsecard is nothing more than playing a card you are known to hold (or will presently be known to hold).

Another (less familiar) "obligatory" falsecard is seen here:

```
              K108
Axxx          □              QJ9
              xxx
```

Declarer needs one trick from this card combination and begins by taking the reasonable play of finessing dummy's eight. If East takes the trick cheaply with the nine, declarer will be out of options; he'll have to put up the King on the next lead. But if East wins the *Jack*, declarer will be left with the chance to continue his plan by finessing the ten next.

Other falsecards are not classed as obligatory, but instead are intended merely to give declarer a push in the wrong direction. A classic example is:

```
              AQ6
2             □              K1083
              J9754
```

This is the trump suit, and declarer, who is known to have five cards, starts with a finesse of dummy's Queen. Say East wins with his King. Declarer will lead to the Ace next, the finessing position against East will be exposed, and the defense will make only one trick. East's best strategy is to refuse the first trick, *falsecarding with his eight*. How would you play now if you were declarer?

Be honest, now. Wouldn't you be tempted to come back to hand and push the trump Jack through, gaining if East had the singleton eight or the doubleton ten-eight? If you were, in fact, to try this, East's holding would suddenly be worth *two* tricks.

The Jack-nine combination is associated with many falsecarding situations. For example:

```
                    ♠ 8532
                    ♡ Q73
                    ◇ AK
                    ♣ Q864
    ♠ K76                           ♠ Q109
    ♡ 52                            ♡ 10986
    ◇ QJ1086        □               ◇ 973
    ♣ 752                           ♣ AJ9
                    ♠ AJ4
                    ♡ AKJ4
                    ◇ 542
                    ♣ K103
```

West leads the Queen of diamonds against N–S's 3NT. Declarer wins and attacks the club suit by leading low from dummy, intending to put in his ten. If allowed to do so, he will inevitably take three tricks. But East inserts his Jack at once (the card he will soon be known to hold)! Declarer's King wins, and he continues with the ten, won by East's Ace. Declarer is now quite likely to lead a club to dummy's eight next, playing East for the doubleton Ace-Jack and West for 9xxx.

There are other combinations of intermediate cards with which you must be especially alert to falsecard. We saw one holding containing the *ten and eight* that lent itself to a falsecard a moment ago. Here is another position, first noted, I believe, by Terence Reese.

```
                    ♠ AJ
    ♠ Q1084         □               ♠ 5
                    ♠ K97632
```

Declarer has arrived in four spades and can afford one trump loser but not two. He leads low toward dummy, planning a finesse of the Jack. West will do nothing to change declarer's mind if he follows with the four, but if the *eight* is played, declarer might think his best chance is to go up with the Ace and lead the Jack, gaining a trick against the ten-eight doubleton with

West, and saving himself from disaster if West has the singleton eight.

One kind of falsecard involves winning a trick with a *higher card than necessary*. This tactic can sometimes produce startling effects.

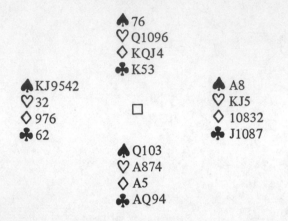

```
              ♠ 76
              ♡ Q1096
              ◇ KQJ4
              ♣ K53
♠ KJ9542                    ♠ A8
♡ 32              □         ♡ KJ5
◇ 976                       ◇ 10832
♣ 62                        ♣ J1087
              ♠ Q103
              ♡ A874
              ◇ A5
              ♣ AQ94
```

South is declarer at four hearts and West hits on a spade lead. East wins and returns his other spade. When a third round is led, declarer ruffs with the ten. If East overruffs with the Jack, that will be his last trick, since declarer will pick up the rest of the trumps by finessing against the King. But suppose that East overruffs with his *King*(!). Now declarer will try to draw trumps by playing Ace and low to the nine, expecting West to hold the Jack. He'll probably suffer a severe shock when East wins.

```
              ♠ K5
              ♡ J954
              ◇ KJ
              ♣ AJ963
♠ J107                      ♠ Q64
♡ Q107           □          ♡ K86
◇ 98754                     ◇ 632
♣ 85                        ♣ KQ107
              ♠ A9832
              ♡ A32
              ◇ AQ10
              ♣ 42
```

South plays 3NT, having opened one spade. He wins the diamond lead in hand and, right or wrong, decides to go after clubs, leading low to dummy's nine. East is discouraged with his spade holding, so he wants to make declarer think that his hopes in clubs will be realized. Therefore, he wins the first club with the *King* and returns a diamond. Declarer will surely win this and continue with a club to the Jack, after which the contract cannot make against best defense. If East wins the first club with his ten, declarer might get discouraged with clubs and switch over to spades, where he'll find the cards lying well for him.

Note that all the falsecards we have seen pass the two *acid tests* of any good falsecard: Each one was played not at random but with a *definite purpose in mind*; and in no case did it matter that *partner* might be deceived as well as declarer. Here is another example of a falsecard that qualifies on both these counts, this time a deceptive *opening lead*.

Bidding:
North	South	
1 ♥	2 ◇	♠ 1063
2 ♥	2NT	♥ K8
3NT		◇ A65
		♣ AK973

H. W. Kelsey presented a problem like this one in his *Killing Defense at Bridge*. The normal lead is the seven of clubs (or perhaps Ace, King, and another), but there is no reason to give partner the count here, since he will play no part in the defense with his near-bust hand. The best lead is the club *three*. The full deal might be:

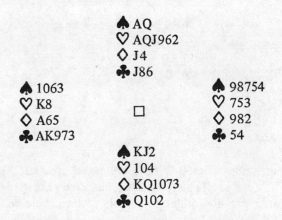

```
                ♠ AQ
                ♥ AQJ962
                ◇ J4
                ♣ J86
♠ 1063                        ♠ 98754
♥ K8                          ♥ 753
◇ A65          □              ◇ 982
♣ AK973                       ♣ 54
                ♠ KJ2
                ♥ 104
                ◇ KQ1073
                ♣ Q102
```

Imagine how you would play as declarer against the *seven* of clubs lead. You would certainly be inclined to expect the actual 5-2 club break, so you'd stake the contract on the heart finesse. Knocking out the diamond Ace would look suicidal. The lead of the club *three* should lead declarer to believe that clubs are 4-3, and he is safe for the contract merely by playing on diamonds.

There are many deceptive maneuvers that do not really involve false-cards, though some of them are intended to give declarer a chance to go wrong. A well-known example is:

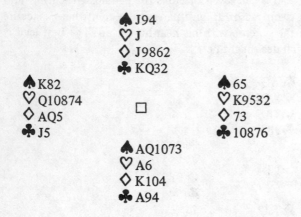

```
              KQ10
   J952         □         A83
              764
```

Suppose E-W are defending 1NT, and West leads this suit. When declarer puts up dummy's King, East should duck automatically. When West gets a chance to lead the suit again, declarer will have to guess whether to play the Queen or ten.

The principle illustrated here is that the defenders may benefit from a *refusal to take a winner* at first opportunity. This is a very common tactic. Often, it takes the form of a defender allowing declarer to win the *first* time he tries a repeatable finesse, reserving a nasty surprise for him later.

```
                    ♠ J94
                    ♡ J
                    ◊ J9862
                    ♣ KQ32
   ♠ K82                           ♠ 65
   ♡ Q10874            □           ♡ K9532
   ◊ AQ5                           ◊ 73
   ♣ J5                            ♣ 10876
                    ♠ AQ1073
                    ♡ A6
                    ◊ K104
                    ♣ A94
```

South is declarer at four spades after E-W have competed in hearts. A heart is led to declarer's Ace. He ruffs his heart loser, and passes the spade Jack. If West wins here, he can do nothing to trouble declarer, who will have time to draw trumps and establish his tenth trick in diamonds. But say West ducks the first spade. Declarer will surely take another spade finesse, and now West can win and, with dummy out of trumps, force the *closed* hand to ruff a heart. South will eventually lose control and come up a trick short.

```
                        ♠ A105
                        ♡ AQ1053
                        ◇ 76
                        ♣ AK10
    ♠ 86432                           ♠ J7
    ♡ J4                              ♡ 962
    ◇ AJ8          □                  ◇ 105432
    ♣ Q53                             ♣ 872
                        ♠ KQ9
                        ♡ K87
                        ◇ KQ9
                        ♣ J964
```

Bidding:

	South	West	North	East
			1♡	Pass
	2NT	Pass	4NT	Pass
	6NT	(All Pass)		

West leads a spade, and when East shows the spade Jack, declarer is known to have all the outstanding face cards. Declarer plays the King of hearts and a heart to the Ace, and continues with a diamond to his Queen. West should be ready to *let this hold* without a flicker. Note the effect on declarer's play. He must now decide whether to return to dummy for another diamond play, or stake his contract on the *club* finesse. If West wins the first diamond, declarer is left with no option but to try the club finesse (which West can see will work like a charm).

The name of the great Italian champion Benito Garozzo is synonymous with deceptive play. In fact, Garozzo seems to have written a book on deception with his exploits *right at the table*. Here is a famous hand from the 1963 World Championship on which he applied the principle of waiting to take a winner to good advantage.

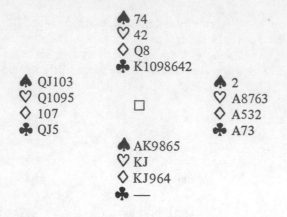

♠ 74
♡ 42
◇ Q8
♣ K1098642

♠ QJ103
♡ Q1095
◇ 107
♣ QJ5

♠ 2
♡ A8763
◇ A532
♣ A73

♠ AK9865
♡ KJ
◇ KJ964
♣ —

Garozzo was East. South for the U.S. team, G. R. Nail of Houston, played four spades doubled, after showing length in spades and diamonds. E-W had bid hearts and West led a heart to the Ace. Garozzo shifted to a trump, won by declarer. Nail now led a diamond to the Queen . . . and Garozzo ducked as smoothly as a man who had never heard of the diamond Ace! When a diamond was continued, he ducked again, and there would have been no justice if poor Nail had not been led astray. In fact, he judged to pass the diamond eight, hoping it would drive out West's "Ace," and Garozzo's magnificent play had created a second diamond trick out of nothing.

Bringing off a master stroke like this should be a goal for all ambitious defenders to pursue.

□   □   □

AT THE TABLE

One

Playing in a Sectional Pair game, you are opposed by a youthful married couple. Traditionally, husbands and wives are supposed to be notorious for letting all the little frustrations of their marriage surface at the bridge table, and this pair seems to be no exception. After the first board of the round, which goes in your favor, there is a tirade. My experience has been that wives are usually more quick to fuss, but this time it's the young husband, obviously the dominant force in this partnership, who applies the time-honored "criticize-partner-before-she-can-criticize-you" technique.

Perhaps it's a tribute to the game of bridge that it can become such an ego trip for those who play it. I know of no other game that can evoke such primal emotions in the players. The intimacy that binds two people playing bridge together is deceptively strong. If partner makes an error, there is a natural urge on the part of our ego to compensate for a presumed loss of esteem by delivering a vocal blast at him for his ineptitude. Everybody within earshot will therefore be aware that the disaster was not our fault.

When two players happen to be bound in marriage as well, the insecurity that partner's error may bring on can be even stronger than usual. Given that the matrimonial bonds provide married couples with an exemption from the normal social restraints that compel civility to one's partner, it's no wonder that the stories of husband vs. wife over the green baize are legendary. A well-known expert playing with his wife was once heard to mutter: "To think this is the mother of my child!"

Since harsh criticism can ruin any partnership, my theory is that it's better, if your hopes are high, to work up a regular partnership with someone with whom you have no strong emotional attachments. There have been many successful partnerships based on a "pitcher-catcher" type of relationship, with one personality clearly dominating. But surely, *distance* between partners, detachment that nurtures mutual respect, must be a desirable state of affairs.

Back at your table, the young husband is still ranting, though his wife, a rather pretty girl, was abashed some time ago. Repelled by it all, you feel like you would like a chance to teach the guy a little humility. Fortunately, the next hand offers you a chance, in the guise of this problem.

```
Dlr: West        ♠ 874
Vul: E-W         ♡ AQ4
Matchpoints      ◇ K942
                 ♣ J63
  ♠ K10
  ♡ KJ10765      □
  ◇ J83
  ♣ A8
```

Bidding:	Husband South	You West	Wife North	East
		1 ♡	Pass	Pass
	2 ♠*	Pass	3 ♠	Pass
	4 ♠	(All Pass)		

*Intermediate—good suit and around an opening bid.

You decide to lead the club Ace, and for once this turns out well. Your partner signals with the club nine, and you continue with a club to his King. On the third club, declarer plays the Queen. Plan your defense.

Play the card you're known to hold. Ruff with the spade *King*! The full deal:

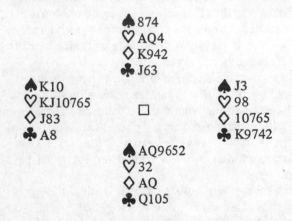

If you ruff with the ten, declarer will have no trouble picking off your trump King later, playing you for that card because of your opening bid. But when you ruff with the King, one of those strange things we mentioned happens. Declarer wins your heart return with dummy's Queen, and *passes the spade eight to your ten*, naturally playing East for J10x. Down one.

Sure enough, as you leave the table, the Mrs. is giving her better half a hard time about not guessing the trump suit! And after the first board, you figure she's entitled.

Two

The first chess-playing computers were introduced several years ago, and since then they have achieved a high degree of sophistication. Not so in bridge. If somebody ever tells you that you and your partner are "playing like machines," it may well be a backhanded compliment. There are plenty of mechanical bridge players on the market, but as a rule they are as yet woefully inadequate. Their technical ability (compared to that of a good human player) is severely limited, they display nothing in the way of creativity or imagination, and (needless to say) they lack an appreciation for the personal and psychological elements of the game.

There is an often-heard analogy describing the difference between chess and bridge that lends itself well to the problems involved in programming a bridge-playing computer. It is said that if you put somebody on a desert island with annotated volumes of all Fischer's games, you could return to fetch him after ten years or so, and you'd have a mighty fine chess player. Supply the same castaway with a complete library of bridge books, though, and he wouldn't be much good at bridge no matter how long he labored. The partnership and human side of bridge count for too much, not to mention the ability to learn from experience.

Of course, things will get better. Probably much better, and sooner than you and I imagine. However, I'm confident it'll be awhile before any collection of nuts and bolts will be able to defend the following deal successfully.

Dlr: South   ♠K105
Vul: N-S   ♡Q109
IMPs   ◇J4
          ♣AQ965

♠Q942
♡762
◇Q1053   □
♣103

Bidding:	South	West	North	East
	1 ♡	Pass	2 ♣	Pass
	3 ◇	Pass	4 ♡	Pass
	4NT	Pass	5 ◇	Pass
	6 ♡	(All Pass)		

You, West, decide on a trump lead. Partner follows low, as dummy's ten wins. At trick two, declarer leads a diamond to his King. Plan your defense.

□   □   □

There is a beautiful swindle available. Drop your diamond *Queen* under the King! The full deal is:

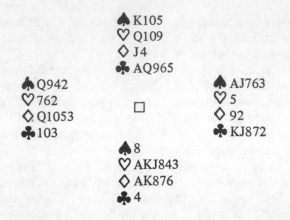

```
                    ♠ K105
                    ♡ Q109
                    ◇ J4
                    ♣ AQ965
♠ Q942                              ♠ AJ763
♡ 762                              ♡ 5
◇ Q1053          □                ◇ 92
♣ 103                              ♣ KJ872
                    ♠ 8
                    ♡ AKJ843
                    ◇ AK876
                    ♣ 4
```

Suppose, first, that you follow with a routine diamond three. Declarer will continue with the Ace and another diamond, ruffing in dummy. The Ace and a club ruff will put him back in hand to ruff a fourth diamond, establishing his fifth one, and he can ruff still another club to draw trumps and take his twelve tricks. Pretty routine.

Now say that West plays his diamond Queen at trick two. Declarer has problems. He'll think it is suicide to try to cash the diamond Ace, and will probably decide his best chance for a make is to set up clubs, playing for a 4-3 split and the King onside. This will not come to pass.

If declarer is a sportsman and not a machine, he'll congratulate you for an inspired defense.

Three

Around 1968, when the original Dallas Aces were in training to return the Bermuda Bowl (the symbol of world bridge supremacy) to America, they devised a system to scrutinize their bad results. It was hoped that careful analysis would show what types of errors the team was making most frequently and provide a way to measure progress. The Aces' system worked like this: The team sat in judgment of itself; questionable results were discussed in open forum, and the pair involved might be assessed a "charge." A *black* charge was levied for a loss caused by a demonstrably wrong play or unreasonable decision in the auction—in other words, a clear error. However, a *white* charge was assigned if the losing action was deemed only a misguess—a reasonable, if unsuccessful, decision the other players conceded they might well have made the same way. A *gray* charge was applied in doubtful cases.

Maybe you and your teammates do the same thing in a less formal way. Post-game charge sessions can be fun and constructive as well. My team usually repairs to the local tavern after each match we play. It's agreed that each acknowledged black charge costs the offender a fine, and the money goes into a pot that pays for the beer and pizza, or whatever. This arrangement usually turns out to be equitable, since the worse you play, the more you generally feel like drinking.

Of course, you need to be a fair analyst before you start handing out charges right and left. The easiest mistakes to overlook, of course, are the ones you make yourself . . .

Your team just won the monthly Board-a-Match event at the club. Nevertheless, here you all are in the bar having your usual charge session. So far, *your* debit sheet is spotless, but now the discussion turns to Board 24. The evidence is:

```
Dlr: West          ♠ 92            ♠
Vul: none          ♡ KQ108         ♡
Board-a-Match      ◇ 8             ◇
                   ♣ AKJ432        ♣
   ♠ 85                              ♠ KJ7
   ♡ A93                             ♡ 6542
   ◇ AJ9652        □                 ◇ Q103
   ♣ 98                              ♣ Q76
                   ♠ AQ10643
                   ♡ J7
                   ◇ K74
                   ♣ 105
```

				You
Bidding:	South	West	North	East
		Pass	1♣	Pass
	1♠	2◇	3♣	Pass
	3♠	Pass	4♠	(All Pass)

Partner led the diamond Ace and followed with the heart Ace. You contributed the diamond three and heart two. Partner now switched to the nine of clubs: King, seven, five. Declarer passed the nine of spades, winning. He led a spade to the Queen, drew the last trump, and made the rest without difficulty, for an overtrick in his contract. This was a halved board, since essentially the same thing happened at the other table.

Does anyone deserve a charge?

☐   ☐   ☐

West may deserve a white charge, since there is a (double-dummy) defense that will always hold the hand to four: Ace and another diamond, then a third diamond, forcing dummy to ruff, when he's in with the Ace of hearts.

But you, sad to say, merit a black charge. When partner shifts to a club, handling the trump suit is beyond doubt declarer's only remaining problem. Therefore, you should have dropped your club *Queen* on dummy's King! Declarer would now be very nervous about taking the double finesse in trumps. From his point of view, he would run into a club ruff if *either* spade honor were wrong. He'd probably settle for a spade to the Queen, ending with just ten tricks, and you'd have scored up another win.

Put fifty cents in the pot, mister.

☐   ☐   ☐

Four

There wasn't any tournament close to home this weekend, but you couldn't stand to finish in 452nd place on the ACBL's *Top 500* list when you could have achieved 451st. So here you are playing in the Reykjavik Sectional. And in the Swiss Teams, there may be a chance for you to defeat declarer in a cold (no pun intended) contract.

Dlr: North   ♠ AKJ94
Vul: both   ♡ A10
IMPs   ◊ 652
           ♣ QJ5

                 ♠ Q1085
                 ♡ KJ9
     ☐   ◊ Q73
                 ♣ 942

Bidding:

	South	West	North	East
			1 ♠	Pass
	2 ♡	Pass	2 ♠	Pass
	2NT	Pass	3NT	(All Pass)

West, your partner, leads the six of clubs, and dummy's Queen wins the first trick, declarer following with the eight. What do you think declarer will lead at trick two, and how do you plan the defense?

□   □   □

Quite possibly, declarer will attack hearts (holding a spade play in reserve). The bidding indicates he has at least a five-card heart suit, probably headed by the Queen, and you can tell that he'll strike gold if he tries this.

You would much prefer that declarer try to get the tricks he needs from the *spade* suit. So, if declarer calls for the heart Ace at trick two, drop your *King*. Note that this play cannot cost you a trick—if declarer's holding is Qxxxx, you are due only one trick regardless. But declarer will give up on hearts and look for tricks elsewhere when he sees your heart King. The full deal is actually:

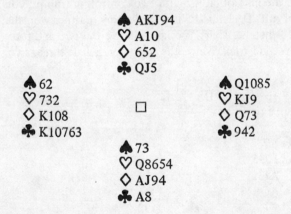

```
              ♠ AKJ94
              ♡ A10
              ◇ 652
              ♣ QJ5
♠ 62                        ♠ Q1085
♡ 732                       ♡ KJ9
◇ K108                      ◇ Q73
♣ K10763                    ♣ 942
              ♠ 73
              ♡ Q8654
              ◇ AJ94
              ♣ A8
```

Declarer is likely to try a diamond to the nine or crank out three rounds of spades after your diabolical falsecard, and in either case you will eventually defeat him. The chance to make a play like this might even be worth the trip to Reykjavik!

□   □   □

Five

That art of drawing inferences at the table must be tailored to your opposition. It can be embarrassingly wrong to base an action on a delicate inference drawn from an opponent's play if he is a poor player. In the same way, a potential downer to knowing all about deceptive defense is that your opponent must possess enough imagination to fall for one of your devious plots before you can expect to enjoy seeing it work.

Playing in the Life Masters Men's Pairs, an event full of good players, you run into this defensive problem:

```
Dlr:  North        ♠ A7
Vul:  none         ♡ 1095
                   ◇ AJ32
                   ♣ AQ106
      ♠ J865
      ♡ AQ6
      ◇ Q754        □
      ♣ 97
```

North opened 1NT, South responded three hearts, North raised to four hearts. You, West, led the nine of clubs; with two controls in trumps, you hoped for an eventual ruff. Declarer ducked in dummy, partner won the club King and returned the club eight. Declarer played the two and four, and dummy won the second trick. Next, the heart ten is led: three, two. Plan your defense.

□   □   □

The full deal was:

```
                   ♠ A7
                   ♡ 1095
                   ◇ AJ32
                   ♣ AQ106
      ♠ J865                    ♠ K10432
      ♡ AQ6                     ♡ 83
      ◇ Q754        □           ◇ 1086
      ♣ 97                      ♣ K83
                   ♠ Q9
                   ♡ KJ742
                   ◇ K9
                   ♣ J542
```

This famous deal actually comes from one of a series of exhibition matches, played in 1968 between the Omar Sharif Bridge Circus and teams representing several U.S. cities. Four hearts was reached at both tables in the match vs. New York, with the nine of clubs opening lead ducked by declarer.

At one table, Garozzo, East for the Circus, played low smoothly! Declarer ran the ten of hearts to the Queen, and another club was led. Deceived by the play to the first trick, declarer ducked again, and now Garozzo took the King and gave partner a club ruff, for down one.

At the other table, East won the first club and returned a club. Declarer lost a finesse to the trump Queen, and West shifted to a spade. Declarer, Sharif, diagnosed the position, rose with the spade Ace, and took a diamond finesse to dispose of his losing spade. The trump Ace was his only other loser.

There was a chance for deception at the second table as well as the first. West could have won the first round of trumps with his *Ace* and shifted to a spade. Declarer would have assumed the heart Queen was well-placed, so he would have won the spade Ace to take a second *heart* finesse, expecting to lose only three tricks. This would have led to a well-earned down *two* for the defense.

◻   ◻   ◻

Six

The first ACBL National Tournament I ever attended was in Atlanta in 1971. That was the year Benito Garozzo and Giorgio Belladonna came over from Italy to capture the National Men's Pairs event. Both players were members of the Italian Blue Team, perennial winners of the world team championship, and in 1971 they were in the midst of a fantastic run in pairs' tournaments. For several years, Belladonna and Garozzo were said to have been *undefeated* in pairs events, a pretty unbelievable feat considering that the entry in a typical National Championship event in the U.S. may be 500 pairs.

I too played in the Atlanta event (with somewhat less success than the Italians). The table occupied by Belladonna and Garozzo, surrounded by kibitzers, was somewhat suggestive of an arena, and one of my biggest thrills in bridge was going into the "pit" against the two great players. The hands, as it turned out, were of no special interest, but I remember being scared to death anyway. The leonine Belladonna was an intimidating presence at the table. I fully expected to be the luckless victim of a coup like the one he pulled off in the 1967 Bermuda Bowl. See if you can do as well:

Dlr: South
Vul: E-W
IMPs

♠ J86
♥ J108
◇ QJ4
♣ QJ82

□

♠ AK3
♥ KQ2
◇ K10953
♣ 106

Bidding:	South	West	North	East
	1♠	Pass	1NT	2◇
	2♥	Pass	2♠	Pass
	4♠	(All Pass)		

West, your partner, leads the eight of diamonds. Low from dummy, you play the three, and declarer's Ace wins. At trick two, declarer leads a trump to partner's ten and dummy's Jack. How should you defend?

□ □ □

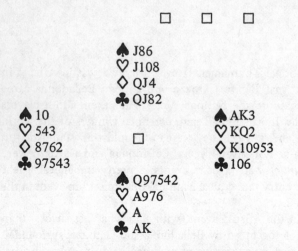

♠ J86
♥ J108
◇ QJ4
♣ QJ82

♠ 10
♥ 543
◇ 8762
♣ 97543

□

♠ AK3
♥ KQ2
◇ K10953
♣ 106

♠ Q97542
♥ A976
◇ A
♣ AK

Your only real chance for a set is to win and shift to the heart *Queen*.

Declarer must have all the missing high cards to justify his jump to game, so you need two heart tricks to beat him. The lead of the Queen of hearts may create the impression that you have Qx. In that case, declarer needs to duck, win the second heart, and plan to discard his other hearts on dummy's clubs. If he pursues that line, you can embarrass him by cashing your heart King when you win your other high trump.

The 1967 hand (it's Board 18 of the Finals, U.S. vs. Italy) was almost exactly similar, except that the contract was doubled. And Belladonna did shift to the heart Queen, successfully fooling the American declarer, and picking up a big swing to Italy when the same contract was made at the other table.

chapter nine

SAVING PARTNER

PRELIMINARIES

I borrowed the title of this chapter from an old *Bridge World* article of the same name by Terence Reese. Reese's theme and mine are the same: Since partners are well known for stubbornly doing the wrong thing, there is value in anticipating your partner's problems and doing what you can to keep him on the straight and narrow path to best defense.

Many defenders seem afflicted with a double fault. First, they give little thought to their *partner's* perspective of the defense and the problems he may have, and expect him to play double-dummy all the time. Second, they'd rather furnish partner with five easy ways he could have known to avoid the error he just made *after the hand is over*, than to spend some effort *during* the play trying to prevent him from making the error to start with. A bad defense can really bring out the truth in a bridge player's character!

There will be countless times when your partner has a problem (and many other times when he'll think he has one even when you know he really doesn't). If he goes wrong, you should always ask yourself if there was anything at all you could have done to save him. More often than not, the answer will surprise you. There are many little ways to make life easier for your partner. For example, say partner leads the nine of spades against declarer's heart contract, and you sit behind dummy's Axx with Jxxxx. If dummy plays low, you should do likewise.

Putting up your Jack in third seat here will accomplish nothing constructive, since the lead of the nine marks declarer with all the remaining honors; but if declarer wins the King, partner might be led to believe you have the Queen as well, and continue the suit in vain. Similarly:

	Q106	
7 (led)	□	K853

Suppose you can, in one way or another, judge that partner's lead is "top-of-nothing." If declarer puts up dummy's Queen, play low. If you cover with the King, partner, as before, won't know what is going on. He may think your holding is as good as KJ9x.

Quite often, keeping your partner from making an error will require that you make a judicious discard for his benefit.

Dlr: South
Vul: none
Matchpoints

```
                  ♠ Q109
                  ♡ KJ72
                  ◊ Q9
                  ♣ 8654
   ♠ A43                        ♠ 62
   ♡ A1053            □         ♡ Q984
   ◊ 10                         ◊ A8752
   ♣ KJ973                      ♣ Q10
                  ♠ KJ875
                  ♡ 6
                  ◊ KJ643
                  ♣ A2
```

Bidding:

South	West	North	East
1 ♠	Pass	2 ♠	Pass
Pass	3 ♣	Pass	Pass
3 ♠	(All Pass)		

You may not agree with the bidding (or the opening lead, which was the club seven), but try to cope. Declarer won the first club and played a diamond to the ten, Queen, and Ace. East's club ten was allowed to win the next trick, so he continued with a diamond, which West ruffed. Next came the club King. At this point, East knew that declarer had two clubs and five diamonds in addition to his presumed five-card spade suit, therefore a singleton heart. He made the thoughtful discard of the heart *Queen*, which prevented West from ducking his Ace when declarer got around to leading a heart. Of course, West might have chosen to grab the setting trick anyway, but East's play made it impossible for him to go wrong.

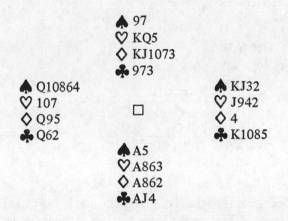

Declaring 3NT, South was inconvenienced by the opening lead of the spade six, East playing the King. Declarer won immediately and led a diamond to the King and a diamond back. Applying the Rule of Eleven, East could tell that South had no other spade higher than the six, so the suit was ready to cash. Just in case partner was in doubt, however, East was careful to make his discard the *spade Jack*. When West got in with his diamond Queen, he took his spades with alacrity. Without East's discard, West might have shifted to a non-spade on winning the diamond Queen, playing East for an Ace, and declarer for AJx of spades.

Sometimes, one defender will have information about the hand that is unavailable to his partner, and it may then be up to him to take charge of the defense instead of leaving partner to guess his way along. "When you know what to do, do it!" is a good rule for these situations.

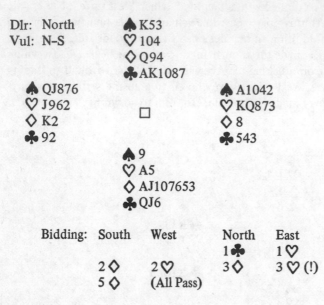

Dlr: North
Vul: N–S

North
♠ K53
♡ 104
◇ Q94
♣ AK1087

West
♠ QJ876
♡ J962
◇ K2
♣ 92

East
♠ A1042
♡ KQ873
◇ 8
♣ 543

South
♠ 9
♡ A5
◇ AJ107653
♣ QJ6

Bidding:	South	West	North	East
			1♣	1♡
	2◇	2♡	3◇	3♡ (!)
	5◇	(All Pass)		

This is a hand from rubber bridge. West led the two of hearts, to the Queen and Ace. Declarer led the club Jack to the King, and ran the nine of diamonds to West's King. West realized that partner needed the spade Ace for the defense to have a chance, so he shifted to the spade Queen, ducked in dummy. Luckily, East was wide awake. Knowing from the opening lead that declarer had to have a heart remaining, he *overtook* the spade Queen and cashed the setting trick with his King of hearts.

If West's Queen of spades had been allowed to hold, he would have had to guess where to cash out, and East's devil-may-care three heart bid would probably have misled him into leading another spade.

Oddly, making things easier on your partner may occasionally require feeding him some *false* information. When we discussed deception in the last chapter, it was stressed that the ideal falsecard fools the opponents without fatally deceiving your partner. Well, if deceiving him is the best way to accomplish your objective, go ahead. He'll forgive you.

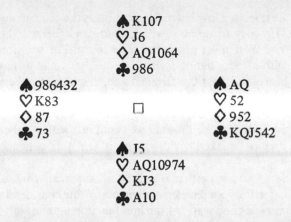

♠ K107
♡ J6
◇ AQ1064
♣ 986

♠ 986432   ♠ AQ
♡ K83   □   ♡ 52
◇ 87   ◇ 952
♣ 73   ♣ KQJ542

♠ J5
♡ AQ10974
◇ KJ3
♣ A10

N–S reach four hearts after East opens one club as dealer. West leads the club seven. If East is looking ahead, he will play his *King* on this trick. From East's vantage point, declarer will make his game easily (probably with overtricks) unless West can win a trick in trumps. Even so, as the cards actually lie, West must then shift to spades if the defenders are to eke out a one-trick set. The play of the club King, which ostensibly denies the Queen, is intended to make West think there is no future in clubs, so that he will find the spade shift automatically.

True, a good West should shift to spades regardless, but East is trying to make it especially easy for him. Plays like this preserve your partner's supply of mental energy for the time he must be able to think a really difficult problem through clearly.

A classic example of fooling partner for his own good is seen here:

♠ KQ5
♡ 6
◇ Q876
♣ QJ976

♠ 10942   ♠ J63
♡ A9852   □   ♡ QJ104
◇ 94   ◇ K1053
♣ K4   ♣ 85

♠ A87
♡ K73
◇ AJ2
♣ A1032

South is in 3NT and West leads a low heart. Say East plays the ten and declarer wins the King. He goes to dummy with a spade and finesses the Queen of clubs to West. West must now guess what to do. The solution looks simple enough with all four hands in view, but declarer could just as easily have KQxx of hearts and East the diamond Ace, in which case West must shift to a diamond.

In fact, East can save partner by playing his heart *Jack* at trick one. Now when West wins the club King, he might as well continue with another low heart. Since declarer is "marked" with the heart ten, this play can cost nothing.

Our last example of saving partner is a little off the beaten track, because it deals with preserving your partnership's *morale*. Being considerate of your partner's *feelings* is a good way to keep him functioning smoothly. This hand came up in the 1968 Olympiad Finals, United States vs. Italy, and was the subject of a wry commentary by Edgar Kaplan in *Bridge World* magazine. Kaplan was East, playing with Norman Kay, who has a reputation as the most thoughtful and considerate of partners.

```
Dlr: South        ♠ QJ54
Vul: none         ♡ 96
                  ◇ A84
                  ♣ AJ102
    ♠ 1093                    ♠ 62
    ♡ K8532         □         ♡ QJ104
    ◇ J10                     ◇ K6
    ♣ Q85                     ♣ K7643
                  ♠ AK87
                  ♡ A7
                  ◇ Q97532
                  ♣ 9
```

D'Alelio and Pabis Ticci for Italy reached six spades on the N-S cards. South cue-bid both clubs and hearts after the trump suit was agreed on. Nevertheless, Kay found a heart lead, the only one to beat the slam.

Kaplan's account of the deal relates how happy he was to see this lead—he knew the slam was down for certain, since the lead of the three marked South with a heart loser, and the diamond King was a certain entry for the defense. However, Kaplan gently reproached himself for his play at trick one, the heart *ten*. He should, he wrote, have been more solicitous of his partner's feelings by playing the *Queen* of hearts, so that Kay would not have to wait an extra nerve-wracking moment to see how his daring lead away from the heart King had turned out! We should all have such partnership rapport, I think.

☐   ☐   ☐

AT THE TABLE

One

For a long time, the practice of hiring partners for ACBL tournaments was mildly stigmatized (although one's motivation for retaining a professional player might be merely to *learn* some more about the game, or something else entirely legitimate). The League's position was to hold its nose and hope that "play-for-pay" would just go away. Instead, professionalism in League events became so widespread that the League was obliged to recognize officially a "problem" that before it had tried hard to pretend didn't exist.

So now there are several League-approved organizations for professional players. Anyone who receives compensation for playing in an ACBL event at the Regional level on up *must* belong to one of the organizations. The organizations are allowed to advertise in the ACBL *Bulletin* and otherwise promote themselves, and most are trying ambitiously to extinguish that strange, vaguely shady aura that accompanies the idea of paying someone to apply to his skills at bridge.

I joined one of the organizations, not wanting to rock the boat, although I'm sure I wasn't the only one who silently wondered whether the League really had the legal right to insert itself into the private relationship between a professional and his client. The organizations, however, do provide several benefits and services, and the regulations allow people who only give frequent "playing lessons" in local club games to continue to do so "unofficially."

Playing with a pupil at the club, incidentally, will give you a good workout in visualizing and assisting with your partner's problems. Most pupils need plenty of this kind of help, and that may be what they're paying you for.

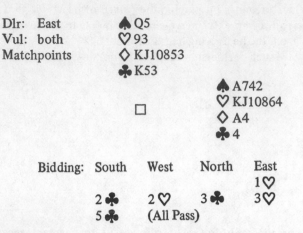

Dlr: East   ♠ Q5
Vul: both   ♡ 93
Matchpoints   ◊ KJ10853
      ♣ K53

              ♠ A742
              ♡ KJ10864
      □   ◊ A4
              ♣ 4

Bidding:	South	West	North	East
				1♡
	2♣	2♡	3♣	3♡
	5♣	(All Pass)		

West, your wide-eyed pupil partner, leads the two of diamonds. How should you defend?

    □   □   □

Not many pupils would have enough "imagination" to pick a diamond lead from Qxx(x) on an auction like this, so the diamond two must be a singleton. Be careful to *cash your spade Ace* before giving partner his ruff, however. If you carelessly return a diamond at trick two, partner will have to guess where the setting tricks lies, and anybody, not just a pupil, would be inclined to lead your bid suit. Declarer's hand is:

      ♠ J
      ♡ A5
      ◊ Q976
      ♣ AQJ972

One big plus I can think of from the ACBL's regulation of professionalism is that it may discourage some of the half-assed "pros" I've seen. The proliferation of play-for-pay has brought them out of the woodwork. A funny thing about bridge is that the best amateurs are as good as the best pros. A pro is simply someone who has decided to make bridge his vocation as well as his avocation. Anybody who wants to can declare himself or herself a professional, and if you can only get somebody to pay you, that makes you one for sure.

So while there are a great many sensitive and reputable professionals, there are also a few fly-by-night operators. I bring this up because, when I was declarer on the hand above, East (who was charging West $25 a session) returned a diamond at trick two, got a heart return, and then castigated partner for not setting the contract with a heart opening lead!

His license should have been revoked, I thought.

□   □   □

Two

In the last chapter when we talked about partnership rapport, I surmised that insecurity was the primary cause of that popular bridge pastime, yelling at partner when he seems to have made an error. You can insist that when *you* jump on partner's case, it's only because you're filled with righteous indignation at seeing this lovely game defiled, but my guess is that it's really a fragile ego seeking compensation for a presumed loss of face. Having consented to play with this person who's just made some egregious error, you just can't stand the clear implication that you're fully capable of the same egregious error, or worse!

The tendency to climb all over partner for his mistakes can be explained in other ways as well. Look at this hand:

Dlr: South
Vul: both

♠ AQ1053
♡ 10
◇ K1054
♣ J85

♠ 94
♡ AJ9763
◇ 732
♣ Q9

□

The game was rubber bridge. South opened 1NT, North responded three spades, South converted to 3NT, and all passed.

West, a stronger player than his partner, led the heart seven. East covered dummy's ten with the Queen and declarer won the King. Declarer then played the spade King, a spade to the Ace, and the Queen of spades, on which he discarded a small club. If you were West, what would you discard?

□   □   □

Discard the heart Ace, waking partner up to the fact that your suit is solid, so that with a minor-suit Ace, he will win it immediately and put back a heart. The full deal:

```
                ♠ AQ1053
                ♥ 10
                ◇ K1054
                ♣ J85
  ♠ 94                        ♠ J862
  ♥ AJ9763        □           ♥ Q52
  ◇ 732                       ◇ 96
  ♣ Q9                        ♣ A742
                ♠ K7
                ♥ K84
                ◇ AQJ8
                ♣ K1063
```

In practice, West somewhat greedily discarded a low diamond on the third spade. Declarer then led dummy's club Jack and went up King when East ducked. Four diamond tricks rounded out the notrump game.

Now, of course, West favored partner with some unprintable comments on that duck of the club Ace, which (he said) violated every known principle of notrump defense. He had a right to be upset, I suppose, but I suspect he was as mad at *himself* as he was at East, and he just had to take his frustration out somewhere. Deep down inside, he just knew he *should* have thrown the heart Ace away on the third spade. His partner had punished him for his tiny error, and that was the underlying cause of his anger.

How do I know so much about the workings of West's subconscious mind? I'll never tell!

□   □   □

Three

In the highest echelons of bridge expertdom, the men stand alone.

In 1972 a quartet of some of the best women players in the United States reached the Semifinals of the Vanderbilt Knockout Teams, an admirable achievement that has not since been duplicated. Only a handful of women players have ever competed in the Bermuda Bowl, the world Team Championship; and none have competed for the U.S. since Dorothy Hayden (now Dorothy Truscott) in 1965. However, if you think this means that all women are soft touches at the bridge table, guess again. The very top tournament players may be men, but I'd guess that the average standard of play among all women is higher. There may even be more fine women players overall, and some of them are very tough indeed.

Playing in a Regional Swiss Teams, you sit down for a match against Carol Sanders and Betty Ann Kennedy. Mrs. Sanders, Nashville, and Mrs. Kennedy, Shreveport, are current holders of the Womens' World Pairs title, as well as two-time winners of the Venice Cup, the Womens' World Team championship. Each has won multiple national championships. They are noted for their steady and effective partnership, which has ground down many opponents of both sexes.

This will be a match in which you may have occasion to do some partner-saving, because, in addition to their exceptional talents at bridge, both ladies are literally dreams walking! If they focus their beautiful winning smiles on partner, there is no telling what aberration might befall the poor man.

This is the first deal of the match:

```
Dlr:  North        ♠ 10532
Vul:  E-W          ♡ AJ4
IMPs               ◇ K10
                   ♣ KJ75
                              ♠ Q96
                    □         ♡ 1097
                              ◇ AQJ4
                              ♣ Q64
```

Bidding:	Sanders	Partner	Kennedy	You
	South	West	North	East
			1♣	Pass
	1♡	Pass	1♠	Pass
	1NT	(All Pass)		

Partner leads the four of spades. Dummy plays low, you try the nine (fervently hoping partner does not have AKxx), and declarer's Ace wins.

Declarer leads a heart to dummy's Jack, cashes the heart Ace, on which partner plays the Queen, and continues with a heart to the King, partner discarding a diamond. Now a further heart is led, and partner lets go of another diamond. Plan your defense.

□   □   □

Partner already has those stars in his eyes, so you had better discard your *Queen of clubs* on the fourth heart.

Declarer has five heart tricks and the spade Ace, so the contract is cold if she also has the club Ace or spade King. Assuming partner has both of those cards, your side has seven tricks to cash: three spades, three diamonds, and the club Ace. But partner cannot know you have the diamonds completely sewed up. If declarer leads a club after finishing with the hearts, he may duck, thinking the only chance for a set is for declarer to misguess. Since Mrs. Sanders has a habit of guessing right in these situations, you must prevent partner from ducking. Your discard of the club Queen will give him no choice but to go up with his club Ace and try to cash everything in sight.

□   □   □

Four

Toiling in an Open Pairs qualifying session, you could use a good result to improve your chances of not playing in the Consolation.

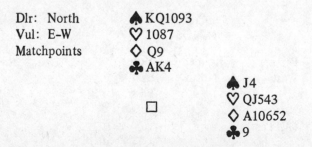

```
Dlr:  North        ♠ KQ1093
Vul:  E-W          ♡ 1087
Matchpoints        ◇ Q9
                   ♣ AK4
                            ♠ J4
              □             ♡ QJ543
                            ◇ A10652
                            ♣ 9
```

Bidding:

South	West	North	East
		1 ♠	Pass
2 ♣	Pass	2 ♠	Pass
3 ♣	Pass	4 ♣	(All Pass)

Partner thinks it over and leads the six of hearts. North's bidding looks a little questionable; he might have passed three clubs or raised two clubs to three. There should be a chance to set them at the four level. But how should you plan the defense?

☐   ☐   ☐

Chances are that partner has found a heart lead from K96. But this good start for the defense may be wasted unless you exercise a little care. The full deal is:

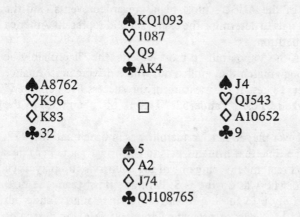

```
              ♠ KQ1093
              ♡ 1087
              ◇ Q9
              ♣ AK4
♠ A8762                    ♠ J4
♡ K96                      ♡ QJ543
◇ K83          ☐          ◇ A10652
♣ 32                       ♣ 9
              ♠ 5
              ♡ A2
              ◇ J74
              ♣ QJ108765
```

Say you play the heart Jack at trick one and declarer wins the Ace. He'll probably lead his spade toward dummy. Partner will win this, but he may be tempted to try to cash out with King and another heart. He may feel reluctant to lead away from his King of diamonds. No doubt he should place you with the diamond Ace when the opponents stopped short of game, but he may just neglect to count. All of us do occasionally.

Since you know something that partner doesn't, that your side can only cash one heart trick, you must try to get him to switch to diamonds. The way to do this is to play your *Queen* of hearts at trick one. West may cash the heart King when he gets in, but since he "knows" that declarer has the heart Jack, he will have no choice but to try a diamond lead next.

(Even if you play your heart Jack at trick one, you might come out all right. An expert West would probably lead his *nine* of hearts to your Queen upon winning the spade Ace, and you could shift to diamonds. Nevertheless, even if playing with Garozzo, you should keep him from making an error if you can.)

☐   ☐   ☐

Five

The truest form of competitive bridge is a *Knockout* event, in which teams of four players play long matches head to head. The winning team advances to the next round, while the losers are eliminated. There are brackets and seeding. The Vanderbilt Knockout Teams, held at the Spring National tournament, is one of the ACBL's most highly regarded events, and the winners qualify for Trials to determine the team that will represent America in international competition.

If you mention the Vanderbilt to most experts, they'll probably be reminded of some tough match they pulled out with a driving performance in the fourth quarter. I guess it's a measure of the success I've "enjoyed" in this event that when I hear "Vanderbilt" I think of . . . animals in the playing area!

The first time I ever played in a Vanderbilt was in Cincinnati in 1972. It was about the same time that bringing pets to the bridge game became a popular fad. Well do I remember seeing one of the country's top players (it was Andy Bernstein, who was on the U.S. Bermuda Bowl team the next year) stride purposefully into the big room for his first-round Vanderbilt match, loyally trailed by a pair of prancing white poodles. Upon reaching the table, the poodles both hopped resolutely into kibitzers' chairs, prompting one of Bernstein's opponents to state that he had played bridge with some dogs in his time, but this was ridiculous.

Perhaps somebody's dachshund misbehaved at the most inopportune time, or maybe the League feared that someone would bring his elephant to the game—whatever, the Board of Directors passed a regulation outlawing animals in the playing rooms (with the exception of seeing-eye dogs) not long afterward. And not so much as a white mouse has been seen since.

Playing in a tight Vanderbilt match, you need to solve this defensive problem to keep things close.

Dlr: North
Vul: both
IMPs

♠ Q1053
♥ 53
♦ AQ4
♣ KQ105

♠ AK7
♥ K842
♦ 109763
♣ 9

Bidding:

	South	West	North	East
			1♣	Pass
	1♠	Pass	2♠	Pass
	4♠	(All Pass)		

West, your partner, leads the Jack of hearts, which is won by declarer's Queen. A trump is led to dummy's ten, partner following low. How should you proceed after winning the king?

□   □   □

The full deal was:

♠ Q1053
♥ 53
♦ AQ4
♣ KQ105

♠ 8
♥ J1097
♦ J852
♣ A876

♠ AK7
♥ K842
♦ 109763
♣ 9

♠ J9642
♥ AQ6
♦ K
♣ J432

At the other table, in the same position, your opponent returned his club. South falsecarded with the club three, concealing his deuce, and West *ducked*, preserving communication if partner had led from a *doubleton* club. (East, to his credit, was ethical enough *not* to bang down his club without a momentary pause, lest he give partner an improper clue to the winning action.)

You defended better at your table and it gained you 12 IMPs. You *cashed your spade Ace* before leading a club. Since partner knew you had no further trump entry, he was left with no choice but to win immediately and return a club, for down one. Nicely done.

□ □ □

Six

Most tournaments have, in addition to the main events in the afternoon and evening, morning side games for the early risers. At the Nationals, it is possible in theory to play three (maybe even more) sessions a day for ten days running. Even at the rate of two sessions a day, stamina can soon become a factor, particularly for those in the Championship events. Personally, two sessions daily for three or four days are more than enough to wear me out, but there are a few iron men who seem able to ignore, or perhaps even thrive on, the emotional stress that accompanies tournament competition.

Playing in a morning game at the San Antonio Nationals, your partner is a guy who thinks he's Thomas Jefferson. Among his other gifts, Jefferson was known for needing no more sleep than a bird; but your partner looks more than a little bleary-eyed. Instead of asking how many sessions he's played so far in the tournament, you resolve to be on the lookout for chances to save him from a sleepy error.

Dlr:
Vul:
Matchpoints

♠ 92
♡ Q4
◇ KJ10864
♣ A53

♠ J6
♡ AJ9653
◇ 97
♣ J109

Bidding:	South	West	North	East
	1 ♠	Pass	2 ◇	Pass
	3 ♠	Pass	4 ♠	(All Pass)

West, your partner, leads the two of hearts. Dummy plays low and your Jack wins. You decide to shift to the Jack of clubs. Declarer eyes this card and plays the four; partner contributes the eight and dummy's Ace wins. Now declarer plays off the Ace and King of spades and continues with a low one, won by partner's Queen. What are your thoughts about the defense from here?

   If partner has the King of clubs, as declarer's hesitation suggests, declarer must hold the Ace-Queen of diamonds for his jump rebid. So the defense must cash whatever tricks it can right now. The danger is that partner is about to underlead his King of hearts again, trying to put you on lead for another club play through declarer's Queen. This will cost you a winner, since you know from the bidding and partner's opening lead that declarer almost surely has no more hearts.

   In order to force partner to *cash his club King*, you must pitch your *Ace of hearts* on the third spade. Such a spectacular discard ought to be sufficient to wake even your partner up to the right play!

```
                    ♠ 92
                    ♡ Q4
                    ◊ KJ10864
                    ♣ A53
  ♠ Q104                         ♠ J6
  ♡ K1072            □           ♡ AJ9653
  ◊ 53                           ◊ 97
  ♣ K862                         ♣ J109
                    ♠ AK8753
                    ♡ 8
                    ◊ AQ2
                    ♣ Q74
```

(Based on a hand of Terence Reese)

chapter ten

THE EXPERT'S ERROR

PRELIMINARIES

I expect that the title of this chapter has every reader intrigued, and you are curious to know just what kind of error I think you might be capable of making. Well, for starters answer this question: *What, in your opinion, is the most important quality of mind required for success at bridge?*

While you're thinking about it, take a look at this deal, which is based on various deals described by several bridge writers. I consider it one of the all-time classic themes in bridge history.

<pre>
                        ♠ 6
                        ♡ AQ103
                        ◇ Q84
                        ♣ KQ1043
    ♠ Q852   ♠ A109743
    ♡ 9842   □   ♡ KJ765
    ◇ 93   ◇ 62
    ♣ 875   ♣ —
                        ♠ KJ
                        ♡ —
                        ◇ AKJ1075
                        ♣ AJ962
</pre>

After an auction you don't want to hear, South declared 7NT doubled. West understandably failed to lead a spade away from the Queen. He started the heart nine. Declarer unhesitatingly won dummy's Ace and raced off six rounds of diamonds, discarding two hearts and the six of spades. Next came the club Ace, on which dummy played the four; the Jack of clubs, overtaken with the Queen; and two more of dummy's high clubs. With two cards to go, the situation was:

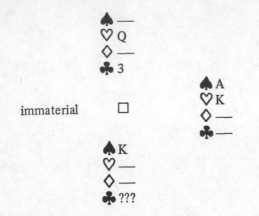

When declarer led dummy's three of clubs, East woke up with a start. He knew that declarer had a club left in hand, but he didn't know which one it was. He hadn't had any clubs to start with and the suit had seemed insignificant to him, so he hadn't paid much attention to the club plays. After much futile thought, he threw the heart King.

And declarer produced the two of clubs! Dummy remained on lead to trick thirteen, which was won by the heart Queen.

An expert makes relatively few *technical* errors. He has an extensive learned knowledge of the game that can serve him well, a sense of the cards that helps him make the right play instinctively in ambiguous situations, good judgment born of long experience at table, and probably enough stamina to play well through long, arduous sessions. But, like anyone else, he is fully capable of being distracted, losing touch with the table for a moment and thereby making some silly error he knows enough to avoid. Most of the mistakes *any* player, not just an expert, makes are just lapses. Believe me, I speak from (long and bitter) experience.

So the answer to our big question is . . . ferocious *concentration* is the most important attribute for a good bridge player to possess. Perhaps as much as half of whatever success you achieve at bridge will depend on this one factor. If you could always *play up to your own capabilities*, I guarantee you'd be the most feared competitor on your block.

There is a famous tale about Terence Reese, one of the world's great players, who is well known for his intensity. Reese was playing rubber bridge one day, the story goes, and while he was mulling over a tough problem in dummy play, a nude model(!) entered the room, danced around the table, and left. After the hand, they asked Reese if anything unusual had happened during the play, and all he said was: "Just the play of the spade suit." Reese's friends, it turned out, had bet a large sum that he would be so wrapped up in the game that the model could pass by unnoticed.

Could be that your powers of concentration aren't quite as spectacular as Reese's. Personally, if any nude models came in while I was declarer, the game would have to be temporarily adjourned. But you see what I mean about the importance of keeping your mind on the game. A winner applies himself strictly to the task of playing well, is determined to play slowly and carefully, and notices every little detail in the play.

There are ways that you can *improve* your concentration at the bridge table. To do so, you must try to *save* your precious mental energy so that you can apply as much of it as possible to the game. Do you post-mortem incessantly between hands, instead of letting your mind have a moment's respite to prepare for a fresh problem? When you are dummy, do you follow partner's declarer play closely, perhaps trying to spot an error in his technique? Do you spend a lot of time on easy hands, worrying about some obscure chance of trouble? Do you spend time and energy trying to solve a "problem" that is really no more than a total guess? If you're guilty of any of these practices, you aren't harnessing your mental energy at the table as well as you could.

Defensive play seems to be a particularly rich source of lapses. The defenders, after all, operate in a cloud of uncertainty on many hands. The play is usually under declarer's control, and it is easy to make a play on defense without really having tried hard to imagine its consequences. We'll discuss some other ways to sharpen your concentration presently. For now, we can look at a few hands that demand close attention and appreciation of the minor details on defense. Studying such hands is a good way to learn the value of being alert at all times.

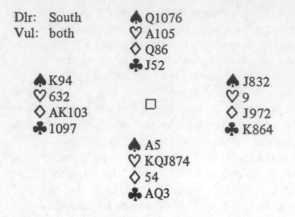

Dlr: South
Vul: both

♠ Q1076
♡ A105
◇ Q86
♣ J52

♠ K94
♡ 632
◇ AK103
♣ 1097

□

♠ J832
♡ 9
◇ J972
♣ K864

♠ A5
♡ KQJ874
◇ 54
♣ AQ3

This deal comes from the 1983 Blue Ribbon Pairs. Four hearts was reached at about every table, and West invariably laid down a high diamond and then switched to the ten of clubs.

Declarer won the Queen and correctly led his other diamond. West won and got out with a diamond to dummy's Queen, declarer pitching his spade loser. A spade was now led to the Ace, and declarer returned to dummy by leading the trump seven to the ten. East's singleton nine fell on this trick. Now declarer ruffed a spade high and led his trump four, and the spotlight came to rest squarely on the West players. Those eagle-eyed spot watchers who had been paying close attention put up their *six* of trumps(!), blocking the suit and denying declarer the third entry to dummy he needed to establish and cash a spade trick.

At several tables, when West austerely followed with the *three* of trumps, declarer finessed dummy's five(!), ruffed a spade dropping the King, and got back with the heart Ace to score a valuable overtrick.

A common error that afflicts experts and lesser players alike is called a "fixation." We saw (in Chapter One) that making some assumptions is a frequent task for any good defender. Many of these assumptions can be simple ones, and made without any deep thought. A fixation occurs when a player defends the entire hand on the basis of an early assumption without rechecking its validity in light of the way the play has gone. Here is a simple example:

Dlr: South
Vul: both

```
                    ♠ KJ
                    ♡ QJ953
                    ◇ K105
                    ♣ A73
  ♠ A93                          ♠ 87652
  ♡ A86                          ♡ 742
  ◇ 986          □               ◇ 73
  ♣ J1094                        ♣ K86
                    ♠ Q104
                    ♡ K10
                    ◇ AQJ42
                    ♣ Q52
```

Bidding:	South	West	North	East
	1◇	Pass	1♡	Pass
	1NT	Pass	3NT	(All Pass)

This was at matchpoint duplicate. West led the Jack of clubs, ducked to East's King, and declarer won the club return with his Queen. He played the heart King, ducked, and followed with the heart ten, which West won. At this point, with his mind firmly fixed on establishing a club trick while he still had the Ace of spades, West led another club, and declarer claimed the rest, making five.

West's defense was based on a fixation instead of the evidence of the bidding and play. Once East showed up with the club King, he could have no more than another Jack. Declarer did not have four hearts (no raise) or four spades (no one spade rebid), so he had to have at least four diamonds. Therefore, declarer had no fewer than ten tricks ready to cash, and eleven if he held a five-card diamond suit. West should have realized that under no circumstances could he do better than cashing the spade Ace and folding his cards.

A less-obvious example of a fixation is seen in this hand, which was dealt in a home team game, and appeared in one of my *Bridge World* articles.

```
Dlr:  North        ♠ 53
Vul:  none         ♡ KJ76
IMPs               ◇ KJ854
                   ♣ 107
♠ K102                          ♠ A974
♡ Q9542                         ♡ A108
◇ A76         □                 ◇ Q1093
♣ J3                            ♣ 65
                   ♠ QJ86
                   ♡ 3
                   ◇ 2
                   ♣ AKQ9842
```

Bidding:

	South	West	North	East
			Pass	Pass
	1♣	Pass	1♡	Dbl.
	2♣	2♠(!)	Pass	Pass
	3♣	(All Pass)		

After West's enterprising two spade bid had pushed South to the three level, he led the two of spades. East won and shifted to a trump. Declarer won and tried to sneak the spade Jack through, but West took his King and played the trump Jack. Declarer then ran off all his trumps. And East, seduced by partner's lead of the two of spades, thought it safe to throw a spade away, handing declarer his contract.

A careful East would have analyzed the hand like this: "Declarer is a cinch to make his contract if he has a heart or diamond void, and he will also succeed if his pattern is 3-1-2-7 or 3-2-1-7. After leading his red-suit singleton and locating the Ace of that suit, he will not misguess in the other red suit. Since there is nothing I can do in hearts or diamonds to affect the outcome (except, perhaps, to pitch the diamond *Queen*, in case partner has it in mind to duck a diamond lead), I can only be sure to hold on to all my spades." As it was, East had a fixation about the lie of the spade suit, and it caused him to lose the hand.

The next theme has been written up several times as a good example of how it pays to avoid hasty play.

Dlr: North   ♠ AQJ4
Vul: none   ♡ QJ3
              ◊ KQJ
              ♣ 876

♠ K1093   ♠ —
♡ K4   ☐   ♡ A10876
◊ 109643   ◊ A8
♣ 104   ♣ QJ9532

              ♠ 87652
              ♡ 952
              ◊ 752
              ♣ AK

Bidding:

South	West	North	East
		1NT	2♡
2♠	Pass	Pass	3♣
Pass	3♡	3♠	(All Pass)

Three hearts would have been uphill work, but despite his "slow" heart trick, North thought he had too many cards in spades and too few points in clubs to defend. Since the game was matchpoint duplicate, he chose to push on to three spades, hoping that one of the three-level contracts would make.

West led the heart King, continued a heart to the Ace, and ruffed the third heart. The defense then took the diamond Ace and played another diamond, but declarer was able to enter his hand twice with high clubs for two winning trump finesses, and he lost no more tricks, making three spades on the nose.

At first glance, it seems that no one did anything wrong. But in fact, West might well have beaten the contract by discarding a club on the third heart instead of ruffing. With only one *club* entry to his hand, declarer would probably end up conceding two trump tricks, for down one. (Nine tricks could still be made, but only with double-dummy play.)

Remember this hand the next time you are about to ruff in an "obvious" situation. If you ruff first and think about it later, you may have just made an error!

☐   ☐   ☐

AT THE TABLE (and concentrating hard)

(You may find these problems easy to solve when they are presented on paper and in a quiz format. Nevertheless, you might miss one *at the table* if you weren't paying really close attention.)

One

The last time I walked into the local bridge club for a duplicate game, I noticed that Harley Walters, our perennial kibitzer, had already taken his preferred position. There he was, seated expectantly in the North-West chair at Table One, his cane leaning against the wall nearby. Needless to say, I felt motivated enough to hustle over to where the entries were being sold, so I could assure myself of a North-South position—at another table. And, preferably, in some far-flung corner of the room. Not that I mind a kibitzer. Having someone watch me play usually makes me concentrate a little harder, so as to avoid any "accidents." A lot of people, though, dislike having somebody look over their shoulders. Fearful of the specter that all their decisions will be silently second-guessed, they imagine their concentration may ebb, if ever so slightly.

Nobody, however, relishes the thought of having Harley as a kibitzer. There are supposed to be rules for kibitzers, like watching one hand only, and keeping absolutely "bridge-faced" (which is twice as impassive as poker-faced), all of which Harley cheerfully ignores. He has a reputation to maintain as the club comedian, and his brand of wit is truly devastating. From his vantage point in the kibitzer's chair, he dispenses all sorts of drollery, most of it invented at the expense of some poor pair of novices just beginning to cope with the perils of duplicate bridge. If, for instance, one of these wretched souls misguesses a two-way finesse, Harley will sit up in his chair, chuckle, and roar "You're a real player, George. You better get you a mirror next time." This invariably produces smiles and laughter from everyone (except maybe George) at the table where Harley is watching, not to mention every other table in the vicinity.

Like a dedicated kibitzer, Harley never plays bridge himself, although if he did, we'd find out rather quickly whether he could take it as well as dish it out. But alas, he always says he is content just to watch "the experts." So that from the safety of the kibitzer's seat, he favors us with his nimble ripostes.

Playing in a Chicago game, you have an interested kibitzer, chomping intensely on a big brown cigar as he observes the play. The smoke from the cigar, wafting over the table, makes it hard to concentrate, but you're doing your best. Pretty soon, you face this problem.

```
Dlr: West        ♠ AQ
Vul: N-S         ♡ Q10
                 ◇ QJ1093
                 ♣ A943
                              ♠ KJ972
                 □            ♡ K63
                              ◇ K5
                              ♣ 762
```

Bidding:	South	West	North	East
		Pass	1◇	1♠
	1NT	Pass	2NT	Pass
	3NT	(All Pass)		

West, your partner, leads the eight of spades, and dummy's Queen is played. Plan your defense.

□   □   □

There are many possible hands declarer could hold, but realistically, if he has the Ace of diamonds your chances look gloomy. He cannot be wide open in hearts, else he would never have ducked the first trick, and even if his hearts are only Jxx, he will have the diamond Ace and club King, and nine tricks.

No, if you beat this contract, it'll be with spades. Most probably, declarer has 10xxx and partner led from the doubleton eight. Say you take the King of spades and return the suit. Declarer wins the Ace and leads the diamond Queen, losing to partner's hypothetical Ace. Partner has no more spades, so he must give declarer back the lead to finish setting up the diamonds.

The right play should be getting clearer. To have a chance, you must *duck* the Queen of spades! Notice that, with his 10xxx, declarer is always entitled to two spade tricks. But if partner has the diamond Ace, your duck will leave him with a spade left to lead, so that you can get your suit established while you still have the diamond King. The full deal:

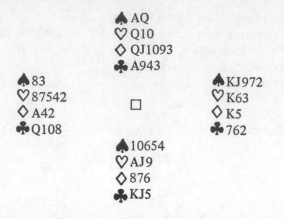

Your super defense paid a double dividend. You defeated the contract. And when you played your nine of spades on dummy's Queen, your cigar-smoking kibitzer snorted, got up, and walked out!

□ □ □

Two

The French statesman Talleyrand (1754-1838) once admonished a youthful colleague: "Young man, you don't play whist? You are laying up for yourself a dull old age." Bridge, I suppose, is a young person's game. Not so much as a pursuit like competitive swimming, where a youngster may peak before the teenage years end—good judgment distilled from long hours at the table mean too much in bridge. But Terence Reese wrote that when a master passes fifty, though his technique and judgment may be as good as ever, he is less able to maintain the long periods of concentration needed to perform well at the highest level.

As against that, bridge is such a stimulating mental exercise and there is so much interaction between the players, that it seems as though this game is perfect for those who want to nurture their mental acuity. Bridge should be the Senior Citizens' Official Game (and the ACBL does run some events that are flighted by age, or open only to older players).

One of the regular patrons of our local club is Elinor Murdoch. Elinor was born in 1901. Back in the early 1930s, when contract bridge was in its infancy and your author was no more than a gleam in his father's eye. Elinor was winning National Championships. Today, full of vitality and competitive spirit, she's as hard to beat as ever and would no doubt tell you that her long career at the bridge table has helped keep her mind remarkably sharp and agile. I hope I play this game as well at 83. (Actually, I hope I'm still around at 83.)

And, in other geriatric news, the immortal Oswald Jacoby won the Reisinger Teams, perhaps the most demanding National Championship event of all, not long ago at the callow age of 81!*

Playing in a local matchpoint duplicate, you face a mean defensive problem. Handle this hand correctly and you defend as well as one of the oldest players in our club, who found the right answer at the table.

Dlr: South
Vul: N-S
Matchpoints

♠ AQ10542
♥ Q5
♦ Q5
♣ 963

♠ J7
♥ 86
♦ AJ97632
♣ J7

Bidding:	South	West	North	East
	1 ♥	Pass	1 ♠	3 ♦
	3 ♥	Pass	3 ♠	Pass
	4 ♣	Pass	4 ♥	(All Pass)

West, your partner, leads the diamond King and a diamond to your Ace, declarer following. What should you do at trick three?

☐　　☐　　☐

The unthinking play is to lead a club up to dummy's weakness. Anyone who wasn't on top of the situation would make that play routinely. The thinking return is the Jack of spades. That shows some foresight (and some concentration). The full deal was:

*The world of bridge was greatly saddened when Mr. Jacoby died June 27, 1984. His passing was practically the end of an era.

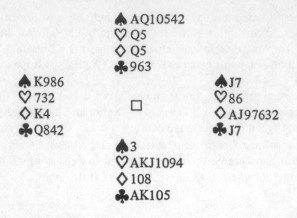

♠ AQ10542
♡ Q5
◇ Q5
♣ 963

♠ K986
♡ 732
◇ K4
♣ Q842

□

♠ J7
♡ 86
◇ AJ97632
♣ J7

♠ 3
♡ AKJ1094
◇ 108
♣ AK105

The bidding marks declarer with at least ten cards in the "rounded" suits, probably six hearts and four clubs. His hearts are likely solid and he is a favorite to have the Ace and King of clubs for his free rebid at the three level. If you return a club, declarer wins and runs six rounds of trumps, forcing partner to reduce to four cards. If he blanks the club Queen to hold Kxx of spades, declarer's clubs will run. And if partner keeps two clubs and two spades, declarer will guess to finesse the Queen of spades (not so hard a play when he knows you have a weak hand for your jump overcall and at most two spades), and dummy will take the rest. Either way your side will concede an overtrick.

The effect of your spade shift will be to ruin declarer's link with dummy, making any squeeze against West impossible. (A spade switch will also work fine if declarer's clubs are headed by the Ace-Queen. The only way a spade play could lose is if declarer's clubs are Kxxx and his singleton spade is the *King*, and with that hand, his bidding would be too aggressive.)

Incidentally, how old are you anyway?

□   □   □

Three

You won't find too many people who make their living playing rubber bridge for money. Nowadays, more of the better players prefer the tournament circuit instead, where they can collect a hefty fee as a paid partner just by sitting down at the table. They need not risk losing any of their own money.

It takes a special temperament to play rubber bridge (or Chicago) for stakes. I know I certainly don't have it. I just can't stand the injustice of seeing the opponents, whom I expect to beat in the long run, score up a cold grand slam or reach an ironclad 3NT, making six, on four or five straight hands. The winning money player must be able to face the run of bad luck, the temporary setback, with courage and equanimity.

Another drawback is that the good player's edge at bridge is less than in poker or other card games. Not many players are good enough to buck the odds. Of course, playing for a small stake is a good idea, even in a social game. You'll keep your mind on the game if you have a little incentive. In fact, it is said that there is no better way to learn this game than to play for stakes higher than you can afford. Your concentration, and your whole game in turn, is likely to improve dramatically!

Playing in a rubber bridge set game for half a cent a point, which means you could lose thirty or forty dollars if things don't go well, you have a chance to get down by a lot on the very first deal. As West, you hold:

♠ Q103
♥ A983
♦ Q1096
♣ K5

Bidding:	South	West	North	East
	1 ♠	Pass	4 ♣	Pass
	6 ♠	(All Pass)		

What is your opening lead?

☐   ☐   ☐

With what looks like a certain trump trick, it is tempting to try to get by with the heart Ace. But the auction sounds forbidding. South's failure to use Blackwood suggests that he isn't worried about controls. He must have a void somewhere, and it may be in hearts, where you have length. A trump lead is out, and the desperation club King could be the only lead to let a pushy slam make. So you settle on the ten of diamonds.

♠ J854
♡ KQJ64
◇ K
♣ Q63

♠ Q103
♡ A983
◇ Q1096   ☐
♣ K5

Dummy's King wins, and declarer leads a trump, scowling when your partner shows out. He plays off the Ace and King of spades and puts you in with a third spade, partner pitching three small diamonds. You have to lead something again. What will it be this time?

☐   ☐   ☐

This problem is based on a hand from one of H. W. Kelsey's excellent books, *Improve Your Bridge*. In a definitive discussion of common errors at the bridge table, Kelsey devotes a whole chapter to lapses in concentration. At this point in Kelsey's narrative, West played another diamond, still nervous that the heart Ace would be ruffed. But declarer sluffed dummy's two little clubs on the Ace and Jack of diamonds, and ruffed out West's King of clubs to make the slam. The full deal was:

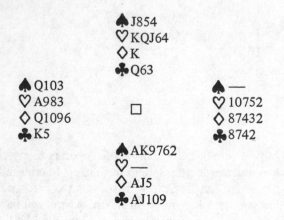

♠ J854
♡ KQJ64
◇ K
♣ Q63

♠ Q103   ♠ —
♡ A983   ♡ 10752
◇ Q1096   ☐   ◇ 87432
♣ K5   ♣ 8742

♠ AK9762
♡ —
◇ AJ5
♣ AJ109

If West had been applying himself efficiently, he would have seen that the correct defense was simply a matter of counting declarer's tricks: five in spades; the Ace-King of diamonds; two diamond ruffs at most, since East had played four diamonds; the club Ace. Ten tricks. Even if declarer scored one heart trick, he would still have to concede the setting trick to West's King of clubs. So, as Kelsey points out, the lead of a *low* heart by West could not give away the slam even if declarer had a singleton heart!

Are you a quarter richer or three dollars poorer?

□   □   □

Four

If there's one quality shared by most bridge players, it's endurance. The marathon bridge game is a well-known institution. Tournament players are no exception to the rule of not knowing when to quit. For those who would rather play bridge than relax (or party) after the day's main event is over, many tournaments now offer a never-get-enough team-of-four, otherwise known as the Midnight Zip Swiss, or, less formally, the "Pajama Game."

For some people, this can be escape. An afternoon and evening of intense competition and concentration can create an emotional high in many players. They find it hard to forget the day's hands (especially the bad ones) and find the path to sleep. Well, if you're not going to sleep, you might as well play some more bridge. Others find that the less-serious approach to the Midnight game is a way to relieve tension. To be sure, the bidding and play can loosen up, so to speak, as the hour gets very late and Morpheus beckons (or the effects of a few trips to the bar begin to tell).

You're not sure just how you wound up playing in the Midnight Swiss, but, while wondering what you're doing here, you're trying hard to keep your mind on the game. It's only 2:45 AM, after all. You may be the only person in the game who's awake, much less thinking.

Sure enough, the opponents sadistically bid a close vulnerable game, which you must find a way to beat.

```
Dlr: South        ♠ A62
Vul: both         ♡ 73
IMPs              ◇ 108643
                  ♣ KQ10
     ♠ K95
     ♡ 10964          □
     ◇ AQ2
     ♣ 542
```

The bidding, at least, is uncomplicated. South's 1NT opening is raised to 3NT, and everybody passes. You, West, lead the four of hearts. Partner wins the Ace, felling declarer's Jack, and he continues with the heart two to declarer's Queen. Declarer now leads a club to the King, partner dropping the nine, and plays a diamond to his Jack and your Queen. What is your next play?

□　□　□

If you thought to lead another heart, you were fixed by a fixation. This is IMPs, remember, and there is no chance to set up enough tricks to beat the contract by continuing hearts. You will get only two hearts and two diamonds. To have a chance, you must shift to a spade away from your King, hoping partner owns the spade Queen. The full deal is:

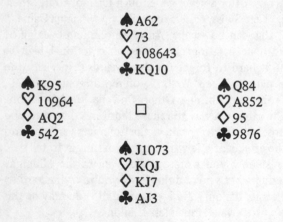

```
              ♠ A62
              ♡ 73
              ◊ 108643
              ♣ KQ10
♠ K95                        ♠ Q84
♡ 10964                      ♡ A852
◊ AQ2          □            ◊ 95
♣ 542                        ♣ 9876
              ♠ J1073
              ♡ KQJ
              ◊ KJ7
              ♣ AJ3
```

If declarer plays dummy's Ace on your spade switch, the defense will have five tricks available when you win the diamond Ace. If he ducks to partner's spade Queen, a switch back to hearts will beat the contract; you'll get your two hearts and two diamonds, *plus a spade*.

□　□　□

Five

Your bridge club had a festive get-together during the Yuletide season with a little bridge to follow. Stuffed full of a sumptuous buffet, you're not concentrating at peak efficiency; but then, neither is anybody else. Some of your opponents seem to be concentrating strictly on how much good cheer their egg nog will hold, which makes them a lot worse off than you are. Anyway, Christmas party or not, it would be a shame to blow an easy hand like this one.

Dlr: North
Vul: N–S
Matchpoints

♠ 109
♡ KQ964
◇ A83
♣ J63

♠ K8732
♡ A53   □
◇ J94
♣ 98

Bidding:

	South	West	North	East
			Pass	Pass
	1NT	Pass	3♡	Pass
	3NT	(All Pass)		

You lead the three of spades. Partner obliges with the spade Ace and continues with the Queen. Plan your defense.

Surely you had the presence of mind to notice the spots, even in your condition. You should overtake partner's Queen of spades with your King and lead the spade eight to force out declarer's Jack. Your heart Ace will serve as a sure reentry to cash two more spades, putting the contract down one. The deal:

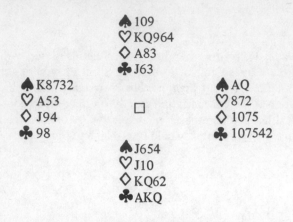

Your defense would cost a trick, perhaps even the contract, if partner had a third spade, but in that case the disaster would be his fault, not yours. With AQx of spades, his correct play at trick one would be the *Queen*.

If you got this one right, go back for one more piece of fruitcake as a reward.

□   □   □

Six

At the other end of the spectrum from the easy-going Christmas game is the pressure cooker of the Spingold Knockout Teams. A good way to see your concentration improve is to play in prestigious events like this one, in which you would dearly love to do well. In an event like the Spingold, with tough opposition and much at stake, you will naturally give it all you've got. You'll be determined to miss nothing, and you may acquire some good habits at sharpening up your presence of mind.

You'll find that there is a special problem keeping your concentration in an event like this. The players are apt to operate very slowly and very carefully. This is good in a way, because you will be able to rest when your opponent goes into a protracted huddle trying to decide what to do. But if the wait is particularly long, you may be apt to let your mind wander too far. You must be careful not to lose your perspective of the deal during a long delay.

Playing in the Spingold round-of-16 (and with hopes of making the quarter-finals), you run into this hand:

Dlr: East
Vul: both
IMPs

♠ J8
♡ J972
◇ A7532
♣ KQ

♠ A632
♡ 5
◇ KJ1098
♣ J52

□

Bidding:

	South	West	North	East
				1♡
	1♠	Pass	2NT	Pass
	3♣	Pass	3♠	(All Pass)

You, West, lead the heart five against their spade partial. Partner wins the first trick with the heart ten, and continues with the King. Declarer considers the hand for some time, and finally ruffs with the five of trumps. Plan the defense.

□   □   □

The full deal is:

♠ J8
♡ J972
◇ A7532
♣ KQ

♠ A632
♡ 5
◇ KJ1098
♣ J52

□

♠ 97
♡ AKQ10643
◇ Q
♣ 987

♠ KQ1054
♡ 8
◇ 64
♣ A10643

If you can honestly say that you wouldn't overruff and worry about it later, I think there is much hope for you as a bridge player. The correct and winning play, as it happens, is to discard a diamond. When declarer has a two-suited hand, best defense may be to make him use up all his trumps so that he cannot make tricks in his second suit. That is the case here. If West holds onto all his trumps, control will eventually pass to the defenders, and they should earn a one-trick set. But if West overruffs the second heart, declarer will be able to keep control, and with the clubs coming in, he'll be able to make nine tricks.

Perhaps you are wondering, as I did, why East didn't open four hearts with his hand. But you must admit he did give your side a chance to get a plus score, provided you found the way to beat three spades.

chapter eleven

HIDE AND SEEK

PRELIMINARIES

In this chapter, we will look at three of the more exquisite and difficult aspects of defensive play. While the plays discussed here are simple in principle, the execution of one of them at the table should be a goal for all aspiring players. I think I'd rather pull off an Anti-discovery play on defense than some abstruse squeeze as declarer. For one thing, squeezes are, by comparison, relatively commonplace. We'll take up these three advanced ideas one at a time.

A *Discovery* play is one solely designed to obtain some needed piece of information. In a broad sense, the act of counting out the distribution of the concealed hands in order to place a missing card could be considered a Discovery play. However, the term is usually applied to a gambit that is accomplished in just one trick. Discovery plays are most often employed by *declarer*, who is more apt to be in control of the play. For example:

♠8652
♡K5
◇AQ32
♣A75

□

♠AQ743
♡842
◇76
♣KQ4

Playing rubber bridge, South arrives in four spades and the heart Queen is led. The defenders score two fast heart tricks and shift to a club. Declarer wins and should take an *immediate diamond finesse*. If it loses, he must hope for the spades to split 2-2 with the King onside. But if the diamond Queen holds, he can afford to take a safety play in trumps by cashing the Ace first, *then* leading to the Queen. By making his diamond play early, declarer discovers what his expectations must be in trumps.

Now, a Discovery play by a defender is less common, but there is the occasional chance. One or two positions, in fact, have become standard in the literature.

Dlr: South
Vul: both

♠A96
♡963
◇86
♣KJ1054

♠832
♡108752
◇AQ4
♣87

□

♠K5
♡KJ4
◇J10953
♣932

♠QJ1074
♡AQ
◇K72
♣AQ6

South declares four spades in a matchpoint game. West leads the five of hearts, and East should play his *Jack* as third hand. Declarer must hold the heart Ace (since West wouldn't underlead that card), so the Jack can cost nothing, and it may gain—East will discover who has the *Queen* of hearts. When declarer produces the heart Queen, East will be inclined to shift to the Jack of diamonds when he wins his trump trick.

If the Jack of hearts were to force the Ace, East could be sure of cashing at least one heart trick when he got back in. Note that the insertion of the Jack from KJ works best when East can be sure of a quick reentry. The benefit of the play can be lost if East is never in again to clarify the situation for partner.

This same idea can be applied in a similar position:

Defending a spade contract, West decides to lead the two of clubs, and dummy plays low. Knowing declarer has the club Ace, East might put in his *ten*, learning whether there is a potential club trick to be established.

At times, you may need to maneuver to let partner have a chance for a meaningful signal.

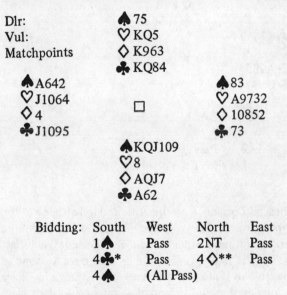

Bidding:

	South	West	North	East
	1♠	Pass	2NT	Pass
	4♣*	Pass	4◊**	Pass
	4♠	(All Pass)		

*Gerber—Ace-asking.
**"Sorry, they didn't deal me any."

West made the odds-on lead of his singleton diamond. Declarer won East's ten with the Ace and led the King of spades. West, of course, was careful enough to *hold off* with his Ace twice. On the third round of spades the Ace finally won, and East got to discard the nine of hearts. A heart to the Ace and a diamond ruff held declarer to his contract. This may seem pretty straightforward, but believe it or not, a player who would get a crop of votes as The Greatest Of All Time won his trump Ace prematurely on a similar deal in the World Championship some years ago, and a beatable contract slipped through as a result!

We said that Discovery plays by the defense are rare. That may explain why the *Official Encyclopedia of Bridge* perhaps too hastily seized upon this deal as its illustration of such a play. The deal comes from the 1961 British International Trials.

```
Dlr: East        ♠93
Vul: both        ♡A872
IMPs             ◇7642
                 ♣KJ7
♠AQ107                        ♠84
♡KQ94            □            ♡J1063
◇QJ3                          ◇K10
♣A2                           ♣108653
                 ♠KJ652
                 ♡5
                 ◇A985
                 ♣Q94
```

Bidding:	South	West	North	East
				Pass
	Pass	1♡	Pass	2♡
	2♠	Dbl.	2NT	Pass
	3◇	Dbl.	(All Pass)	

West led the King of hearts. Declarer won the Ace, and led a spade to the Jack and Queen. According to the *Encyclopedia*, West now laid down the Ace of clubs, hoping to learn if his partner had the club Queen. When East signalled low in clubs, he was likely, on the bidding, to have a diamond honor. So West was now able to lead a *low* diamond, preventing a blockage of the suit. The text implies that the defenders soon managed to clear three rounds of trumps, holding declarer to six tricks, for an 800 penalty.

Without detracting from West's originality, declarer must have misplayed if he went three down. Once West releases the club Ace, declarer can always make seven tricks by entering dummy twice in clubs to ruff hearts in his hand. (It does not help West to ruff the second club.) Declarer might, in fact, have done even better if he had ruffed a heart at trick two instead of making his spade play.

The defenders *can* get 800 after West wins his Queen of spades. He must immediately continue with the Ace of spades and another. East can overruff dummy, and return to the club Ace for another overruff. West must still get his two trump winners. This line of defense should break even at worst, since East must have at least *one* trump higher than dummy. A diamond switch at trick *three* will also earn a three-trick set.

The basic concept of discovery in the play is really nothing unusual. We have talked a little about the techniques of counting and logical inference that are commonly used in play and defense. Players are always on the lookout for clues to what their opponents have, and as we have just seen, they may take positive action to get the clues they need. If you are a defender, you should be aware of the times when declarer goes out investigating for these clues. If you could somehow manage to feed him some false or confusing information, you might stand to benefit. This is the idea behind an *Anti-discovery* play. Your plan is to plant a misconception, a seed of doubt, in declarer's mind.

Here is a noted example of an Anti-discovery play, by Garozzo. The occasion was the 1973 World Championship.

```
Dlr: West          ♠ KQ62
Vul: both          ♥ K987
                   ◇ 1064
                   ♣ 63

♠ 74                              ♠ 83
♥ QJ1062           □             ♥ A54
◇ A85                             ◇ K97
♣ Q107                           ♣ A9542

                   ♠ AJ1095
                   ♥ 3
                   ◇ QJ32
                   ♣ KJ8
```

	Chagas	Belladonna	Assumpcao	Garozzo
Bidding:	South	West	North	East
		Pass	Pass	1◇ *
	1♠	2♥	3♠	(All Pass)

*This was the proper opening bid in the Italians' system.

West led the heart Queen, and when it held, switched to a trump. Declarer drew another round and led a diamond from dummy. Garozzo *went up with the King of diamonds* and led a low club. Do you see the idea? If East could convince declarer that he had *both* the Ace and King of diamonds, declarer might be apt to misplace the club honors. Unfortunately, Garozzo's universal reputation for trickery betrayed him; the Brazilian Chagas solved the problem by simply taking the opposite-from-indicated view. He put up the club King and made his contract. Both players received warm applause.

An Anti-discovery play may involve *refusing* to take a winner. On this deal, declarer tried for a Discovery play but the defenders thwarted his effort.

```
Dlr:  North        ♠ QJ52
Vul:  none         ♡ 96
IMPs               ♢ K52
                   ♣ AQ105
      ♠ K                        ♠ 876
      ♡ AJ10542         □        ♡ Q83
      ♢ J1096                    ♢ A874
      ♣ 74                       ♣ K86
                   ♠ A10943
                   ♡ K7
                   ♢ Q3
                   ♣ J932
```

Bidding:	South	West	North	East
			1♣	Pass
	1♠	2♡	2♠	3♡
	3♠	(All Pass)		

West began with the diamond Jack, which rode to declarer's Queen. South decided that West rated to have one black King for his overcall and East needed the other one for his raise. He therefore led a low club to dummy's Queen, hoping to smoke out the location of that King. However, when East followed with the club seven, East was able to *duck* in tempo. Declarer was then induced to take a losing spade finesse and he later lost an unexpected club as well, to finish down a trick. If East had won the first club, declarer would undoubtedly have played to drop the singleton King of trumps from West.

(Declarer's plan was a little faulty. Once he decided that the black Kings were split, his first play should have been the spade Ace. If the spade King turned up onside, he could feel confident that the club finesse would work.)

Even if there is no chance to furnish declarer with some totally *false* information in his quest for clues, you can at least try to conceal the *truth* about what you have from him. There are many opportunities for *Concealment*, and I think the subject has received rather less attention from bridge writers than it deserves. This hand, which was reported by Terence Reese in *Bridge World*, was played in the famous money match between experts Jeremy Flint and Jonathan Cansino and the Sharif Bridge Circus. The stakes for this memorable encounter were one English pound per point(!), which meant that a vulnerable game made against you could cost you a couple of thousand dollars. There were, in addition, numerous side bets.

```
Dlr:  South        ♠ 5
Vul:  N-S          ♥ 72
                   ◇ A108763
                   ♣ Q532

♠ A7642                          ♠ KJ109
♥ 853                            ♥ KQ1064
◇ K92        ☐                   ◇ 5
♣ 64                             ♣ 1098

                   ♠ Q83
                   ♥ AJ9
                   ◇ QJ4
                   ♣ AKJ7
```

Bidding:	South	West	North	East
	1♣	Pass	1◇	1♥
	2NT	Pass	3♣	Pass
	3NT	(All Pass)		

This wasn't a very good contract. The defense started with four spade tricks, but only four, owing to the blocked suit. South, Cansino, pitched the heart nine on the fourth spade. Now, East (it was the indefatigable Garozzo again) switched to a *low* heart in spite of South's discard. He hoped to make declarer think that West had a heart honor in addition to his spade Ace. In that case, declarer might play East, who had overcalled, for the bare King of diamonds! This was a typically good shot by Garozzo, though it went for nought when declarer guessed the diamond situation correctly and made his game.

There was an odd hand from the finals of the 1972 Vanderbilt Knockout Teams. A *Bridge World* report noted that a defender went out of his way *not* to conceal his holding from declarer. I suppose you might call this a "non-concealment" hand. At any rate, the information declarer got was intended to do him ill.

```
Dlr: West        ♠ 8
Vul: N-S         ♥ A1073
IMPs             ♦ A10876
                 ♣ 743
    ♠ Q                        ♠ 10763
    ♥ KQ95                     ♥ 642
    ♦ K95        □             ♦ 32
    ♣ K10962                   ♣ AQJ8
                 ♠ AKJ9542
                 ♥ J8
                 ♦ QJ4
                 ♣ 5
```

At one table, West opened one club. East's one spade response discouraged South, and E-W were able to buy the contract for three clubs, off the five obvious tricks and down one. In the other room, E-W were playing a big club system. West couldn't open one club (which would have promised 17 or more HCP), nor were the alternative openings attractive, so he passed despite his ample high-card strength. South got to open four spades in fourth seat, ending the auction.

West led the heart King. Declarer won and guessed well by leading to his spade *King*. After taking two more high trumps, he led the heart Jack to the Queen. West shifted to the club nine, and declarer ruffed the second club, as West followed with the *ten*. Now, a trump was led to East's ten. If East had returned a third club here, West would have gratuitously dropped his *King*. Note the effect on declarer. He would have seen West, who failed to open the bidding, show up with the heart King-Queen, the spade Queen, and now the club King. If you were South, would you not view the diamond finesse as a lost cause and lead a diamond to the *Ace*?

That's just what West had in mind. Unfortunately, East failed to play his part, returning a *diamond* instead of another club. However, the fact that declarer wound up making his contract doesn't detract from West's excellent defense.

□　□　□

AT THE TABLE

One

Almost all Knockout events are seeded, some according to the average master point holdings of team members, others by way of "victory points" earned in one or more qualifying sessions.* Once in a while, though, you might enter a KO like the one you're playing in today, with pairings determined by a random draw. Needless to say, your team, which is better than fair, bought the strongest team in the whole event for your very first match. Is it not always so? Well, no matter. If you want to win this event, you'll have to beat them sometime.

The first couple of boards at your table are played without incident, but then comes a possible swing deal.

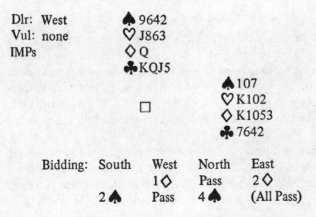

Dlr: West
Vul: none
IMPs

♠ 9642
♡ J863
◇ Q
♣ KQJ5

♠ 107
♡ K102
◇ K1053
♣ 7642

Bidding:	South	West	North	East
		1◇	Pass	2◇
	2♠	Pass	4♠	(All Pass)

*In seeding nationally-rated events like the Vanderbilt and Spingold, previous high finishes in national competition are taken into consideration.

West, your partner, leads the four of diamonds. How do you feel about affecting the outcome of this hand with your meager collection?

Not many people would be up to it, but you must *refuse to cover the Queen of diamonds* (and do it smoothly if your play is to be effective). The full deal is:

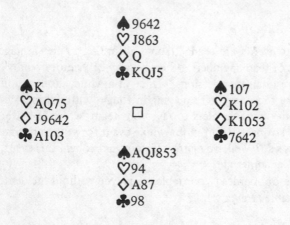

The fact is, there is nothing whatever to be gained by putting up your King of diamonds here, and you will give away some valuable information if you do cover. Declarer will infer that you have the Ace or King of hearts (since partner would have surely tried a top heart on opening lead otherwise), and if he sees you play the diamond King, he will have no trouble picking off your partner's singleton King of trumps, making his contract exactly.

Your team can win this match, but only if you play well enough. At the other table, your colleagues made ten tricks in spades, but they stopped in a part-score. So there is a fair-sized swing riding on whether you gave declarer a chance to go down in his game. Did you deserve to win 6 IMPs or lose 6?

Two

We talked before about the qualities that are most needed for success at bridge—card sense, stamina, and so forth. There are other intangibles I could have mentioned. It can be shown that *confidence* is a factor. There is a phenomenon in tournament bridge whereby one pair or team often puts together a *string* of successes over a period of a year or two. When you consider how tough it is to win just *one* National Championship, there can only be one explanation: When you capture one important event, you start feeling your oats a little—the assurance you gain provides you with some momentum for succeeding events. As I write this, the New York pair of Marty Bergen and Larry Cohen is having a great run. They concluded the year at the Fall Nationals by winning *two* major pair events. Edgar Kaplan and Norman Kay, one of the longest-lived and successful partnerships in America, dominated the National Team Championships for a period of years, and then lapsed into what was, for them, a lean stretch. But they came back to win the 1982 Reisinger Teams, and swiftly added a Vanderbilt title, a third in the Spingold, and another Reisinger victory in 1983.

In an arena as intensely competitive as tournament bridge, the most important intangible asset is a driving *will to win*. Bridge is like any other pursuit. You get as much out of it as you are willing to put in. Those with an irrepressible desire to excel have an edge. Just as Jack Nicklaus often seems able to *will* his golf ball into the hole, there are bridge players who somehow find the way to get good results. The quote attributed to expert Victor Mitchell comes to mind: He once testily informed an opponent, "I won't *allow* you to play well against me."

In a local Sectional, you sit down against an acquaintance named Joe, a super-serious type. Will to win is fine, but this guy has gone off the deep end. To be sure, he's only an average Senior Master, but he takes bridge far more seriously than does, say, Ira Rubin. The game dominates his every waking moment. Job, home, and family have all been relegated to backseat status next to his pursuit of excellence at this subtle, elusive game (and, incidentally, a larger collection of master points).

Joe's collection of bridge books is already larger than the average attorney's law library, and threatens to grow larger as he adds all the newest titles. He attends all tournaments within a 500-mile radius, and has never been known to miss a local duplicate. He makes his dates three months in advance, and the standing joke is that the club would go out of business without him. He had to add a wing to his house to store the vast accumulation of hand records and convention cards.

If Joe guesses a two-way finesse, he can hardly put a lid on his exultation, and one can almost hear the faint sound of trumpets soaring over the table. If he goes down in slam, his life expectancy is shortened by at least six months. All in all, he suffers more over one session of play than does a prisoner on Devil's Island in a month. His molars must really take a beating while he sleeps.

There was that time you played Joe's team in a local Knockout. Halfway through the match, he went into a long anguished huddle trying to make some contract that obviously had no chance. After a while, Joe's partner tried to take him off the hook. "Come on, Joe," he said solicitously. "It's just a game." But Joe looked up quickly. "Don't tell me it's just a game," he growled. "It's *not* just a game." And he flagellated his brain for a few minutes more, trying to bring home the contract that had no chance. You get the idea about Joe?

There is nothing for Joe to get agitated about on the first deal. On the second one, he is declarer.

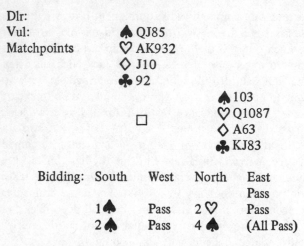

Dlr:
Vul:
Matchpoints

♠ QJ85
♡ AK932
◇ J10
♣ 92

♠ 103
♡ Q1087
◇ A63
♣ KJ83

Bidding:

	South	West	North	East
				Pass
	1♠	Pass	2♡	Pass
	2♠	Pass	4♠	(All Pass)

West, your partner, leads the heart Jack. Joe must be suspicious of the lead, because he draws two rounds of trumps ending in dummy (instead of trying to set up hearts immediately) and calls for a low club. Plan your defense.

□ □ □

You should put up your King of clubs. This is a free shot since declarer is about to take a winning finesse if he has the club Ace-Queen. When your King holds, lead a low diamond. Declarer's hand is:

♠ AK974
♡ 65
◇ K85
♣ Q105

Joe will place you with the Ace-King of clubs and the Queen of hearts, and he will remember that you passed as dealer. So he is a heavy favorite to misguess the diamond situation and play low on your lead.

Joe's play of the hand deserved a better fate. He planned to find out how the club honors lay, so he would have a better idea where the *diamond* honors were. As it is, when he realizes what you've done to him, all he may gain is a few more points on the old blood pressure.

□   □   □

Three

Enroute by air to a big tournament in Miami, you find yourself in coach with three other travelling bridge players. The stewardess is able to produce a deck of cards, so you pass the flight trying to make a little expense money in a high-rolling rubber bridge game. An early deal:

Dlr: South   ♠ J63
Vul: N-S   ♡ A932
                 ◇ J642
                 ♣ A5

                          ♠ AQ7
                 □   ♡ K6
                          ◇ Q1083
                          ♣ J1092

South opened one heart, North offered him a "limit raise" to three hearts, and South went on to the heart game. West, your partner, thinks for a while, then leads the two of spades. Dummy's three is played. How should you defend?

☐ ☐ ☐

You should put in the spade *Queen* at trick one, as a discovery play. If you play Ace then Queen, you risk finding that partner led from 10xxx, and declarer will avoid a second spade loser. (This is a loser he may find impossible to get rid of otherwise, since you have the minor suits all sewed up).

It might be wrong to win the spade Ace and shift, since partner could hold the spade King after all and declarer may have KQx of clubs, good for a spade discard. If the spade Queen holds, you can continue the suit. But if declarer wins the King, you may have escaped disaster. You will be content to defend passively for the remainder of the hand, letting declarer be the one to lead the spade suit again. The full deal is:

```
                    ♠ J63
                    ♡ A932
                    ◇ J642
                    ♣ A5
   ♠ 10842                        ♠ AQ7
   ♡ 85              ☐            ♡ K6
   ◇ K75                          ◇ Q1083
   ♣ Q876                         ♣ J1092
                    ♠ K95
                    ♡ QJ1074
                    ◇ A9
                    ♣ K43
```

Careless defense will be costly this time. In fact, at Miami Beach rates, it'd cost you one night's lodging in the Sheraton Bal Harbour.

☐ ☐ ☐

Four

When the ACBL initiated the six-session Blue Ribbon Pairs in the early Sixties, it was meant to be a championship for the elite, a tough game from start to finish, and an event in which it was an honor just to play. But times have changed, the qualifying guidelines have become very liberalized, and I'm concerned.

There are a great many Flight B events being run nowadays (open only to players with less than a certain number of master points; 750 is often the dividing line). I can't help but feel that the exclusion of Blue Ribbon qualifiers from these events threatens the BRP's prestigious status. In 1983, in Bal Harbour, I felt that the field was the worst yet. The first day, I'll swear that half the pairs we met had qualified by finishing second in a Flight B or Ladies' event. It now seems that the first two qualifying sessions merely consist of culling out these weaker pairs, essentially turning the Blue Ribbon into a four-session event. If qualifying pairs from lower flighted games are going to be accepted, *perhaps the Blue Ribbon itself should be flighted.* Personally, I hate to see one of the few remaining bastions that reward those who display the talent and dedication to *excel* at the bridge table go by the boards.

Sorry, I got carried away. Back to the hands. Playing on the second day of the Blue Ribbon, there are a lot of matchpoints riding on your defense of this deal.

Dlr: North
Vul: both
Matchpoints

♠AKQ5
♥94
♦AJ62
♣J73

♠ 97
♥ KJ82
♦ 943
♣ Q1062

□

Bidding:	South	West	North	East
			1◇	Pass
	1♠	Pass	2♠	Pass
	3♣	Pass	4♠	(All Pass)

You, West, lead the two of clubs. Partner wins the King and tries to cash the Ace, but declarer ruffs. He draws two rounds of trumps, partner following low–Jack. Next, a heart is led to the three, Queen, and your King. You can get out safely at this point by forcing declarer to ruff another club. Now declarer lays down the heart Ace. What are your thoughts about the remainder of the defense?

☐   ☐   ☐

The only problem declarer could have left is in diamonds. If partner has the diamond King, it will always be worth a trick, but declarer could be on a guess for the diamond Queen. If so, he will postpone his guess until after he ruffs a heart in dummy. If he does lead a third round of hearts, you should drop your *Jack*. Look at the full deal:

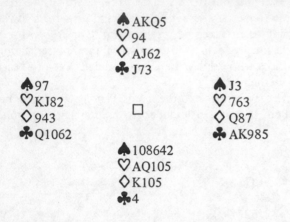

Declarer knows you have four clubs (from the opening lead) and two spades. If you can convince him that you have only three hearts, he is likely to go wrong in diamonds. (With only three hearts, you would have four diamonds, and the odds would be 4 to 2 that *you* held the diamond Queen.)

Your face would be red if declarer turned up with *five* hearts to AQ10xx, but in that case, he might have bid his second suit, he might have played the hand differently, and partner might have signalled count on the first heart lead.

If you defend well enough to go right on this one, you should be a favorite to reach the Blue Ribbon Finals tomorrow.

☐   ☐   ☐

Five

After you had won a few events and your fame at bridge began to spread, you started getting phone calls from players wanting advice. It's strange to pick up the receiver and hear a strange voice say: "You hold three to the King, four to the Ace . . ." without an introduction or often even a hello.

Since you were a good listener and usually offered sage counsel, the calls kept coming. Sometimes the other party just wanted somebody to give heed to his woes. Like the other morning (about 1:30 AM), when you heard about this situation:

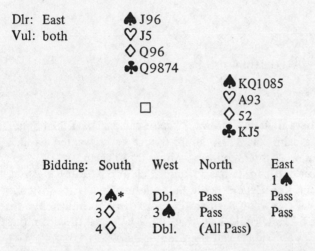

Dlr: East
Vul: both

♠ J96
♥ J5
◊ Q96
♣ Q9874

♠ KQ1085
♥ A93
◊ 52
♣ KJ5

Bidding:	South	West	North	East
				1♠
	2♣*	Dbl.	Pass	Pass
	3◊	3♠	Pass	Pass
	4◊	Dbl.	(All Pass)	

*"Michaels"; a two-suiter (usually 5-5 or better) with hearts and a minor.

"I don't know why these things always happen to me," said the distraught voice on the other end of the line. "It was matchpoints. Partner led the Ace and seven of spades to my Queen, declarer following with the three and four." (Plan your defense from here, reader.)

"I figured with that dummy I might as well punt, so I continued with the spade King, and declarer ruffed. He led a diamond to the Queen, a heart to his King, and gave up a heart to partner's Queen. Partner tried to cash the club Ace, but declarer ruffed. He ruffed a heart, drew trumps, and claimed. The full deal was . . . "

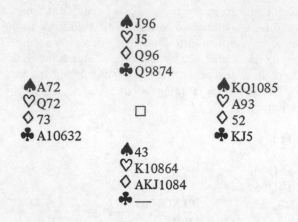

♠ J96
♡ J5
◇ Q96
♣ Q9874

♠ A72
♡ Q72
◇ 73
♣ A10632

□

♠ KQ1085
♡ A93
◇ 52
♣ KJ5

♠ 43
♡ K10864
◇ AKJ1084
♣ —

"Why did partner have to double anyway?" came the wail over the phone. You took over in a calm voice. "He doubled because he wanted a top," you said. "Look, at trick three you can assume that declarer is 2-5-6-0. If he has a club loser or if partner has a trump trick or the heart King, you will always set them. But declarer could be on a heart guess for his contract, as in the actual case. You need to find some way to induce him to misguess the hearts." "How could I do that?" the voice asked with more composure. "Easy," you said. "Lead the *King of clubs* at trick three. Declarer will place you with the Ace of clubs too, so he'll figure partner for the heart Ace."

A lengthening silence. And then a click.

□   □   □

Six

This is a deal from the 1970 World Pairs tournament in Stockholm.

Dlr: West   ♠ 10872
Vul: none   ♡ A762
Matchpoints   ◊ 96
            ♣ A43

♠ 3
♡ QJ108   □
◊ AK75
♣ Q975

Bidding:	South	West	North	East
		1 ◊	Pass	2 ◊
	2 ♠	Pass	3 ♠	Pass
	4 ♠	(All Pass)		

You, West, decide to lead the Queen of hearts. Dummy wins the Ace and partner plays the three. At trick two, declarer leads the six of diamonds; Jack, Queen, . . . Plan your defense.

□   □   □

Declarer's failure to draw trumps suggests that he has a problem in the trump suit. Perhaps partner has the spade King and South is uncertain whether to finesse or play you for the King singleton. You should win the diamond *Ace* and return a low one. This is safe enough (since partner's play of the diamond Jack promises the ten), and you would just as soon declarer think your partner has two diamond honors. Then he'll be more apt to put the spade King in your hand. The full deal was:

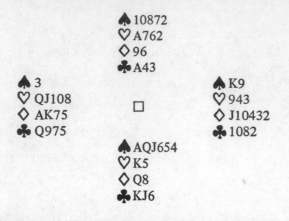

♠ 10872
♡ A762
◇ 96
♣ A43

♠ 3   ♠ K9
♡ QJ108   ♡ 943
◇ AK75   □   ◇ J10432
♣ Q975   ♣ 1082

♠ AQJ654
♡ K5
◇ Q8
♣ KJ6

In 1970, Eddie Kantar actually did find this excellent defense. But the story had no fairy-tale ending for Eddie. When he wrote the hand up in *Bridge World*, he told how his partner was also deceived and played *low*(!) on the second diamond, assuming that declarer started with the doubleton King-Queen. Declarer was pleased to win his diamond nine, and wound up making *twelve* tricks on a red-suit squeeze!

chapter twelve

DUPLICATE DEFENSE

PRELIMINARIES

In *matchpoint duplicate* competition, each hand is played several times (but by different players) under conditions that are exactly duplicated—same dealer, same vulnerability, same lie of the cards. This allows for a meaningful comparison of the results after the game is over, and the winners are those who made the most of what cards they had to work with on each hand. In theory, skill at the game, not the luck of the deal, becomes the primary factor in determining who has the best score.

In a matchpoint contest, your true competitors are really the players who hold your cards the other times the deal is played. It is important to remember from the start that, at matchpoint scoring, *the number of points* by which you outscore them is unimportant. Just ten points is enough! Whether you win or lose depends on *how many* of your competitors you can outscore on each deal, by even the smallest of margins. This consideration profoundly affects the strategy of the game, with every pair trying hard to get the most from each deal, in an effort to achieve that small but crucial edge.

Matchpoint defense is probably the most trying part of tournament bridge. In a rubber game, you are concerned with a single objective—the defeat of the contract. This may simplify your thought processes considerably. As we saw way back in the first chapter, playing good defense involves making some assumptions about declarer's holding, consistent with the bidding and play. If you hope to defeat the contract, your options may be very limited. We saw that there may even be only one hand declarer can reasonably hold that will give you a chance for a set.

But at duplicate, the important thing isn't really the defeat of the contract (although you will often be delighted if that is the outcome), but how your score stacks up against the scores achieved by the other pairs who held your cards. Your goal may therefore range from squeezing out a second undertrick, to holding declarer to just one overtrick, to going all out to beat the opponents' sacrifice 700 when your side could have made an easy vulnerable game. Since your score will be compared with others, every trick is potentially vital, and, unlike rubber bridge, you can't afford to relax even when the fate of the contract is not in doubt. You can see that making assumptions and setting a "trick target" at matchpoints is a tricky business, because you must often consider the significance of extra overtricks and undertricks. There is much greater room for error.

Quite a lot has been written about matchpoint defense, so I don't propose to go into a more extended discussion of the principles involved. It suffices to say that if you are strictly a rubber bridge player, you may be surprised (maybe chagrined) to find that matchpoint conditions dictate that you make plays that would be clearly wrong at any total-point form of scoring.

Here is a typical matchpoint headache, in problem form:

```
Dlr: South      ♠ J5
Vul: N-S        ♡ 1074
                ◊ AQJ94
                ♣ 654
                              ♠ A7
                              ♡ 8653
                    □         ◊ 732
                              ♣ QJ102
```

South opened one spade, North responded 1NT; South rebid three spades, North raised to four spades. West, your partner, led the King of hearts. Declarer won the Ace and knocked out your Ace of trumps. At rubber bridge, your continuation would be automatic. Partner must have the club Ace if you are to win four tricks, so you return the club Queen. Perhaps declarer's hand is:

♠ KQ10962
♡ A
◇ K85
♣ K87

It helps to be a realist, though, at matchpoints. The hand above would be pretty sketchy for declarer's three spade rebid. More likely, he has a little more robust hand, with the club Ace:

♠ KQ10962
♡ A2
◇ K8
♣ A87

or:

♠ KQ10962
♡ A2
◇ 108
♣ AK8

In either case, you need to cash partner's heart trick or lose it. Since the odds favor declarer's holding one of the better hands, you should return a heart. Your chances of beating four spades do not justify a club return.

This next deal shows how a good matchpoint defender must be alert at all times.

Dlr: South
Vul: both

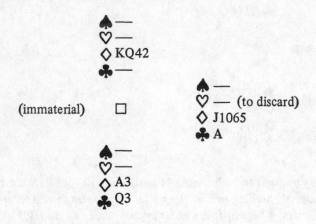

Bidding:

	South	West	North	East
	1♠	Pass	2♣	Pass
	2♠	Pass	4♠	(All Pass)

West led the Queen of hearts and East won the Ace and returned a heart without giving the matter much more than a shrug. Declarer won, ruffed his low heart, and ran all his trumps, arriving at:

No matter what East did, South was bound to make the rest.

Declarer was likely to have six spades, since he did not rebid two of a red suit over the two club response. Unless he had opened an 11-count, he held the diamond Ace. He was known to have the heart King, and if he had *either* another heart that dummy could ruff or the Queen of clubs, at least eleven tricks for declarer could be counted. Even if East wasn't up to visualizing the possible minor-suit squeeze against him, there was no reason not to grab the club Ace at trick two; and at matchpoints, it was clearly too dangerous not to cash out.

Quite often, defense at matchpoints requires that you evaluate the contract and plan your defense according to how good a position your side has achieved in the bidding.

Dlr: East
Vul: ???

	♠ J76	
	♡ Q832	
	◊ J832	
	♣ 75	
♠ Q4		♠ AK1082
♡ A7654	□	♡ J109
◊ K4		◊ A95
♣ A1032		♣ 64
	♠ 953	
	♡ K	
	◊ Q1076	
	♣ KQJ98	

For the time being, we won't specify the vulnerability. Say East opens one spade, South makes a rather pointless two club overcall, and West doubles for penalties. West leads the Queen of spades and continues the suit to the King and Ace. East shifts to a low diamond, and the defenders play three rounds of that suit, West ruffing. Declarer is down one already.

At rubber bridge, West might go for the throat by underleading his heart Ace now. It is certainly possible for East to have the King of hearts, and if he can get in, a fourth round of spades will promote West's ten of clubs for a sweet four down.

If the contest is matchpoints, the *vulnerability* becomes a prime consideration. Suppose that *neither side is vulnerable*. West should be content to cash his heart Ace, for a certain down three. His score of +500 will be enough to beat the +420s, +430s, and +450s of all the pairs who score a game on the E-W cards (and there will be plenty of them; South may avoid the sketchy overcall at many tables, leaving E-W to bid their normal game).

Now say that *E-W are vulnerable, N-S are not*. West should consider underleading his heart Ace, hoping for down four, +700. This time +500 will be worth a bottom, if all the other E-W pairs are scoring up various vulnerable games (620, 630, and so forth). West might reason that, even at those tables where South overcalls two clubs, many Wests will bid two hearts instead of doubling, and E-W will proceed to game.

On the actual deal, declarer would get out for down only two, −300, if West adopted this defense. But the loss of 200 points would cost E-W very few *matchpoints. Either* +500 or +300 would probably be worth the same bottom score when the matchpoint scores were tabulated. And you can't score worse than a bottom!

At least you had a clear-cut *opening lead* as West on this deal. It won't always be so. The awkward problems of matchpoint defense in general carry over to the opening lead, the toughest part of bridge at any form of scoring. The broadest and best advice is: Remember that your aim may not be the defeat of the contract. So, your opening leads should tend toward the more conservative. You want to avoid giving away a crucial trick. You cherish the safe lead, you avoid the spectacular. For instance, say they bid: 1NT-2NT-3NT against you, and you must make the opening lead from:

♠K53
♡763
♢9852
♣Q64

At rubber bridge or IMPs, you might go out after them with a spade lead, hoping to find partner with length in the suit plus an entry or two. This would be somewhat speculative at matchpoints, though, and might cause a disaster, perhaps by picking up the whole spade suit for declarer. Most matchpoint players would prefer a passive diamond lead.

What would you lead, at matchpoints, in this situation?

Bidding:	South	West	North	East
	2♣	Pass	2♠	Pass
	3♡	Pass	3♠	Pass
	3NT	Pass	4♡	Pass
	4NT	Pass	5♢	Pass
	6NT	(All Pass)		

You are West, with:

♠ Q6
♡ 763
◇ J10974
♣ A64

Declarer should have some sort of spade fit to bid the slam in notrump, your spade holding suggests that dummy's suit will come in, and there is nothing about your heart holding that indicates declarer will have trouble running that suit as well. Chances are you may need to cash your club Ace just to hold them to six. The N–S hands could be:

♠ KJ10753
♡ 1082
◇ A82
♣ 5

☐

♠ A8
♡ AKQJ5
◇ KQ5
♣ KQ9

You would, of course, lead the Jack of diamonds at IMPs or rubber bridge.

South's defense on the part-score deal below is a good example of an experienced matchpoint player's thought processes.

Dlr: East
Vul: both

♠ J842
♡ 98
◇ J964
♣ AQ4

♠ K7
♡ A53
◇ Q108
♣ KJ983

☐

♠ 95
♡ KQ42
◇ A53
♣ 7652

♠ AQ1063
♡ J1076
◇ K72
♣ 10

After two passes, West opened one club, and East, perhaps because he was a passed hand, chose to respond with a slightly eccentric 1NT. All passed, and South led a spade. Declarer put up dummy's King, winning the trick as North signalled with the eight. He led a heart to his Queen (North playing the nine to show count), and tried a club, to the ten, Jack, and Queen. The two of spades came back, and South won and considered his position.

Prospects for a good matchpoint result looked gloomy. East's 1NT had shut N-S out of the bidding,* and it looked as though they could take nine tricks in spades. At most tables, South reasoned, East would respond one heart, allowing the other Souths to overcall one spade and wind up in a spade partial.

South knew that he could set the 1NT contract one trick by putting partner back in with a spade for a diamond return, but he decided he needed +200, a *two-trick* set, to score well in the matchpoint column. Therefore, he did not cash out the rest of the spades, but shifted immediately to a low diamond! Declarer played dummy's ten, and won North's Jack with his Ace. But when he knocked out the club Ace, North was able to cross to partner with a spade, and South underled the King of diamonds again. Understandably, declarer misguessed by playing the eight from dummy, and the defenders had their +200, and a cold top.

South's strategy would have been unthinkable at rubber bridge or IMPs. He would have given away a sure set had declarer guessed right on either of the diamond plays. But South was willing to take that risk at matchpoints because he felt he was headed for a poor result if declarer made his contract *or went down only one trick.*

☐   ☐   ☐

AT THE TABLE

One

Some two-session matchpoint events are "playthrough." The entire field plays both sessions, and your combined score for the two determines your overall placing. On other occasions, the first session will be for the purpose

---

*We think South might well have entered with a (takeout) double over 1NT.

of *qualifying* a part (usually, about one-half) of the field for a second, Final session. Since the competition in the Finals is always tougher, only a *percentage* of your score from the qualifying session is carried over and added to your Final session score. The results in the Finals are usually compared across *two* sections of pairs instead of the usual one, so that more matchpoints are at stake, and the comparison is more meaningful.

ACBL tournaments offer plenty of events of both kinds, so it really doesn't matter that some people prefer playthrough and some like Qualifying-Final. The usual argument for Q-F is that the qualifying set weeds out the hopeless pairs and makes the Finals a better test. As for me, I've always thought that there was nothing wrong with putting two solid sessions together to win a playthrough. I suppose I'm biased, having watched too many 210 games in the afternoon Qualifying dissolve into a struggle to come in average at night.

The best thing about a playthrough event is that you need not worry about failing to qualify and suffering the ignominy of being consigned to the Consolation, or "Goats," for the evening. When playing in the Goat game, my usual preoccupation is something like figuring out a way to meet that nice-looking brunette at Table 5 across the aisle. My incentive to play tough bridge is apt to have long since caught the last train for the coast.

After having your usual two boards below average in the afternoon, you find yourself you-know-where after dinner. On the second round, you have a matchpoint decision on defense.

Bidding:	South	West	North	East
	1 ♠	Pass	2 ◇	Pass
	2 ♣	Pass	3 ♣	(All Pass)

You, West, hold:

♠ 6432
♡ K1062
◇ 5
♣ A942

What opening lead do you choose?

□ □ □

It's a guess. Anything could be right. If partner has the diamonds under control, a trump to stop ruffs could be your best start. Either a club or heart lead might initiate a successful forcing game. As for the singleton diamond, that would be my last choice against a part-score. With four trumps, you should be far from sure you want to take a ruff. (But if North had raised to *four* spades with a confident air, the singleton lead could be the only way to beat them.)

Knowing that it doesn't pay to spend a lot of time trying fruitlessly to solve a "problem" like this, you produce the two of hearts after a minimum of thought. The dummy hits with:

♠Q75
♡953
♢KQJ94
♣K5

♠6432
♡K1062
♢5   □
♣A942

For once, you chose the right lead. Partner wins the heart Ace, and continues with the Queen and Jack, declarer following all three times. How should you defend? How should you defend at rubber bridge?

□   □   □

At rubber bridge, overtake partner's heart Jack and *underlead* your Ace of clubs. Surely declarer holds the diamond Ace and the top spades as part of his opening bid, so your only chance for a set is that South has the club Jack, not the Queen, and he misguesses on your club lead.

At matchpoints, overtake and *cash* the club Ace. This play will give up on *beating* the contract, but *that is not your objective*. You only wish to outscore the other pairs in your direction, most of whom will end up defending the same three spades as you. At many tables (especially in the Consolation), the opening lead will be less effective than yours. The other Wests may try the singleton diamond, or a trump, or lay down the club Ace and switch to a diamond. In any case, declarer will wind up making four or five. Holding him to just three, therefore, should be worth an excellent score to you.

Your well-judged opening lead has earned you a good matchpoint result on this deal already, and it would be overkill to underlead the club Ace now. You have little to gain by doing so, and possibly a lot to lose. If declarer had the club Queen, or if he guessed right holding the Jack, you would never get your club Ace, and the advantage you had gained would be thrown away.

□   □   □

Two

One of the fringe benefits (maybe, just plain benefits) of playing in bridge tournaments is that you meet lots of interesting people. We have tall and short players, fat ones and skinny ones. There are the loud and the reticent, the friendly and the hostile, the nondescript and the unique. Some play their cards with the speed, if not the remorseless accuracy, of an IBM computer. Others take so long that you may feel like calling for a stethoscope to check them out for signs of life. Quite a menage, we have.

Some very dynamic personalities inhabit the tournament bridge world. There are a few who are so dynamic they're obnoxious. You know the kind of person I mean—the type who lacks tact and subtlety. He may be able to handle AJ10 opposite Kxx to perfection, but the other kind of finesse he ain't got. He's constantly having to extricate his foot from his mouth, like that time last January when you were standing there having a promising conversation with an attractive member of the opposite sex, and he came over and immediately cramped your style by asking what you wound up getting your spouse for Christmas.

I'm sure that *you* wouldn't ever commit such a faux pas. You're probably sensitive and discreet to the point of being devious. Just in case, though, we could take a look at your bridge and perhaps get a clue to your personality. This defensive problem requires a little more subtlety than usual. If you see the answer, your ability to use your imagination and look beyond the obvious at the bridge table might indicate you're sentient in other areas as well.

Dlr: South   ♠ Q9762
Vul: none   ♡ J9
             ◇ AJ53
             ♣ Q2

♠ J853
♡ Q104   □
◇ Q107
♣ J109

Bidding:	South	West	North	East
	2NT*	Pass	3♣	Pass
	3♡	Pass	3♠	Pass
	3NT	(All Pass)		

*21–22 HCP

You, West, lead the club Jack: two, five, Ace. Declarer cashes the Ace–King of spades, partner following, crosses to the club Queen (four from East), and plays Queen and another spade to your Jack, discarding a heart and a club. Your partner discards the seven and two of hearts. What do you lead at this point? (Remember, it's a matchpoint event.)

□   □   □

The full deal is:

           ♠ Q9762
           ♡ J9
           ◇ AJ53
           ♣ Q2

♠ J853   ♠ 104
♡ Q104   □   ♡ K762
◇ Q107   ◇ 964
♣ J109   ♣ 8754

           ♠ AK
           ♡ A853
           ◇ K82
           ♣ AK63

Declarer must hold the heart Ace to have 21 HCP, and he has the heart eight too, since partner signalled with the seven. If you fail to lead a heart, South will surely take a diamond finesse and make *six*, and the outcome should be the same if you play a low heart. But suppose you lead the heart *ten*. What a diabolical card! Declarer is now *safe for eleven tricks* (after it goes: Jack, King, Ace) by setting up his eight of hearts. From his point of view, this line may be hard to resist; a diamond finesse would only gain if the suit were split 3–3 with the Queen onside, and a losing diamond finesse would allow the defense to win three tricks.

Well, how subtle did you turn out to be?

□   □   □

Three

At poker, all kinds of gamesmanship are permitted, even encouraged, as an integral part of the game. But in bridge, skill in choosing the right bid or play is what matters. Especially in tournament bridge, a well-defined code of ethics (the "Proprieties") is more or less strictly observed. For instance, it is considered unethical to take inference from partner's mannerism, vocal inflection, or hesitation. Such extraneous happenings fall into the category of "unauthorized information." You are entitled to information available from partner's bids and plays *only*, not from, say, the amount of time it takes him to make up his mind what to do.

Playing in a matchpoint game, a Sectional Masters Pairs:

```
Dlr: West          ♠ AQ32
Vul: none          ♥ 965
                   ◇ J1094
                   ♣ QJ
♠ K7
♥ AK842            □
◇ K862
♣ 106
```

Bidding:	South	West	North	East
		1♥	Pass	2♥
	Pass	Pass	Dbl.	3♥
	3♠	Pass	4♠(!)	(All Pass)

You, West, lead the heart Ace. Partner looks worried, goes into a long tank, and plays the three. Declarer drops the Queen. What do you lead to trick two?

□   □   □

Whatever partner's reasons for huddling, he has placed you in an uncomfortable position. You must try hard to *ignore* his hesitation in choosing your next play. Of course, any ethical player would avoid a play that partner's mull clearly made more attractive. But basically, you want to strive to take the same action you feel you would have taken had partner acted in tempo. The Proprieties are designed to handle any subsequent problems; for instance, if the opponents feel that your partner's huddle made it *too* difficult for you to consider your problem objectively, and the action you eventually chose *might* have been influenced (even subconsciously) by the huddle, they can ask for redress on the deal. This is how problems resulting from a hesitation are routinely handled today.

Back to our problem deal. Consider the *bridge* aspect of your play to trick two. North's raise to game is very strange. Not every North will even reopen the bidding over two hearts. So you must assume that very few (if any) N-S pairs will bid four spades at other tables, reducing this to a rubber bridge situation. If they make even four against you, you get a bottom score.

East is marked with a weakish raise on the bidding, so your chances for four tricks look slim. For sure, you won't cash another heart. Even if your partner has the diamond Queen and club Ace, which is really more than you can look for from him, the contract will still be made. By far your best hope is that partner has the doubleton Ace of diamonds, and the full deal is something like this:

```
              ♠ AQ32
              ♡ 965
              ◇ J1094
              ♣ QJ
♠ K7                        ♠ 96
♡ AK842          □          ♡ J1073
◇ K862                      ◇ A3
♣ 106                       ♣ 98543
              ♠ J10854
              ♡ Q
              ◇ Q75
              ♣ AK72
```

In that case, you can beat it with a diamond switch and ruff. True, your diamond shift away from the King could cost an overtrick if declarer's hand is:

♠ 108654
♡ Q
♢ AQ3
♣ K972

but that is irrelevant, because your matchpoint score is likely to be the same (a bottom) whether they make four *or* five. *You must take your best play to beat this hand.*

Is it OK to shift to a diamond after partner's slow play? His three of hearts could be interpreted as a suit preference signal for clubs (but maybe not after he thinks about it for so long). With a choice of equally attractive plays, a super-ethical West might now feel obliged to take the action partner's huddle did *not* suggest in a situation like this. He'd lead clubs (or passively continue hearts) since partner's *reluctant* low heart could imply "doubtful" interest in clubs.

Luckily, you really have no options here if you want to set the contract. So a diamond shift is all right. You aren't compelled to stop playing bridge regardless of what table action occurs.

☐   ☐   ☐

Four

The local club duplicate game is the backbone of the ACBL. The majority of the League's membership consists of the thousands of players who regularly sit down each Monday or Wednesday or Saturday evening for a good game of bridge against the same old weekly adversaries. It may be at a country club, perhaps at a small bridge club in a shopping center, sometimes in the private dining room of a restaurant, even in the upstairs room over the local drug store. There are several thousand ACBL-affiliated clubs in the U.S. and abroad.

Having knocked about at bridge professionally for several years now, I confess to an odd but budding thought in the back of my mind. I'm beginning to cherish a secret ambition to retire to some little town with one of those small but friendly bridge clubs, where I can put aside the tournament rat race for a less intense setting and be content just to enjoy a common interest with some good friends. Bridge is bridge, wherever people sit down to play.

Playing in the Tuesday night game at your club, you find yourself tested by this deal:

```
Dlr: West        ♠A10
Vul: E-W         ♡K952
                 ◇KJ
                 ♣KJ874
                              ♠J853
                              ♡AJ10
                 □            ◇Q10542
                              ♣2
```

Bidding:	South	West	North	East
		1♠	Dbl.	2NT*
	Pass	4♠	Pass	Pass
	5♡	Pass	Pass	Dbl.
	(All Pass)			

*Conventionally, a limit raise in partner's suit

West, your partner, leads the King of spades, won by dummy's Ace. At trick two, declarer calls a low trump from dummy. Plan the defense.

□   □   □

Since it appears you could have made five spades (losing just a spade and a diamond), you need to beat five hearts doubled 700 to avoid a very poor matchpoint result. If declarer has the heart Queen, partner surely holds both minor-suit Aces for his four spade bid. Therefore, go up with your Ace of hearts, though you seem to be sacrificing a trump trick, and return the two of clubs. Partner will win and give you a club ruff, after which you can put him back in with the diamond Ace for (hopefully) a second ruff. If there is a spade trick to be had, that will mean the desired four down. The full deal is:

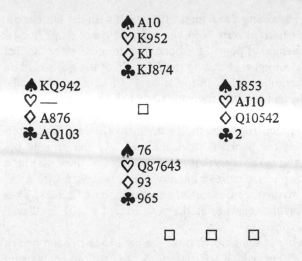

Five

Comparing scores with the other players during the course of a matchpoint game is supposed to be strictly taboo. But if there is time to kill before the next round is called, and some particularly fascinating board has already been played by both sides, you'll probably overhear a clandestine discussion before the players move on to meet other boards. Of course, it would be reprehensible to furnish somebody information about a board they had yet to play, intentionally or not, which is what the prohibition against score comparison is designed to prevent.

I used to be willing to apply the old precept of "It's not what you do, it's what you get caught doing" when it came to an innocent discussion of the hands between rounds. Then came the 1977 Blue Ribbon Pairs in Atlanta and one of the worst things that ever happened to me at the bridge table. I got caught.

We were a moving E–W pair for the opening session. Looking up the row of tables, I spotted Norman Kay and Edgar Kaplan sitting N–S and immediately looked forward to playing against this world-class pair. After a few rounds passed, it was our turn to move to their table, and I did so and sat down, while partner took a quick side trip to the water cooler. Our opponents on the previous round had missed a good grand slam, and, hoping to quell my nervousness and ingratiate myself with the famous opponents all at once, I blurted out, "Did you bid that grand slam?" Edgar and Norman had (I assumed) played the board two rounds before. Kaplan frowned. And at that moment, I saw to my horror that the guide card on the table was an unfamiliar color. In my anxiety, I had crossed into the wrong section! And I had unwittingly revealed that there was a grand slam available to N–S on a board that hadn't yet reached Kaplan and Kay.

Edgar had no choice. He called the Tournament Director, who ascertained the number of the board I had mentioned. My unfortunate opponents were given average-plus on that board, deprived of their chance to bid seven for a certain better score, while my pair was socked with a full board penalty (the standard procedure) for comparison of scores. Thus ended my days of saying *anything* at the table except stuff like "Pass," "One spade," and so forth.

You were playing at the club, and on the next-to-last round one of the boards was passed out, which left time for a surreptitious comparison of scores. One of your opponents wanted to know what you did on Board 9, where East had a decision to make on defense, and he couldn't wait until you got to the bar after the game to find out.

Board 9
Dlr: North
Vul: E–W

♠ AJ
♡ KJ
♢ 1052
♣ AQ10953

♠ K72
♡ AQ962
♢ K8
♣ 872

Bidding:	South	West	North	East
			1 ♣	Pass
	1 ♠	Pass	2 ♣	Pass
	2 ♠	Pass	3 ♠	Pass
	4 ♠	(All Pass)		

West, your partner, leads the four of diamonds: two, King, Ace. Declarer plays to the table's Ace of trumps and continues with the trump Jack. You take your King. What should you lead next?

"I hastened to return a diamond in this position, like any normal human being," your opponent said, "and declarer took the rest!" You remember the other hands . . .

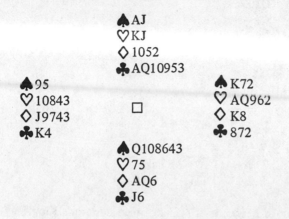

```
              ♠ AJ
              ♡ KJ
              ◇ 1052
              ♣ AQ10953
♠ 95                        ♠ K72
♡ 10843          □          ♡ AQ962
◇ J9743                     ◇ K8
♣ K4                        ♣ 872
              ♠ Q108643
              ♡ 75
              ◇ AQ6
              ♣ J6
```

"So what happened at your table?" "We held them to five," you said. "I cashed the Ace of hearts before leading back a diamond."

The more your opponent thought about it, the more he was convinced you were right. If West had led from the diamond Queen (he would have led the *Queen* with both Queen and Jack), your play would cost nothing, since you would still score four tricks by taking your diamond ruff after cashing the heart Ace. But if declarer had the Queen of diamonds, there was nothing to do but prevent unnecessary overtricks by cashing out.

□   □   □

Six

And after the last round, there was the usual migration en masse down the block, toward the blinking red neon that still announced "FOOD-BEVERAGES." In a babble of voices, the players trooped underneath it into the little bar we have adopted as our own, and carelessly flung ourselves into waiting chairs or pulled up stools to the bar. Here we would argue, laugh, analyze, commiserate with one another, and consume shocking quantities of Marvin's beer and pizza long into the night, like some carefree bunch of bridge-playing Bohemians. What's a bridge game without the post-mortem? For most of us, it's as much fun as the game itself.

One of the younger players claimed the floor to air a disaster that had befallen him on Board 15.

Board 15　　　♠KQ10964
Dlr: South　　♡95
Vul: N–S　　　◇QJ6
　　　　　　　♣A8

♠J8
♡A10863　　　　□
◇A104
♣Q95

Bidding:　South　West　North　East
　　　　　1♣　　Pass　1♠　　Pass
　　　　　1NT　　Pass　3NT(!)　(All Pass)

As West, he led the six of hearts. East's Jack forced declarer's King, leaving the location of the Queen in doubt. Declarer thought things over and pushed out a low diamond at trick two. How should West defend?

□　　　□　　　□

We all knew the hand, so it was apparent he must have won the diamond Ace and exited "safely," perhaps with a diamond. This was no big success, since the full deal had been:

　　　　　　　♠KQ10964
　　　　　　　♡95
　　　　　　　◇QJ6
　　　　　　　♣A8
♠J8　　　　　　　　　　　♠52
♡A10863　　　　□　　　　♡QJ4
◇A104　　　　　　　　　　◇8752
♣Q95　　　　　　　　　　♣J763
　　　　　　　♠A73
　　　　　　　♡K72
　　　　　　　◇K93
　　　　　　　♣K1042

A heart continuation would have fared much better. "Well, how was I supposed to know?" our tyro demanded petulantly. "I knew declarer had the spade Ace, since he failed to lead a spade early; the heart King; and the diamond King. Why couldn't he have held:

♠ A73
♡ KQ2
♢ K93
♣ J742

or some such hand? If he has that, I give away a trick if I lead another heart." Nobody said anything, which was a little strange. So finally I said, "You should have laid down the heart Ace. You gave yourself no chance for a good board."

My young colleague shook his head, so I had to elaborate. "If declarer has the hand you were playing him for, he's always going to make 4NT. But most pairs would be in spades on the hand—let's face it, North's raise to 3NT is a shot in the dark— and ten tricks is the limit in the suit contract; declarer must lose a club, diamond, and heart. So you're locked in for a bad result if South has the hand you gave him. Cashing the heart Ace might cost a trick all right, but probably not many matchpoints. Give yourself a chance for a good score. Play him for the hand he actually held, and lay down the heart Ace. You can't let him make 4NT with *that* hand because, again, only ten tricks are available at spades."

"But," my friend appealed, "how could I play declarer for the hand he had? Why did he lead a diamond, giving himself a chance to go down, when he had nine top tricks to cash?" "He made a matchpoint play," I answered. "He knew that, with ten tricks at spades cold, he needed to make ten at notrump. He had to hope you had the diamond Ace and you misjudged the situation." "Well, I did," the young man said sheepishly, and finally smiled.

Everybody laughed. We ordered another pizza, with anchovies, and the talk turned to Board 22. Now, that was an interesting setup . . .

...I talk of dreams/which are the children of an idle brain/
begot of nothing but vain fantasies... — Shakespeare, *Romeo
and Juliet*

I really don't dream about bridge very often. The game is such a compelling
pursuit and so dominates the conscious thoughts of any true bridge en-
thusiast, that there is little left for the subconscious to do in the way of
dreams.

Once in a while, though...

My bridge dreams are usually pretty disoriented. My subconscious
must want to rebel against the logical, well-ordered nature of the game
that I usually find so appealing, because it can produce a vision that turns
the game upside down and into a farce. There have been times when, snor-
ing away, I've picked up some powerhouse hand and bid myself straight
into 6NT. And then, when they made the opening lead and the dummy hit
the table, I'd look down and find my lovely hand had dissolved madden-
ingly, to be replaced by a sorry collection of sixes and eights. The dummy
itself may undergo an unexpected metamorphosis. At worst, I may suddenly realize that it contains less than thirteen cards, if, like a pasteboard
Cheshire Cat, it doesn't fade away altogether. Even in a dream, it's embarrassing to go down nine or ten in a voluntarily-bid slam.

There are dreams we all have: collective, archetypal images, like being unclothed in a public place. They symbolize some of the more elementary human fears that often turn up in dreams. I've played whole matches, with interested kibitzers around the table, without a stitch on. In frantically trying to cover up my indecentness, I keep dropping my cards on the floor, which only makes matters worse when I have to retrieve them.

Carl Jung wrote that dreams are a cathartic. Your unspoken worries and unfulfilled ambitions are revealed and your desires and fantasies emerge from deep within. Any type of behavior goes in dreams, especially deviations that society normally forbids. I suppose some bridge players may need the release that dreams can provide, and not just because the game can be so difficult. Bridge is a game you're supposed to play impassively. Emotional behavior or a lapse in self-control can damage your partnership, upset your concentration, and cost you some self-esteem. The successful players seem to think only positive thoughts, and they exude confidence and intimidation at the table. Is it any wonder, then, that in a dream they might embrace the aberrant behavior, the disastrous lapse that supposedly is unthinkable?

I'll bet even the best players are occasionally visited with dreams of adversity and frustration, ominous shadows that prepare them for whatever perversity of fate may lurk at the next table. I'll show you what I mean. This is a hand I defended in a match against the Blue Team, about 4 A.M. one Saturday morning.

```
Dlr: East        ♠ K42
Vul: N-S         ♡ 43
                 ♢ K853
                 ♣ K942
♠ QJ5                          ♠ 976
♡ 10                           ♡ KQJ9875
♢ Q10972         □             ♢ 6
♣ Q1073                        ♣ 86
                 ♠ A1083
                 ♡ A62
                 ♢ AJ4
                 ♣ AJ5
```

I am West. I vaguely recall that my partner opens three hearts, and N-S go way overboard, reaching six spades. I lead my ten of hearts, partner plays the five, and declarer, South, takes his Ace. He cashes the Ace and King of spades, and then, belatedly, he plays a heart from the table. Partner puts on his seven, and declarer contributes a heart I can't quite make out but which I am sure can beat a mere seven. So I slam down my Queen of spades, and there is an angry roar from the other side of the table.

I now lead a club, which runs to declarer's Jack. He ruffs his losing heart, comes to the club Ace, and plays ten of spades and a spade, squeezing me in the minors. I've done it, achieved lasting infamy. A quadruple compression play! I ruffed by partner's good trick with my own natural trump trick, endplaying myself into rectifying the count so I could be squeezed.

I wake up in a cold sweat.

Why can't there come a day (or night) when things will change? I'll be a hero. I'm playing for the U.S. in the Bermuda Bowl, and they bid seven spades against me.

Dlr: South
Vul: both

	♠ Q7	
	♡ AK6	
	◊ 432	
	♣ KQ1098	
♠ 642	□	♠ 95
♡ Q1075		♡ J984
◊ Q105		◊ J9
♣ 642		♣ AJ753
	♠ AKJ1083	
	♡ 32	
	◊ AK876	
	♣ —	

I'm East. North has responded in clubs, so I double for a club lead and they redouble. A bad sign. South must have a club void. Sure enough, partner leads the two of clubs, confirming my fears. Declarer, Garozzo, calls low from dummy, and I play—the *ACE!* Declarer ruffs, draws trumps, and goes to a high heart. He cashes the King and Queen of clubs, discarding two diamonds, and leads the ten of clubs. I play low, and, sure that West has the club Jack left, he ruffs! We beat it a trick and win the Bowl. I am carried around the table on the spectators' shoulders, while thousands cheer and shout my name.

> ...Dreams are true while they last, and do we not live in dreams? – Alfred Lord Tennyson

GLOSSARY

ACBL The American Contract Bridge League, the organization that sponsors and franchises most of the tournament bridge played in North America.

Board-a-Match A type of scoring used in team-of-four competition, in which one point is awarded for winning a hand (by any margin), and one-half point for tying it.

Club duplicate A duplicate game, run locally by one of the approximately 5000 clubs affiliated with the ACBL.

Convention card A printed card through which you and your partner fulfill the obligation to make known what methods you have agreed to use in the auction and in defensive carding.

Gold points Master points awarded for overall placings and section tops in Regional and National competition. A quantity of these are required for Life Master ranking.

IMPs International Match Points, a type of scoring used in team-of-four competition. The difference in total points scored on each deal is converted to IMPs according to the following scale (which was established by the World Bridge Federation):

Difference in points	IMPs	Difference in points	IMPs
20-40	1	750-890	13
50-80	2	900-1090	14
90-120	3	1100-1290	15
130-160	4	1300-1490	16
170-210	5	1500-1740	17
220-260	6	1750-1990	18
270-310	7	2000-2240	19
320-360	8	2250-2490	20
370-420	9	2500-2990	21
430-490	10	3000-3490	22
500-590	11	3500-3990	23
600-740	12	4000 and up	24

(If, for example, your team wins 50 points at one table and 200 at the other, your gain would be 250 points, or 6 IMPs.)

Life Master A player who has 300 registered master points, of which at least 50 are *Red* and 25 *Gold*.

Matchpoints (or *Pairs*) The type of scoring used in duplicate competition, in which several results are compared.

National tournaments (More strictly, the *North American Championships*.) Run three times a year by the ACBL, these last ten days and attract thousands of players. Several National Championships are decided at each one.

Red Points Master points won in Regional and National competition. A quantity of these are required for Life Master ranking.

Regional tournaments Large tournaments, lasting several days, sponsored by one of the ACBL's *twenty-five Districts*.

Sectional tournaments Smaller tournaments, usually held over a weekend, sponsored by one of the League's over *three hundred Units*.

Swiss Teams A team-of-four event in which the contestants play a series of short matches. Pairings are determined by pitting teams with similar win-loss records.

Team-of-four A competition in which two pairs play as teammates, seated at different tables and in opposite directions. The same hands are played at each table, allowing for the usual comparison of results.

For those interested in the world of tournament bridge, further information may be had, free for the asking, from:

ACBL
2200 Democrat Road
P.O. Box 161192
Memphis, Tennessee 38186
(901)-332-5586

INDEX

A

Aces, Dallas, 212
Active defense, 27–31
   vs. notrump contracts, 51–55
   on opening lead, 72, 78–79, 85, 163
   compared to Passive defense, 28
   vs. suit contracts, 27–31, 42
All 52 Cards, 164
American Contract Bridge League
   (ACBL), 151, 193, 194, 214,
   229–230, 252, 295, 301, 317
Anti-discovery, 269–270, 277, 280, 282
Assumption, 4–21, 226
   at matchpoint duplicate, 288
Auction bridge, 187

B

Belladonna, Giorgio, 217
Bergen, Marty, 275
Bernstein, Andy, 236
Bid whist, 187

Blocked suits, 246
The Bridge World, 156, 184, 223, 228,
   247, 271, 272, 284

C

Cansino, Jonathan, 271
Card combinations, 131, 179–198
   inferring of, 140–141, 152, 156
Card sense, 141, 156, 179
"Charge" sessions, 212–213
Cheating at bridge, 110
Chess, bridge compared to, 211
Chicago scoring, 35
Cohen, Larry (of New York), 275
Communication, 54, 68, 180, 251
Computers and bridge, 210–211
Concealment, 271–272, 274, 283
Concentration, 243–262
   ways to improve, 245
Contract Bridge Bulletin, 151, 229
Counting, 4–21, 121–135
   declarer's distribution, 122, 124, 129